GLOBAL

AN EXTRAORDINARY GUIDE FOR ORDINARY HEROES

BY LYLA BASHAN

red press

PRAISE FOR GLOBAL

"A timely and essential book! With passion and wisdom, Lyla has written the one-stop guide for teens and college students all over the world to get up to speed on pressing global issues, understand how connected we all are, and most importantly: decide what they will do to make a better world. Educating future leaders should begin with this book."

—PARAG KHANNA, AUTHOR OF *HOW TO RUN THE WORLD* AND *CONNECTOGRAPHY*

* * * * *

"A sweeping yet readable summary of how the international system actually works and how idealistic young women and men can help make the world a better place. As the Dean of a graduate school of international relations, I strongly endorse it as a guidebook to a life spent serving the world."

—ADMIRAL JAMES STAVRIDIS (RET), DEAN, THE FLETCHER SCHOOL OF LAW AND DIPLOMACY, TUFTS UNIVERSITY

* * * * *

"A very readable mix of reflection, guidance and essential information, it is exactly the kind of resource that a college student, recent university graduate or young professional needs as they look toward creative ways to engage successfully on a global stage."

—JONATHAN ADDLETON, FORMER US AMBASSADOR TO MONGOLIA; USAID MISSION DIRECTOR TO INDIA, PAKISTAN, CAMBODIA, MONGOLIA & CENTRAL ASIA; AUTHOR OF *SOME FAR AND DISTANT PLACE* & *THE DUST OF KANDAHAR*

"A truly inspiring guide for future practitioners of diplomacy and development! Lyla draws on her extensive overseas experience to engage a new generation of global citizens and activists about development and diplomatic theory, history, and policy. Woven throughout are heart-wrenching analyses of development challenges and compelling descriptions of how governments, international bodies, NGOs, and concerned citizens can make a difference in improving the lives of those in extreme poverty. This is an extremely practical insider's perspective on how to break into the ranks of development and diplomatic professionals."

–STEPHEN MCFARLAND, FORMER
US AMBASSADOR TO GUATEMALA

* * * * *

"Engaging, well structured, and eminently readable! The issues are clearly explained, distilled into their essential elements (not an easy thing to do given the complexity of this work). This book is a must-read for anyone who is interested, or thinks they are interested, in the field of international development. It should also be a basic resource for career counselors at colleges and universities."

–TESSIE SAN MARTIN, PRESIDENT & CEO,
PLAN INTERNATIONAL USA

* * * * *

"At a time when support for international engagement seems under threat, this book reminds us all – and especially our younger citizens – of the importance of feeling connected to and serving others. Our future depends on the energy and inspiration of ordinary heroes around the world. *Global* is the perfect book for all who want to find meaning and joy in service to our common destiny."

–NEAL KENY-GUYER, CEO, MERCY CORPS

"A guide to one of the best careers in the world—ones which center on deepening knowledge of the way the world works, experiencing all the beauty and heartache the world has to offer, and a chance to help others. What could be a better job than that?! *Global* educates and informs as it provides a practical guide to careers in international development, business and government."

–CAROLYN MILES, PRESIDENT & CEO,
SAVE THE CHILDREN USA

* * * * *

"This book is essential reading for anyone passionate about getting more involved in fixing the planet, international relations, or the true meaning of global citizenship. Written in a breezy, easy-to-read style, it is crammed full of fascinating and useful insights and tidbits that will draw you in and suggest to you exactly what role you can play in making the world a better place for all of us."

–BOB MANDEL, PROFESSOR OF INTERNATIONAL
AFFAIRS, LEWIS & CLARK COLLEGE

About Lyla Bashan

Lyla Bashan is a Foreign Service Officer with the United States Agency for International Development (USAID). Lyla is currently serving in Armenia as the Director of USAID's Sustainable Development Office. This office covers all of USAID's programs in Armenia, which are in the sectors of economic growth, democracy and governance, health and social reform. Directly before Armenia, Lyla served in Washington, DC in the Bureau for Europe and Eurasia and also in the Office of Gender Equality and Women's Empowerment. She has also served in Tajikistan as the Team Leader for Democracy and Governance, Health and Education. Her first USAID tour was in Guatemala as a Democracy and Governance Officer.

Prior to joining the USAID Foreign Service, Lyla was a Civil Servant at the Department of State. There she served as the Conflict Prevention Officer for Sub-Saharan Africa in the Office of the Coordinator for Reconstruction and Stabilization. Before that, she assisted in undertaking one of the US Government's largest foreign assistance reforms by helping to start the Office of the Director of US Foreign Assistance. Once the reforms were initiated and the office established, she served in the office as the Country Coordinator for West Africa. Prior to joining the US Government, Lyla worked for several non-governmental organizations, including Mercy Corps and InterAction.

She has an MA in International Peace and Conflict Resolution from American University and a BA in International Affairs from Lewis and Clark College. Lyla is fortunate to have an amazing husband and two incredible children that join her in adventuring around the world.

For my Mom:
I love you
big as the sky.

CONTENTS

INTRODUCTION

PART ONE: THE GLOBAL SYSTEM

PART TWO: GLOBAL ISSUES

PART THREE: YOUR GLOBAL CAREER

ANNEXES

ENDNOTES

THE WORLD AWAITS

"There were more than 100 countries represented by their most talented (or perhaps best-connected) young artists. Acrobats from China, dancers from Tanzania, painters from Poland... I learned that art and youth and hope and goodwill can overcome political differences."

—Jennifer Lawson, United States Foreign
Service Officer, Paris, France

"I saw field laborers come to our hospital with fertilizer poisoning because they weren't being provided with masks and gloves. Being poisoned kept them away from work for days, or even weeks—and that meant they wouldn't be earning enough to feed their families."

—Janell Wright, Public Health Specialist

"Once you have a greater knowledge of injustices happening in the world, it feels neglectful not to do anything about it."

—Melissa, Freedom University graduate & subject of a New
Yorker *article on undocumented aspiring college students*

"Never doubt that a small group of thoughtful, committed citizens can change the world. Indeed, it is the only thing that ever has."

—Margaret Mead, American cultural anthropologist

"A change is brought about because ordinary people do extraordinary things."

—Barack Obama, 44th President of the United States

INTRODUCTION: CALLING ALL GLOBAL CITIZENS

———•·············•———•——•———•·············•———

I BET THAT YOU REMEMBER the exact moment that it happened. Maybe it was a book you read or a movie you saw. A piece of food; a piece of music; a piece of art. Looking forward to fifth-period Spanish class. Having a secret (or not-so-secret) crush on your school's foreign exchange student. However it happened, whenever it happened, you knew—you *absolutely knew*. There's a big world out there: fascinating, diverse and just waiting for you to go out and explore it. You might not have known, at that exact moment, what that would mean in practice, but you were certain that your life would never be the same again. Maybe you just pointed to a globe and said "There. That's where I'm going to work." Or maybe you had absolutely no idea what to do with your interest other than to nurture it and watch it grow.

If you ask my friend Todd Robinson, he'll tell you his own version of that story. As he puts it, "I always dreamed of travel and faraway places as a child. Some of my earliest memories are of wanting to visit places that I had read about in my books and to learn the different languages. Other kids wanted to drive fire trucks, or arrest the bad guys. I wanted to be an interpreter at the United Nations." Today, his business card reads 'US Ambassador to the Republic of Guatemala'.

If it wasn't the glittering promise of world travel, maybe it was the grim reality of a genuine social injustice that, one day, came crashing into your field of vision. My friend Victoria Stanski will tell you that her moment came on a trip she took as a 12-year-old with her family to South Africa, during apartheid. As she recalls: "Having grown up in California, I couldn't understand why people were being treated differently, *and brutally*, just because of the color of their skin."

Janell Wright, on the other hand, describes her college summer job in rural Honduras as her 'wake-up call'. It was meant to give her some 'real world' experience in a hospital environment before she went off to med school—but she never anticipated just how eye-opening it would be. "I saw field laborers come to our hospital with fertilizer poisoning because they weren't being provided with masks and gloves. Being poisoned kept them away from work for days or even weeks—and that meant they wouldn't be earning enough to feed their families. That's the moment I discovered my passion for *preventative* medicine: teaching vulnerable people how to take steps to ensure that they, and their families, didn't fall prey to avoidable illnesses."

For me, the 'ah-hah moment' was while I was writing a book report in the sixth grade on the Amazon rainforest. I grew up in Oregon, which is stuffed full of the most beautiful mountains, forests and rivers. That book report brought me face-to-face with the idea that there were actually people out there *destroying* the environment, just like the one out my window, the one I loved so much. And not only that, but people out there were suffering as a result: losing their homes, losing their livelihoods. Two questions kept circling around my mind: *Why is this happening? And what can I do to help?*

None of us realized, at the time, that what we were really doing was laying the foundations of a life focused on global social and environmental justice. And yet here we all are today. Victoria works as a program advisor for humanitarian non-governmental organizations, Janell is a public health specialist in Kazakhstan and I'm the Director of Sustainable Development at the US Agency for International Development in Armenia. We all do interesting, challenging work, all in the name of making the world a better place for everyone that lists 'Planet Earth' as their home address.

* * * * *

IF YOU'RE ANYTHING LIKE I WAS, you're looking for a way – any way – to get involved on a global scale. That's lucky, because now, more than ever, we need dedicated and talented people rolling up their sleeves to tackle some of the biggest challenges of our age. And if you like challenges—you're spoiled for choice. Global poverty, growing income inequality, civil war, displaced populations, gender inequality, nuclear proliferation, ethnic wars, infectious diseases, human trafficking, infant mortality, environmental degradation, sectarian violence, land grabs, intergenerational trauma, natural disasters… the list is far longer than it has to be.

These issues may seem overwhelming, but don't be discouraged. We're making progress on lots of things: immunization rates are up; literacy rates are up; absolute poverty is falling. Positive and lasting change takes time to create, but we're definitely headed in the right direction. Here's another thing to celebrate: the list of organizations whose mission it is to put these problems in a museum is huge. There are local organizations and regional organizations. There are national, multinational and international organizations. You might already have an inkling that the landscape of international affairs is varied and complex—but you're about to find out that the landscape of global players (read here: potential employers) is *just as varied and complex*. Collectively, they employ the best talent across a vast range of disciplines—from accountants to zoologists, and everyone in between. What this means for you is that somewhere out there, your perfect job is waiting for you.

Here's my goal. Whatever your starting point, whatever your interest in global affairs—I want to help you turn your passion into a career. Figuring out where to start, and what your options are, can be daunting. Trust me. I know. Then again, there's an old Chinese proverb that says: *to know the road ahead, ask those coming back*. I want to share the wit and wisdom of those who know that road like the back of their hand. You're never too young (or too old!) to start down that road, and believe me it will twist and turn in ways you'd never expect. And that's okay. In fact, it's more than okay, because frankly, you're in for the ride of your life.

Whether you want to work in diplomacy, defense or international humanitarian relief and development – or even if you have no idea where you want to focus your talents – a solid foundation in the key international affairs issues, systems and players will be your best friend. And that's where I come in. I'd like to help you.

Why? Because I'm an ordinary person doing extraordinary work and I want to model that as an achievable career goal. I've been doing this gig for over 15 years, and in that time I've had adventures all over the world. I've been to Timbuktu, Zanzibar and Bali. I've traveled by helicopter, boat and tuk-tuk. I've seen the Monkey King dance, climbed a Mayan temple and summited a volcano. I've been to northern Nigeria where judges enact Sharia law, and to the eastern part of the Democratic Republic of the Congo where there is an active rebellion. I've met with government ministers and foreign ambassadors. I've visited with school children, women's microfinance collectives and victims of human trafficking. When I say that 'you too can join the ranks of ordinary heroes', it's not just because we need you (and we do, by the way). You should know that it's also an awesome career choice to make. If you're looking for a job that will take you beyond the edges of the map, then international affairs is for you.

* * * * *

GLOBAL IS THE BOOK that I wish I could have read 20 years ago when I was starting out on my career in international affairs. Since I don't know how to build a time machine, I wrote this book for other young people who are just beginning their journey towards a life lived globally. For young people who want to learn about how the international system works, and who want to dedicate their lives to making our little blue world a better, more equal, more fair and more peaceful place. For everyone.

I wrote this book with two lenses, one broad and one narrow. Broadly, this book is relevant to everyone interested in tackling the very pressing social, environmental, political and economic challenges of our time. Narrowly, it's *most* relevant to Americans, by which I mean folks from the United States of America. Of course, everyone from North, Central and South America is American—but my personal point of reference speaks to this narrower definition of the term 'American'.

On the other hand, I wrote this book for people who want to be *global citizens*. Global citizenship means defining 'community' in the broadest way possible. It means recognizing the interdependence of different countries and cultures within the world community. What happens out there affects you at home. Your own actions ripple out far beyond our national borders. Everything is connected.

The world out there is as close to you as the shirt on your back, or the smartphone in your pocket. The United States imports goods and services from around the globe (mostly China at the moment), and exports other goods and services (Canada is our biggest overall trading partner). In fact, while folks in North America and Europe make up only 12 percent of the global population, we do 60 percent of the world's consumer spending.

What you put in your shopping cart matters, to more people than you might expect.

Here's a little test: grab your favorite t-shirt and flip the label over. Does it say 'Made in the USA?' Bangladesh? Vietnam? India? Have you ever made the connection between what you were wearing and whether a poor factory worker was paid a decent enough wage to feed her family? We all love a bargain when we're shopping (myself included), but our access to cheap consumer goods very often relies on low wages, poor working conditions and unchecked industrial pollution in developing countries.

Here's another little test: when's the last time you or someone you know complained about the price of gas at the pump? Did you ever think about where it came from? The US is the world's largest consumer of petroleum, and about a quarter of what we use, we buy from other countries. The oil industry is big money. Crude oil (used to make gas and heating oil) is the most-traded commodity on the planet. All the same, our oil addiction is taking its toll. Not just on the environment, but also in terms of the geo-political complexity it adds to our foreign policy. We don't always agree with the actions of the countries that sell us oil—and when you don't want to bite the hand that feeds you, sometimes you end up biting your tongue.

One final test: can you trace the roots of your family tree? Unless you're a member of a Native American tribe, I'm betting that your ancestors were immigrants or victims of slavery. Statistically speaking, it's likely that you know a first or second-generation immigrant. That's because you could fill the seats of *ten Super Bowl stadiums* with the number of immigrants that arrive on our shores *each year*. If you wanted to gather up all the documented immigrants living in the US, you'd need *two hundred Super Bowl stadiums*, and another hundred or so for undocumented immigrants, although this number is harder to pin down. (As you may have noticed, immigration is a hot topic in the halls of the US Government.)

Why does this all matter to you? Because not everyone migrates for the same reason, and not all communities are prepared to welcome migrants with open arms (even though in the long term, communities usually benefit from an influx of new people, new ideas and new skills). Global citizenship means understanding that conflicts and hardship abroad eventually show up at your door—in the form of people seeking both opportunity and safety, but also in the form of diseases, ideology, money, and other factors that neither acknowledge nor respect political borders.

And these days, ordinary people are just as connected around the globe as governments are—in some ways even more so. Technology and travel are increasingly bringing us face-to-face, every day, with people from around the world. Of course, there are a lot of advantages to this. For example, we get a front row seat for different forms of art, literature, music, food, different languages and different perspectives on the ideas that we all think about. Oh, and you get to Instagram your vacation snaps from weird and wonderful places too! The disadvantages, however, are also real: increased racism and xenophobia (fear of outsiders), the spread of infectious diseases (like when the Ebola virus hops on a plane) and increased competition for scarce resources (like fresh water and land to grow crops). And yes, terrorism, too. Not just terrorism on US soil—terrorism everywhere.

If those issues keep you awake at night and spur you into action; if you know a little, and want to know more—then this book is for you.

* * * * *

BEFORE YOU READ ON, let me give you a few tips on how to navigate the chapters that follow. First off, I want you to think of this book as both a reference and a reassurance. Dip in and out of each chapter as you need to—pull out what interests you most, get a good grasp on the basics and get fired up to go learn more about it.

Part One is about the global system. Head there for a crash course (or a refresher) on how you can participate within that system as an effective advocate for the issues close to your heart. A global citizen you may be, but remember that global citizenship starts at home. What the US Government does has a *huge* impact on every aspect of your life—whom you can marry, what you can do with your body, and how much of your paycheck you get to keep each month. As Plato once said: "One of the penalties for refusing to participate in politics is that you end up being governed by your inferiors."

Part One will also talk about nation-states (starting with what in the world a nation-state is!), and how those nation-states interact with the international system. It covers the different organs of government (yep, they're actually called that) that focus on foreign policy and international affairs. It also looks at other forms of cooperation between nation-states and, of course, the role of non-state entities. Next, you'll find a chapter on the global economy—because no discussion on international political affairs would ever be complete without a discussion on money. Orange may be the new black, but green has always been green. Then we'll round off *Part One* with an overview of international development.

In *Part Two*, we'll focus on some of the very pressing global issues that need time and attention today. We'll explore poverty, health, education, work, food, democracy and governance, humanitarian assistance, conflict, gender and the environment. I'll give you a solid foundation on each topic, which you can build upon with further reading (and tips on where to go for this). Bear in mind—what you're about to read is only a sample of global issues. Those I've chosen are some of the most pressing issues and those that I can speak to with a high level of expertise. That said, every global problem is critical, and most of them are inter-related, so I'd urge you to go find out more about things like neo-colonization, torture, the drug trade, LGBTQ (lesbian, gay, bisexual, transgender, queer) rights, disability rights, race relations, nuclear proliferation, free trade, income inequality, the role of multinational corporations as a non-state actor in global affairs, etc.

Part Three is all about you and your global career. It's awesome to have a job where you get to travel the world, help people improve their lives, meet fascinating colleagues and create a lifetime's worth of memories. But first, you'll need to navigate the maze of educational and employment options. Here's where my first-hand knowledge is your new best friend. Remember, there's no perfect path—there's only *your* path. But having a clear view of your options is the best way to start. I've also included a chapter of the wisdom and advice I've collected from friends and colleagues in the sector—because each and every one of us was sitting where you are today, wondering where to begin.

Finally, I've included three *Annexes* with some nitty-gritty information that will help you get started on your journey. Head there to find details on where to find potential future jobs, internships and volunteer opportunities, descriptions of the major international organizations (read: potential future employers), as well as a list of additional websites, books and articles you can use to learn more about the topics discussed in this book.

* * * * *

HAVING TOLD YOU what this book is about, it seems worth mentioning the things this book is *not about*. First and foremost, I try not to takes sides on political issues. I firmly believe that everyone can be a global citizen, no matter how they choose to express that citizenship in the privacy of the ballot box. Moreover, the challenges facing the world today require the best and the brightest—all of them. A poor woman struggling to feed her kids in Bangladesh doesn't care whether or not someone calls you a tree-hugging hippie or a rabid conservative. When it comes to global injustice, results are what matter.

This book also isn't about 'us' being better than 'them'. If you grew up in the US, lucky you. Lucky me, too. Seriously. As the saying goes: if you have food in your fridge, clothes on your back, a roof over your head and a place to sleep you are richer than 75 percent of the world. If you have money in the bank, your wallet and some spare change—you are among the top 8 percent of the world's wealthy. If you woke up this morning with more health than illness you are luckier than the million people who will not survive this week. If you have never experienced the danger of battle, the agony of imprisonment or torture, or the horrible pangs of starvation you are luckier than 500 million people alive and suffering.

But let's agree on one thing: *lucky doesn't mean better.* We don't go out into the world because we are superior. We go out into the world because we want to serve. Because we *can* serve. I didn't grow up in a wealthy family, but I lived in safety, I had a warm bed, enough food to eat and access to quality education and healthcare. I am grateful for my good fortune, and I spend my life working to help those less fortunate than me. It's an honor, and a privilege. Nothing more; nothing less.

It's also important to mention that you're going to learn some unsavory details about some countries, including our own. The fact is: every country grapples with its own social injustice issues. But so too does every country boast its own beauty, resiliency and complexity. I wish I could capture all those aspects in this book; instead, I'll leave it to you to experience and savor them during your career as an ordinary hero.

I have tried to explain processes and issues that are super complex in a simple and straightforward way. Each topic, and each aspect of each topic, has been the subject of dozens (if not hundreds) of books, articles, blogs and Ted Talks. I'm not aiming to be comprehensive. Instead, think of this book as a sample platter in the restaurant of social injustice. You'll get a taste of the big issues and challenges, and as your heart or head are grabbed by particular topics and themes—dive in. Read more, learn more, connect with the organizations that make daily work of those issues.

Another thing (just to be totally upfront about my bias) is that you might find my focus to be a bit 'US Government-centric'. Given my background and job title, I should hope it would be! And, of course, the US Government has a big and important role to play in international development. So too does the vast ecosystem of non-governmental organizations, charities, social businesses, social investors, impact hubs, grassroots organizations, community action groups and others. Each type of organization has its own role to play, its own strengths and weaknesses—but at the end of the day, we're all on #TeamJustice.

The other thing this book is *not* is anything other than my personal opinion. I'm sharing my experience and my insights with you, as are my many friends and colleagues, whose stories you will find throughout this book. Where I, or any of us, express an opinion on matters foreign and domestic, we are speaking as ordinary citizens, rather than as official representatives of any government or organization.

Got it? Great, let's get started!

PART ONE

THE GLOBAL SYSTEM

CHAPTER 1
THE NATION-STATE

THE NUTSHELL...

There are nations, states, and nation-states. Knowing what they are and how they differ is the key to unlocking lots of political conflicts in the world today. Some nation-states are relatively stable. But far too many others are fragile (or even failed) states—which is bad news for ordinary people who are just trying to live peaceful lives.

WHAT KIND OF JOB COULD THIS BE?

International affairs professor • Research assistant at a think tank • Political scientist for a private company • Sociologist at a multilateral organization • US Government Policy advisor

WHAT IN THE WORLD IS A NATION-STATE? And why should you care? These are all good questions, and definitely the right ones to ask if you want to understand how the global system works. And frankly, the global system can (at first) be as confusing as it is interesting.

1

Shall we go back to basics? A nation-state is comprised of two (ideally overlapping) entities: a political entity (the state) and a cultural entity (the nation). Long before we moved on to deeper questions involving chickens and eggs, we were asking ourselves 'which came first, the nation or the state?'

The political backdrop for this question was provided by 17th-century Europe, which was divided into different empires (political entities) that each ruled over a diverse mix of nations (as defined by language and culture).

It wasn't until the Treaty of Westphalia in 1648 that the two ideas of nationhood and statehood were brought together. In this chapter, we're going to look at the idea of the nation-state, and then talk about all the things that happen when that idea breaks down in real life.

THE BIRTH OF THE NATION-STATE

CAST YOUR MIND BACK to the year 1648, when a bunch of powerful men in Europe came together with the very important task of negotiating a peace agreement to end several protracted wars. This agreement was known as the Treaty of Westphalia—and it re-drew the map of Europe into something quite close to its present-day form.

First, it established the concept of the nation-state as an independent entity that has the right to do what it wants within its defined and permanent borders (that are not subject to change when, for example, the princess is getting married to the prince from the neighboring country and needs to offer up a dowry).

Those national borders were created so that political and cultural entities were roughly aligned. Each nation-state was on an equal legal footing, and no country had the right to meddle in the internal affairs of another. Moreover, each monarch was free to determine the religion of their own nation (but freedom of religion wasn't, at that point, guaranteed for those who didn't share in the monarch's religion).

Another outcome of Westphalia was to define the responsibility of a nation-state to its people. In addition to protecting its borders, nation-states were tasked with creating stability and prosperity for their citizens (which, if you think about it, is what we still ask our nation-states to do today).

Finally, Westphalia restricted how different nation-states could legitimately be in conflict with each other. Here's why: while the treaty ended decades of war—religious and ethnic conflict were still a problem. But, gone were the days when a ruler could just nab a neighbor's territory (or throne) to settle a disagreement. Today, when a country's national interest is at odds with that of another, it will still try to exert its power through military force (often seen as a last resort), but usually it first tries what's known as 'soft power', which can be diplomatic, economic or cultural.

Westphalia, as I've mentioned, is when the map of Europe started coming into focus as something we'd recognize today. Some nation-states were established long before 1648 (such as France, Denmark and Portugal). But many others that we know today weren't countries at all back then, but rather were territories within large empires like the Ottoman Empire.

DID YOU KNOW?

The German sociologist, Max Weber, defined the state as a "human community that (successfully) claims the monopoly of the legitimate use of physical force within a given territory." Note he didn't talk about how awesome or crappy the government was… just whether or not it was in control!

3

Of course, the concept of the independent nation-state was, and still is, complicated by the not-insignificant matter of colonization. That's especially true when you pan out from Europe and look at the rest of the world map.

Until the Second World War, various (mostly) European powers claimed sovereignty over other nations or territories in Africa and Asia as part of their empires. Even the US (a former colony itself) has its own history of colonization—just ask a Hawaiian or a Puerto Rican.

It's worth keeping in mind that the colonial legacy still resonates loudly in global affairs. There are good odds that your globe-trotting career will take you to a country that gained its independence only in the 20th century. We'll also touch upon this when we talk about fragile states a bit later—because many of the countries that fall into that category are relatively young countries.

Why the trip down memory lane, you ask? It's because the recognition of distinct sovereign nation-states forms the basis of our current international system. Nations (cultural entities) are represented by state governments (political entities). State governments are in charge of deciding what happens within their territories. There are (at the latest count) 195 sovereign nation-states in the world, and they interact with each other in (ideally) predictable ways through the global system. That all sounds pretty straightforward, doesn't it?

SPOILER ALERT: THINGS SOMETIMES FALL APART

NATION-STATES MAY BE THE FOUNDATION of the global system, but not all nation-states are the same. As I've mentioned, some states have been around for hundreds of years, some for decades and others for just a few years. And when the identity, effectiveness or integrity of a nation-state starts to fray, bad things happen.

A 'DEVELOPING COUNTRY' BY ANY OTHER NAME...

OK, SO I JUST DROPPED A TERM THERE: DEVELOPING COUNTRY. You already know that across the world, there are rich countries and poor countries—but how people refer to them collectively can vary.

We usually talk about rich countries as being *developed*, meaning that their economy is diverse and flourishing, they have high per capita income and high marks on the main socioeconomic indicators (i.e. life expectancy, health, education, etc.).

Developing countries often have all or some combination of weak economies, low per capita income and low marks on key socioeconomic indicators. Those that we call the *least developed countries* are those that are the worst performers (on key indicators) of all developing countries.

Countries that are on the verge of moving from poor to rich are sometimes called *emerging economies*.

Developed countries can also be called *industrialized*, which refers to them having made the transition from 'poor' to 'rich' by developing the manufacturing and service side of their economy.

We used to use the terms *first-world* and *third-world*, but the implicit value judgment involved in 'ranking' countries can seem tone deaf by today's standards.

Truth is: none of the terms are perfect, but it's handy to know what people are talking about when they use them.

When people can't rely on their government for security or economic opportunity, or when one segment of the population decides they want things run differently, that country can quickly descend into chaos.

⤞➤ *National identity*

Let's talk a bit more about why the guys at Westphalia put the *nation* in *nation-state*. It's because they recognized that long before governments grouped people into a 'state', those people were often bound together by a common language, ancestry, and culture. When you think of all the little things that 'make us American' (like our love of baseball and barbecues), you're talking about our *national identity*.

There are many countries in which diverse ethnic groups live peacefully alongside one another. It is also true that the subject of national identity is the root cause of many international conflicts. This is especially true where two nations (who don't like each other) are lumped into one state, or where one nation (as a cultural entity) is spread over territory belonging to two or more different states (and no one can agree where to draw the political line). The Kurdish nation is just one such example of a 'stateless nation': Kurds are scattered across different countries in Southeastern Europe and the Middle East.

Ironically, sometimes it was the presence of colonial powers that helped to unite myriads of different principalities, tribes, etc., into one single national identity and corresponding country. The classic case is Indonesia. Until the Dutch conquered the area and drew a somewhat arbitrary border around some of the islands (but not others), there had never been a sense of 'Indonesia' as a place, or even as a word.

Then there's Africa, where many countries only gained independence during the 20th century. Before that, the continent was organized not into formal states, but lands claimed by various allied and competing tribes. During the colonial period, Africa was carved up between various European empires, and was left with their colonial borders even after the colonial powers withdrew. That means that few African state borders were drawn in a way that reflected shared cultures, ethnicities, religions or any other factors that naturally make up a national identity. The same can be said for the Middle East.

This is one reason why so many countries slid into civil war during decolonization in the middle of the 20th century—conflicts which still roll on today. One such example is South Sudan, the world's newest country, which was created in part because it had a very different national identity from the north of Sudan. In the north, 70 percent of the population is made up of Sudanese Arabs; in the South, the largest ethnic group (30 percent) is Dinka, who live alongside about sixty other ethnic groups.

Add into the mix the question of language, and how that shapes national identity. A lot of times, the national language is the language of the former colonial power. French is spoken as the national language in many states in Western Africa, but not all of it. It's easy to spot the territories that Portugal colonized because those are the places where Portuguese is the official language: Brazil, East Timor, Mozambique, Angola, Cape Verde, Guinea-Bissau, Equatorial Guinea, and Sao Tome and Principe.

European languages in Africa are relics of the colonial age, and also the way that diverse ethnic groups are able to coalesce around one national identity. When the colonizer's language becomes the national language, you can unify different ethnic groups in countries that often have dozens, if not hundreds or thousands, of tribal languages.

National identities can be strong or weak, and they always take time to develop. The US has a diverse and broad national identity, and we've had hundreds of years to develop that identity. Also, our country grew gradually from 13 colonies to 50 states. Delaware became the first state in 1787, whereas Hawaii and Alaska joined the union in 1959! And, of course, while the US grew slowly, we didn't grow in a vacuum. As the US expanded its territory, we pushed Native American populations onto reservations or outright eliminated them—and annexed Hawaii.

African countries that were granted independence (often overnight) during the post-war period didn't have the liberty of slowly developing their national identity. To make matters worse, colonizers had often pitted different ethnic groups against one another in a classic 'divide and conquer' move—cultural wounds that are unlikely to heal quickly (if ever) following independence. This is what we saw between the Hutus and the Tutsis in the 1994 Rwandan genocide. Cultural divisions within a country can be a recipe for disaster when distrust turns into hatred, social exclusion, or even violence. Ideally, the government would try to resolve that tension, build peace, and bring everyone into the political process—but it doesn't always work out that way in practice.

As you read about weak states in the next section, think about what happens when the government works well for some people in the country, but not others, and especially when the difference between these two outcomes falls along ethnic lines. Imagine the social tension that would arise—and what might happen as a result.

⫸→ *Weak states*

Another way that you can sort nation-states is according to how well they are run. There's no such thing as a perfectly-run state. Every country in the world is way too large (even tiny ones like Guatemala, which is roughly the size of Tennessee) and complex to govern perfectly. Also, what do 'perfect' or 'well-run' even mean? And who gets to decide what those terms mean in practice? (The question of 'who gets to decide what is right and wrong?' is at the very foundation of US democracy.) I think we can agree that the US is pretty well-run, but of course there are huge disagreements about the decisions that the government makes. Some people disagree with the Supreme Court's decision on gay marriage. Others, the invasion of Iraq.

Anyway, my point is: there might not be a 'perfectly-run state', but a lot of them do pretty well. Well-run states have strong public institutions: courts, parliament, civil service, regulatory bodies, etc., which effectively counterbalance powerful private groups in society (elites, members of a particular group/tribe/industry, etc.). In theory—this balancing act leads to decisions that benefit *most* people in society, not just a few.

To achieve this, you need a government that is not too corrupt and has clear and coherent policies that provide for the needs of its citizens. Well-run states provide essential social services, like education and access to adequate (or even good!) healthcare. You'll see well-developed infrastructure, like electricity, sewage removal and running water in people's houses, and garbage being collected on trash day. Moreover, you'll see a healthy respect for the *rule of law*—meaning the process by which laws are made, a tendency for people to follow the law, and real consequences for those who don't. Creating a law-abiding society also depends on whether law enforcement agencies are free from corruption, and whether the courts are seen to be impartial and fair.

Be honest: where you live, how easy is it to take all of that stuff for granted? If you answered 'easy', I'd say that's a fairly good indication that you live in a well-run state.

Poorly-run states, on the other hand, don't ace the test when it comes to the factors I just named. Take, for example, the question of infrastructure. Poor infrastructure includes bad roads throughout the country—especially outside of the capital city. Imagine if all of the roads outside of Washington, DC were made out of dirt instead of asphalt (or, if they were paved, they were more 'pothole' than 'road').

Poor infrastructure can also mean a lack of bridges. In some countries, remote villages can be cut off for months on end if they're situated near a big river—especially during the rainy season. Imagine what would happen if you accidentally broke your leg in that village, and you couldn't get to the doctor!

Imagine not having electricity—or having electricity that you can only use during certain times of the day or for certain lengths of time. Many houses in the world don't have running water, or if there is water—you get sick if you drink it. It's estimated that only 2 half of the world's population get water through a piped connection—though the pipe is not necessarily in their house.

Many parts of the world lack the infrastructure for in-house sewage, so people have to go to the bathroom outside (usually not on a Western-style sit-down toilet). Even in the US, there 3 are an estimated 1.5 million people without full indoor plumbing. Poorly-run countries often can't provide garbage collection—so people have to burn it (which smells terrible), bury it, or throw it in the street (hello rats and dogs!).

Another hallmark of a weak state is a lack of adequate education. This shows up as a lack of school buildings, poorly-trained and poorly-paid teachers, and non-compulsory school attendance. Many children don't go to school because their parents can't afford the school uniforms, or because they need their kids to stay home to work in the fields. Girls are often pulled out of school for a myriad of reasons I'll get into later.

The same goes for health care. In poorly-run countries, there are not enough hospitals and clinics, health professionals aren't well-trained, there is not enough equipment or medicine, and you can't guarantee sanitary conditions in medical facilities.

The governments in most poorly-run countries are also corrupt—meaning that government officials steal directly from state funds or state enterprises. That money is then used for things that benefit themselves, their families, or the people that help keep them in office. Where there's high-level corruption, there's usually also low-level corruption. This is where ordinary people have to pay additional, informal fees (bribes) for everyday things like seeing the doctor, sending a child to school, getting a driver's license or getting a business permit.

When corruption eats away at a government's budget, it leaves less money to invest in the country, which compounds the problem of poor infrastructure, a lack of social services, education, healthcare, etc. And when citizens need to pay bribes to access those essential services, then they have less cash in hand to save for a rainy day (which benefits them) and to spend (which helps the economy, and results in more taxable income and therefore government revenue). The result? A population with no safety net and a government that doesn't have the money to provide it. It's a never-ending vicious cycle.

Corruption also leads to other problems for ordinary people. For example, when a corrupt government is bleeding cash and can't pay its military or police force, soldiers will use corruption themselves to supplement their income. Imagine if the police in your town were too busy collecting bribes to enforce the law. I've seen it happen! In Tajikistan, where I served as a diplomat, the police would stop cars just to get a bribe from them. Ironically, the police would never issue tickets for actual driving violations (like speeding), which meant that driving there was scary because no one ever followed the rules!

Corruption also leaves less money for training your police and providing them with the right equipment—meaning that actual criminals are rarely caught. And when they are, if the judicial system is underfunded, then justice becomes a commodity that can be bought and sold. In Guatemala, there is a 98 percent impunity rate for crime (meaning you don't get punished), which means that only two out of every 100 murderers actually go to jail. It happens because courts don't work well, the police force is poorly trained and equipped, and because narco-traffickers (a fancy name for drug cartels) use bribes and violence to ensure the cooperation of police officers and judges.

≫➔ *Fragile states*

Countries can (and do) function when they're weak—but not very well. So what about countries that are barely functioning at all? Yes, they exist! We call them *fragile states*. At the risk of oversimplifying a very complex issue…

How would you recognize a fragile state if you met one in a dark alley? Well, you'd be looking for minimal infrastructure, weak rule of law, virtually no social welfare services, and no security in some, or much, of the country's territory. The state simply isn't present in those areas—either it's too poor, or because an illicit group is in control instead.

Fragile governments are usually able to maintain control of their capital cities. There, maybe things don't work well (e.g. bad roads, corrupt officials, dilapidated schools and poorly-trained teachers and doctors), but it's better than nothing.

In contrast, areas without state presence (even local government) barely function at all. Forget about bad roads, sometimes it's *no roads*. For example, when I went on a work trip to the Democratic Republic of the Congo, I was told that there are only about 300 miles of road in the country's entire 905,968 square mile footprint. To give this some scale: imagine driving from Portland, Maine to Portland, Oregon and only seeing one mile of road the whole time.

In fragile states, communities are often unsafe for the people that live in them. If there are police, they often prey on the local population, demanding bribes, committing extrajudicial (outside of a legal process) killings and aligning themselves with illicit groups. The citizens who live in these areas simply don't see evidence of the government in their daily lives—in the form of schools, running water or medical clinics. Understandably, these areas are home to some of the poorest communities in the world. There, you'll find that non-governmental organizations (NGOs) and other civil society organizations (like the Red Cross or Habitat for Humanity) are doing most of the heavy lifting regarding basic service provision—often in peril of their own safety.

That's because where a central government doesn't have the power (meaning the cash, the skills or the authority) to control a particular region, the power vacuum will be filled by others. Sometimes it's by an NGO or charity, but other times it's by an illicit group—such as narco-trafficking gangs in Guatemala; or

Hezbollah, an Islamic militant group and political party, in Lebanon; warlords in Afghanistan; or tribal leaders in Yemen. Tribal leaders are not necessarily illicit actors, but they also don't officially represent the state government.

Like NGOs, these other groups often fill the role of 'basic social service provider', usually as a way of securing favor with the local population. Mexican drug cartels, including the powerful Sinaloa Cartel, are known for operating drug rehab facilities and building schools and churches in their territories.

But hang on, you say. If the power vacuums in fragile states are filled by groups that do a decent job of providing essential services for the people, what's the problem? Good question. The problem is precisely that states are meant to treat everyone as equals, without favoring a particular ethnicity, caste or social group.

Illicit groups in stateless regions set their own rules; they're free to treat the local population as they please and break the law without facing the consequences. There's nothing to stop them from trafficking drugs, guns and people (as modern-day slaves) with impunity. Terrorist organizations can undertake training, planning and fundraising with impunity. Gangs can extort protection money from businesses, commit murder, and rape women and children with impunity.

In areas without a state presence, there is *zero* rule of law. When there is no rule of law, the potential for ripple effects is enormous. Weak central governments often fall prey to a coup d'état or an insurgent group destabilizing the country; armed conflict and violence are all too common in fragile states.

The most fragile of the fragile states are called *failed states*. A failed state is exactly what it sounds like—a state that has stopped functioning, full stop. Whereas fragile states are often still in control of large swathes of the country (typically including the capital) and the citizens (by and large) recognize the authority of the state—a failed state is one where the central government has no power at all, or has simply stopped existing.

Somalia has long been a textbook example of a 'failed state' because it hasn't had a functioning central government since the early 1990s. Clans, militias, Islamic insurgents and neighboring countries have been vying for power there since 1992. In 2016, it had somewhat successful parliamentary elections, and promising presidential elections in 2017—but it still doesn't have a functioning economy, most of its infrastructure has collapsed, and famine and violence are commonplace.

If you didn't believe me when you started reading this chapter, hopefully by now you'll have realized: running a country is complicated. And running a country *well* is even more complicated. When you get out there into the world, you'll find that there are lots of talented citizens in these countries who have the skills to tackle th eir country's challenges, and you will hopefully have the opportunity to support them in their effort.

Right. So, now that you're an expert on nations, states and nation-states (of every variety), let's head to *Chapter 2* to talk about the different ways you can engage with *your* nation-state.

REMEMBER!

- A nation-state is a political and a cultural entity
- The Treaty of Westphalia transformed global relations
- Developing countries have weak economies and poor socioeconomic performance
- National identity is an important part of the nation-state
- Weak and fragile states are countries that are poorly run
- The effects of colonization are still being felt today.

LET'S TALK COLONIZATION...

THE LEGACY OF COLONIZATION is the crucial backdrop for everything we've just talked about. Keep this in mind because, in your career as a globe-trotting ordinary hero, I guarantee you're going to step off a plane in one of these countries one day. Former colonies tend to fall into the 'developing countries' column—and those are the places that most need the talents of global citizens like you.

Colonization is when a country makes another territory or country its property. The colonial power controls the colony's land, government, economy and people. The practice of colonization dates back to Ancient Greek times, but it was in the late 1400s that Western Europeans started claiming territories across the Americas, Africa, Asia and the Middle East. Japan was also a colonial power over other Asian countries like Taiwan and Korea.

Colonization was a rotten deal for those colonized, to put it mildly. Colonies are conquered and maintained using force and violence. Once installed, the colonial power was usually too busy extracting and exporting the colony's natural resources to bother with investing in the colony, its infrastructure and its people. Worse, indigenous populations were often treated like slaves, forced to work for the colonizers with few or no legal rights. This means that when the colonizer withdrew, newly-independent countries usually lacked the human capital, economy, civil society and infrastructure to be able to effectively run their own countries.

In Africa, colonial powers *intended* to withdraw slowly to help the new countries successfully make the transition to independence. However, they withdrew quickly in response to increasing civil unrest (because of the terrible way they had treated the locals). We'll never know how things might have turned out if the colonial powers had stayed to train local leadership in the new state (just as we'll never know what would have happened had they never colonized those places to begin with).

In many countries that we now consider as 'poorly-run', a dictator took control of the country for a long time after independence. (Some countries held democratic elections right after independence, but then the democratically elected president was overthrown in a *coup d'état,* often by the military.)

These dictators stayed in power for decades, preying on their citizens and using what resources were available to make themselves and their family and friends very rich, rather than investing in the country. In this way, the dictators were just the new face of colonialism. In fact, many post-colonial countries still have dictators or pseudo-dictators in power to this day.

So, next time you hear someone grumbling about how poorly-run a developing country is—remind them that a mere 85 years after US independence, we slid into an ugly civil war, during which we lost more soldiers than in both World Wars combined.

Chapter 2
Your government
and you

The nutshell...
Being a global superhero starts with getting involved with
your government at home: through voting, running for office
and getting involved in civic activism. Civil society and an
independent media are vital to creating a healthy, functioning
democracy.

What kind of job could this be?
Campaign manager on a political campaign • Grassroots
organizer for a community organization • Blogger/journalist
for a news outlet • Campaign communications expert on a
political campaign • Advocacy officer for an NGO

MY ADVICE TO ANY BUDDING GLOBAL CITIZEN IS THIS:
if you want to get to grips with how the world works, then
you've got to start with your own government. You know that

saying 'think globally, act locally'? The two go hand in hand—and the first step towards being an effective global citizen is to be an engaged citizen at home.

Decisions get made in the halls of the US Government that affect the global issues that you care about. Decisions such as whether we go to war, how many aid dollars we send overseas (and what we're allowed to spend them on), whether we sign key treaties that deal with trade, human rights and the environment.

Here's another reason to engage with the US political system: there are billions of people out there in the world who suffer from poverty, conflict, violence and a lack of access to essential services (such as clean water, decent health care and quality education)—and some of them live in the US. Your country needs you to stand up for social justice, and make sure that our society works *for everyone*.

HAVE YOUR SAY!

STILL NOT CONVINCED that being invested in domestic politics is in any way relevant to your career as a global superhero? Allow me to lay some sobering facts at your door.

Your parents pay taxes. If you have a job, *you* pay taxes. If you do, that means you have a direct role in the functioning of the government. That's because the percentage of your paycheck that is withheld for state and federal taxes helps fund community services (including public schools, public hospitals, libraries, roads, bridges, fire departments, police, etc.), national services (e.g. social security and the military) and the government's operational costs (e.g. staff salaries and paperclips).

So just how much money does the US Government need? Are you sitting down? The national budget runs to *trillions of dollars every year.* And does the tax that the government collects fund all of its spending? Nope. Not even close. Since 1789, the government has had at least some level of debt. In the 1950s, we had about $2 trillion. Today, the national debt is almost $20 trillion.

Whether the government should be in debt (and if so, just how much debt is *too much debt*) is an important debate in the halls of government (and despite what anyone might tell you, there are no easy answers).

But what does this have to do with you? Well, the point about taxation is: because you're footing the bill for the government, the government is motivated to look after your needs and your wants (a nice thing about living in a democracy). By voting, you can have your say on how the government spends your money.

The tax-and-spend relationship is the most direct link between a government and its citizens, and as you travel the world, you'll find that different countries define this relationship in their own unique ways. For example, taxes in European countries tend to be a lot higher than in the US, and in turn, those citizens demand a lot more services (like free health care) from their governments.

On the other hand, there are countries (mostly developing countries), where the government's budget is funded mainly from government-owned enterprises and from the sale of the country's natural resources (oil, minerals). In these cases, the government doesn't always need to respond to the needs of its citizens because it doesn't depend on them for funding.

⟫⟶ *Vote, darn it!*

Heard of the Boston Tea Party? Let's figure out why English citizens would chuck tons of perfectly good tea into Boston Harbor in the fine year of 1773. It's because the colonies (as we were then) were sick and tired of *taxation without representation*. In other words, colonists had to pay taxes to the crown but had no representation in the British Parliament, where the laws that affected their lives were being made. Instead of paying the new Tea Tax, they sent 45 tons of the stuff to the bottom of the harbor—an act of defiance that led up to the American Revolution.

The Founding Fathers bequeathed you a unique system of government. The more able it is to represent your views, the

Taxation without representation

The motto 'taxation without representation' is alive and well in the District of Columbia (*aka* Washington DC, our nation's capital). Residents of DC pay taxes, but because DC is a district and not a state, they don't have a voting member of Congress!

more stable it becomes. So ask yourself this: if you're a citizen that pays taxes, shouldn't you also be a citizen *that votes*?

Be honest: what did you get more excited about? Becoming old enough to drive, or becoming old enough to vote? Because frankly, when it comes to your freedom, each is as important as the other.

Here's the deal: for US citizens, once you turn 18, you have the right to vote in open and free elections where the outcome is not known beforehand. (In presidential elections, because of the US's Electoral College system, the winner won't necessarily get the majority of the votes or necessarily the most popular votes, but they can still win.)

You can vote for your preferred candidate at all levels of government and, even though the presidential elections always get the most attention and voter turnout, all levels of government are significant. So make sure to get out and vote in every election, not just for the president. At the local level, we get to vote for our county or municipal representatives, and our city's mayor. At the state level, we vote for the state's governor and state legislators. And at the national level, we elect our Congressional representatives and the President. We also get to vote on ballot measures, like whether to legalize marijuana, whether to reform the education system or to allow physician-assisted suicide. The ballot system varies by state, but it's a great way for you to help shape the laws that impact your life.

Your government will only listen to you if you raise your voice. So if you want clean air, clean water, good schools, safe roads, fair taxes and the right to choose what to do with your brain and your body, then register to vote. Confused about where to start? Your local DMV (Department of Motor Vehicles) office can give you guidance—or check out Rock the Vote, a non-profit organization set up to help young people get engaged in the political process.

⋙⟶ *Get your name on a ballot*

"When you don't have a plan, it can be a lot easier to take risks," according to my friend Rebecca Wall. She's an excellent example of someone whose path to finding a global career was marked by a lot of interesting twists and turns. Today, she's working for the Department of State in Thailand as a Foreign Service Officer. But since graduating from college, she's worked as a waitress, bummed around the world for a few years with a backpack, worked as a waitress, taught English in South Korea, worked as a waitress (again!), got a graduate degree in International Relations, took the law school entrance exam, decided not to go to law school, worked as a waitress, and (wait for it) ran for State Representative in her home state of Pennsylvania. Not necessarily in that order, of course. As she explains: "So there I was, 24, living at home, waitressing and still no plan in sight. I took the LSATs but wasn't sure that law school was the right track for me. So when the opportunity

ARE YOU ROCKING THE VOTE?

"Decisions are made by those who show up," warns Aaron Sorkin (American screenwriter, producer and playwright). He nailed the point—and yet in 2016, one in three eligible voters stayed at home. What does that tell you about who our government is working for?

5

to run for State Representative popped up, I thought *sure, what the heck! It beats waitressing!* So I ran for office. It was a close race. My staff and I ran a great campaign where we knocked on over 60,000 doors and had lots of volunteers and raised oodles of money and got 45 percent of the vote. But we lost." As disappointed as she was, it was a valuable experience, because it gave her a glimpse of what it might be like to make a career out of helping others.

If you're considering a career of civic consciousness, then running for office is one of the most ambitious and most direct ways of making an impact. Being a politician takes a lot of energy, dedication and thick skin! But if you're interested, start now! Start with your student body association or local government and work your way up. If you're old enough to vote, then you're old enough to run for office. We've had state legislators and mayors elected before they were even allowed to drink, and people elected to Congress in their thirties. Presidents Teddy Roosevelt, John F. Kennedy, Bill Clinton and Barack Obama all took office in their 40s. Still think you're too young to throw your hat in the ring?

If you're not inspired to run for office yourself, but still want to be involved in politics, you could work for a political campaign. You can either find a candidate that you want to work for (i.e. someone you believe in!), or you can search for job openings on campaigns and apply for those that sound interesting and match your skill set (whether this is editing speeches or compiling statistics). And, if all else fails, volunteer as an intern for a campaign. There's a good reason why I'm a true believer in internships (you'll find out what it is in *Part Three*)!

INDIVIDUAL ACTIVISM

VOTING IS A GREAT WAY TO MAKE SURE that the government is listening to you—but it's not the *only* way. You can be a civic activist at any time, not just at election time. If you're passionate about issues like human trafficking, conflict, trade, refugees, or gender equality—you can make your voice heard even when your feet are still on US soil. You can take action on issues at a local level (such as your city's budget, domestic violence awareness, environmental regulations affecting your community, or youth homelessness) or national issues (such as gun control or abortion). Activism is a 24/7 hotline to your government. Best of all, your passionate activism can take any one of a number of forms. Here are a few to consider:

⋙⟶ *Exercise your freedom of tweet*

As a citizen, you have the right to voice your opinion about what's happening in government. Anytime. Period. In fact, your freedom of speech is constitutionally guaranteed, more or less from the time you learn to talk. Even before you're old enough to vote, you have the right to contact your elected officials to ask a question or tell them what you think about an issue. If Congress is debating a new bill, you can contact your congressperson and express your views before it becomes law. You can talk to them about any issue really, especially if you feel an issue *should be* on the agenda, and it's not already there.

Bear in mind: they won't *necessarily* listen to you as an individual. But think of what would happen if enough of their constituents (the people they represent) *all* contacted them to deliver the same message. Chances are, they would sit up and take note, because being responsive to their constituents is a great way of ensuring they get re-elected. (Don't forget to keep track of your representative's voting patterns on the issues that matter to you so you can make an informed decision the next time you're in a voting booth!)

Bottom line: if an issue matters to you, no matter what it is, then stand up and be counted. Thanks to the internet, it's really quick and easy to make contact with your representative—whether by email, social media or even by visiting their local office!

⋙⟶ *Take to the streets*

In the US, as in many other countries around the world, citizens communicate directly with their government by holding public protests and rallies. Freedom of assembly is one of the fundamental freedoms guaranteed by the US Constitution. Lucky us!

If you've never been to a protest, let me tell you that it can be a really electrifying experience! Being surrounded by hundreds (sometimes thousands) of other people, who are just as passionate and vocal about an issue as you, generates a feeling of community, of positivity and of possibility. It's the perfect antidote to the sneaking suspicion (that we all feel sometimes) that one person's voice will never change the system. It's also really fun to make colorful signs with catchy slogans! And it's not only about feeling politically empowered—you might meet your new best friend on a march, encounter new ideas you'd never considered, or hear your favorite celebrity speaking up for the issues that are close to your heart. I saw George Clooney speak at a Save Darfur rally, and I listened to the Flaming Lips play at an environmental rally. (Obviously that's not the only reason to join a protest—but it's a nice bonus!)

Do protests work? Some people are a bit cynical when it comes to this question, and I get that. I do. There's no easy answer. Rallies and marches definitely played a vital role in the civil rights movement in the sixties. It's pretty clear that so many people taking to the streets, again and again, had a direct influence on changes in government policy.

On the other hand, the government isn't actually obliged to listen to protesters. For example, before the US invaded Iraq in 2003, thousands of people protested in the US, as did millions around the world, but our government still decided to invade.

In those cases, it's not always clear what a protest ultimately achieves—but that doesn't mean it's not worth doing. At the end of the day, protests are about connection and amplification. What I mean by that is that they are an excellent way to demonstrate the strength of your ideas and feelings in numbers, in the form of actual people on the street. Also, if your protest is large enough, then the media will cover it. Once your protest makes the news, your message will be amplified across the nation—meaning that more people will pay attention. (Just make sure the media is covering your protest for the right reasons: peaceful demonstrations are the best way to get your message across.)

⫸⟶ Join the movement

In recent years, an increasing number of social movements have started harnessing the power of the internet to bring massive numbers of people into a virtual conversation around an issue. Some websites are dedicated to a particular problem (such as lastdaysofivory.com). Others allow you to post and sign any number of petitions around current issues (see for example moveon.org). Still others (such as movements.org) offer themselves as 'skill crowdsourcing' platforms: a virtual water-cooler where you can donate your amazing talents (in areas such as design, translation or social media) to those activists living in closed societies (i.e. under a dictatorship) that need support to strengthen their cause.

Or why not start your own? Leverage the power of social media to raise public awareness around your issue and connect with like-minded people who can amplify your message. Start a Facebook page. Coin a Twitter hashtag. Launch a discussion group on LinkedIn. Remember: strength in numbers isn't always measured in feet on the street—virtual buzz counts for a lot, too.

Decisions are being made every day. So how will you choose to show up as the concerned and engaged citizen that you are? Looking across the landscape of US society, you'll see people who are engaged in activism act in different ways: voting, emailing their Congressional representatives, forming online social movements, etc. Raising their voice in defense of their values and beliefs. Raising their voice in defense of those who cannot. If you don't turn your values into activism, other people's voices will be the ones the government listens to. Think about it.

A LARGE AND CIVIL SOCIETY

ANY GROUP OF PEOPLE (large or small) can organize themselves into political parties, book groups, religious institutions, bowling leagues, universities, knitting groups, Rotary Clubs, trade unions, social enterprises, yoga classes, or businesses. Some of these exist for purely commercial or entertainment purposes; others represent the needs and the interests of citizens (and some do both). For example, there's the World Wildlife Fund, Save the Bay, the National Collegiate Athletic Association and others. They can also be focused on the business sector: for example, chambers of commerce and business associations advocate against corruption and for better services.

When I talk about 'civil society', I mean organizations and institutions that represent citizens but are *not* part of the government. Instead of individual activism, civil society is *organized activism*. No matter whether they are for-profit or not-for-profit, the aim of *every* civil society organization is to influence the government, create positive social change, provide social services and/or represent a particular subset of the population. Healthy civil society is a crucial ingredient in a stable state. How?

Our government consists of a carefully designed set of checks and balances. Each arm of the government holds the other arms accountable. In a way, civil society's most important role is that of an external watchdog: holding the whole of the government responsible for making sound decisions that benefit the majority of the population. That's why civil society is a vital part of any well-functioning democracy (more on that point soon).

How does civil society perform that role? Well, it can be an advocate (putting pressure on the government around a certain issue), a liaison between the government and the people (to foster understanding and dialogue), or even run projects both at home and abroad (this is called 'implementing', in the biz).

Sometimes people use the term 'NGO' (non-governmental organization) as a kind of shorthand for a civil society institution. At last count, the US has almost 1.5 million institutions categorized as non-profits, which include NGOs, non-profit organizations, religious organizations and other voluntary organizations. Want that another way? We've got one civil society organization for every 220 people in the US. You can't even fill up a jumbo jet with 220 people!

THE FIRST AMENDMENT

SPEAKING OF FREE SPEECH, the US boasts a very independent, reliable and inquisitive media that is not controlled by the government. Journalists in the US are free to report on our government and its politicians, even if they write or say critical things about them. Freedom of speech means we have the freedom to access information, and that's vital for maintaining an informed and engaged civil society that holds the government accountable for its actions. (That's why the media is sometimes considered a part of civil society, and why its 'watchdog' function makes it worth mentioning in any discussion of holding our national leaders to account.)

Compared with other countries, our civil society is reasonably healthy and well-protected. It's a hallmark of our stability as a nation-state. In fragile states, the government often sees civil society organizations, the media, and even private business as a threat to its power. When that happens, the government does all it can to limit civil society's ability to function (by cutting off funding or making it nearly impossible to legally register). As a result, ordinary people lose an important means for voicing their concerns, and for getting the support that they need to live secure and decent lives.

When civil society is under threat, you can usually guarantee that so too is a free and impartial media. Want more evidence that the US is relatively stable? Freedom of the press is protected by the Constitution, just like freedom of speech and assembly. In more fragile states, independent journalists (i.e. ones who don't work for government-run media outlets) are intimidated into silence (often through illegal means). In some countries, there are stringent libel laws (and other restrictive media-related laws) where journalists can't legally say anything negative about the government. Some governments use violence, even murder, to silence outspoken journalists.

Civil society and a free press ensure that a broad range of ideas and perspectives are heard, that the government is held to account, and that no one gets left behind—especially those voices that tend to be marginalized within a society. They're like the big spoon that every nation-state needs to keep their democracies well-stirred. As grumpy naturalist Edward Abbey once suggested: "Society is like a stew. If you don't stir it up every once in a while, then a layer of scum floats to the top."

In many developing countries, civil society is more than just a watchdog—it acts as a direct provider of social and welfare services (such as education and health care) where the state is too weak (or too poor) to provide them. For a global citizen like you, working for a civil society organization or NGO can be one of the most effective ways to participate in raising the quality of life for the poor and marginalized of our world.

REMEMBER!

- Start your career in international affairs by thinking globally and acting locally
- Government is accountable to the people who fund it through taxes
- Voting is essential—you can't be a global citizen if you don't vote
- Don't like any of the candidates on offer? Run for office!
- Engage your government through civic activism on social media, in the streets, by contacting your representatives or signing an online petition
- Civil society and the media are an essential part of well-functioning democracies.

CHAPTER 3
NATION-STATES IN
A GLOBAL SYSTEM

THE NUTSHELL...

The global system has many interlocking layers and players. The US Government has a number of arms that deal with foreign policy, including the Department of State, the Department of Defense and USAID. Governments also engage in other forms of international cooperation through multilateral organizations. In recent years, international power dynamics have been increasingly shaped by non-state actors.

WHAT KIND OF JOB COULD THIS BE?

Foreign service officer with the US Government • Intelligence analyst in the military • Public affairs consultant for a private company • Policy advisor at an NGO • Geospatial analyst for a management consulting firm

ACCORDING TO THE US DEPARTMENT OF STATE, there are (as I write) 195 nation-states that are sovereign over their own territory. No state can legally claim sovereignty over another. And frankly, if every single one of them wanted to (now and forevermore) mind their own business and not talk to each other, you could stop reading this book, right now. Seriously. If countries never needed to interact, we wouldn't need to think about global affairs.

But just how likely is that to happen? Sometimes two countries will want to cooperate with each other (for example, by trading goods and services with each other, or swapping tourists in the summer holidays). Other times, two countries will disagree with each other, and need to resolve that disagreement in some way. But of course it's not just two countries—*it's all 195 countries* that need to cooperate, avoid conflict, manage change, share power and promote the collective welfare of the global human community.

For that reason, nation-states need a system they can use to interact with one another—one that is reliable, coherent and rational. Just like each government has dedicated departments for dealing with various domestic issues (think: transportation, education and health), it also has departments that deal with different aspects of the international system.

You might be asking yourself: *Why all those different departments? Why doesn't the President just take charge of all these things?* I hear you. After all, the President is meant to be the main representative of our country abroad, right? Well, it's really a question of practicality. Because the list of international issues we're dealing with on any given day is longer than your arm, no single person can take the lead on all of them. Nor should they, since doing so successfully would require that person to be an expert in a huge range of skill sets (including law, economics, technology, trade, finance or security). Because no one person can do it all, that means good news for you! If there's a globe, there's a job in global affairs waiting for you. Ready? Let's go.

Government foreign policy

Every sovereign government decides its own policies, which define what a country *believes* and what it *does*. Domestic policy covers a government's work within its national boundaries, and includes laws and government programs on education, health care, the environment and taxation. Foreign policy covers the decisions and actions made by the government to achieve its goals in the rest of the world through the international system. Think of it this way: if the world were a playground, a country's foreign policy reflects how it wants to play with the other countries and their toys.

The current stated goal of US foreign policy is to advance freedom for the benefit of the people in the US and the international community by helping to build and sustain a more democratic, secure and prosperous world composed of well-governed states that respond to the needs of their people, reduce widespread poverty and act responsibly within the international system. That seems like a pretty good goal to me!

The President, in coordination with the Cabinet and Congress, determines the US's foreign policy. As you might expect, our ideas about foreign policy evolve over time. For ages, our policy was *isolationist*, which means we tried not to get too involved in what was going on in other countries. With the onset of World War I (and to an even greater extent, World War II), our foreign policy changed to being more *interventionist*, which means we were more likely to get involved in the affairs of other countries.

For reasons we'll discuss shortly, other countries now even *expect* the US to take a lead role in ensuring global justice and peace, which means we have intervened in the affairs of other countries quite a lot. And, when we do—some countries appreciate it, and others resent it.

More recently in the US and across Europe, we see a growing wave of isolationism again due to the (real or perceived) injustices of globalization and global migration. However, in contrast to the late 19th century, the political and economic ripple effects of this shift are being felt far and wide. Simply put: it's easier to be isolationist when you're not already globally connected, as we are today. It is too soon to tell how or if the global order will be reshaped in the next coming years, but suffice it to say that the international system is constantly evolving and complex—more so today than ever before.

* * * * *

So who decides our foreign policy? The President has a lot of the power when it comes to foreign policy, but needs Congressional support because the government budget is agreed upon between the Executive Branch and Congress, and implementing our foreign policy takes money!

In order to implement foreign policy and interact with other governments, each government has a series of international departments and agencies. Elsewhere, departments are often called 'ministries'. In the US, the big three foreign policy bodies are: the Department of State (also known as the State Department); the US Agency for International Development (USAID) and the Department of Defense (DOD). We'll go into more detail on all of those shortly. Before we do, let's talk security.

The National Security Council (NSC) is another body that deals with foreign policy. Its part of the Executive Office of the President, and its job is to advise and assist the President on foreign policy and national security issues. The NSC is hugely important, because it brings together the top civil servants (e.g. senior national security advisors and cabinet members) in one room to talk about global issues. The NSC's job isn't only to come up with policies, but also to help coordinate the implementation of the policies throughout the government.

The *National Security Strategy* is updated every few years, and is available to read online. Another interesting foreign policy read, if you want a blueprint for the United States diplomatic and development efforts abroad, is the *Quadrennial Diplomacy and Development Review*, which is jointly written by the State Department and USAID. Interested in finding out more? Do a quick internet search to find the latest version.

Why are we talking about *national* security in the context of our *foreign* policy? Because absolutely everything is connected. What happens abroad affects our lives at home. This is a lesson the US learned in World War II (WWII), where not caring about 'foreign affairs' in the 1920s and 1930s (after the First World War) set the stage for fascism and gave rise to WWII.

Poverty and war abroad lead to instability whose ripple effects can be felt in our communities. Climate change threatens the livelihoods of everyone on the planet, and it doesn't give a damn about national borders. In this way, it's useful to think about foreign policy as a type of enlightened self-interest: by focusing on global defense, global diplomacy and global development; by working towards more democratic, secure and prosperous lives for everyone on the planet, we safeguard the security and prosperity of the people in the US.

That's why our National Security Strategy includes global defense, diplomacy and development (the three Ds), through the work of the State Department, USAID and DOD. Now let's look at how each works in greater detail.

DEPARTMENT OF STATE

OUR LEAD FOREIGN AFFAIRS AGENCY is called the Department of State. It is the body that formulates and executes foreign policy, and maintains diplomatic relations with other countries.

Diplomatic relations are interactions between governments. Think of it in terms of relationships: some countries are BFFs, some are just friends (with or without benefits), some are more like casual acquaintances, some occasionally disagree, and some are 'frenemies'. Sometimes, two countries will downright despise

DID YOU KNOW?

The Department of State got its name because, in addition to foreign affairs, it was also initially tasked to house key documents, such as the Great Seal, and to maintain national records.

each other and cut off formal diplomatic relations. Even when that happens, however, low-level interactions can still occur (like the movement of goods and people between the two). When things really go sour, one country can impose trade and other economic sanctions on another (an aggressive form of diplomacy meant to punish a country for so-called 'bad behavior').

Diplomatic relations allow states to peacefully co-exist (even if they're not BFFs). One of my colleagues in Tajikistan often talked about the Tajik civil war of the 1990s and the unpopular dictator who remained in power there since he 'won' the civil war. Her insight was that the people let him stay in power because 'a bad peace is better than a good war'. This is true of most contexts— even a bad diplomatic relationship is better than war.

⫸──▶ Diplomacy in action

One of the most famous cases of diplomacy maintaining a bad peace is called the Cuban Missile Crisis. The clue is in the name: it was a crisis about missiles in Cuba. This was one of the many crazy and scary confrontations between the US and the Soviet Union during the Cold War. We'll discuss the Cold War shortly, but for now: the Cuban Missile Crisis was the closest we've ever come to outright nuclear war.

It was the fall of 1962, and Fidel Castro had overthrown the Cuban Government in a communist revolution. The US was un-happy about this because he was an ally of our Cold War nemesis, the Soviet Union. (Google 'Bay of Pigs' to find out the extent to which we tried to show our displeasure!) The Soviets, with their new buddy in the Western Hemisphere, saw an opportunity to get the upper hand by putting nuclear missiles in Cuba, a mere 90 miles off the coast of Florida. Needless to say, things didn't turn out as the Soviets had hoped—a political and military standoff kicked off when the Americans sent a naval blockade to stop the missiles from reaching Cuba.

Luckily, after almost two weeks of this tense stalemate – the world on the brink of nuclear war – the Americans and Soviets reached a diplomatic settlement. The Soviets agreed to not station nuclear missile on Cuba, and we agreed not to invade the island. Nuclear war averted! Diplomacy in action!

⇢ *Types of staff*

The Secretary of State (who is the head of the Department of State) is the President's primary foreign policy advisor, and their office is in the main State Department in Washington, DC. Thinking about your future career in international affairs? Well, many State Department employees are *Civil Servants* who work in Washington, primarily on foreign policy issues. I was a State Department Civil Servant for several years and thought it was a great gig!

The State Department also has a *Foreign Service,* who are the State Department employees that work abroad in embassies, consulates and other diplomatic missions. Foreign Service Officers are also known as *diplomats.* The head of the Embassy and the big boss of all of the diplomats within a foreign country (excluding active combat military personnel) is called the *Ambassador.* The *Deputy Chief of Mission* (DCM) is the second in charge after the Ambassador and acts as the Ambassador in their absence (at which point they're called the *Charge d'Affaires*).

According to the State Department: *The mission of a US diplomat in the Foreign Service is to promote peace, support prosperity and protect US citizens while advancing the interests of the US abroad.* In a nutshell, diplomats are responsible for

6

undertaking the activities that help us achieve our foreign policy goal. How do they do this? One way is through meetings: lots and lots of meetings! The Ambassador and the DCM regularly meet with high-level host country officials, which could include the president or prime minister. Foreign Service Officers regularly meet with ministers (i.e. heads of government departments and agencies in a country) and their staff. Diplomats also meet with members of the business community, civil society and members of the international community.

US diplomats also support US citizens living in the host country with a range of support services. One of these services is that each Embassy has a number that US citizens can call if they're in trouble or lose their passport—remember this next time you travel abroad!

In addition to its Civil Servants and Foreign Service Officers, the State Department (and all other government agencies) also hires independent contractors to work directly for the US Government. Government contractors working for the government do not have the same benefits as direct hires but often have similar rights and responsibilities.

ONE IS NOT ENOUGH

The US Government doesn't have one Foreign Service—it has four! The biggest and most well-known one is at the State Department. The second largest is the USAID Foreign Service. Both the US Department of Agriculture and the Commerce Department also have their own Foreign Services. Other US Government agencies and departments, including (but not limited to) the Department of Justice, the Drug Enforcement Agency, and DOD, also send their employees to work abroad, but not through a formalized Foreign Service. Check out *Chapter 16* for more information on the Foreign Service—including how to join it!

No discussion about the Foreign Service would be complete without mentioning the local staff. Foreign Service Nationals (FSNs) are citizens of the host country, and they are absolutely the backbone of the work of each mission. While US Foreign Service Officers do 'tours' in foreign countries (lasting 1–4 years each), FSNs often work for the US Embassy for *decades*. They provide essential continuity regarding the institutional knowledge of US Government agencies and departments abroad and have the best understanding of their own country's history, culture, politics, etc. They're our insider knowledge and our cultural translators all wrapped up into one—and our work wouldn't succeed without their support. It's funny to think that some of our most important foreign policy team members aren't even from the US!

⟫⟶ *Political appointments*

Like other government agencies, including USAID and DOD, the State Department also has some employees who are *political appointees* (rather than career government employees). Political appointees are nominated by the President and serve for a limited amount of time (usually for the duration of the President's administration). My sister-in-law was a political appointee at the Federal Emergency Management Agency (aka FEMA) during Hurricane Katrina. As the Deputy Director of Communications, she stayed in New Orleans for over two months, helping the government and the media communicate about what was going on.

Most Ambassadors are career Foreign Service Officers, but some are political appointees. Usually, the Ambassadorships that are political appointees are given to strong allies of the administration and are often perceived as 'rewards' for political support or substantial financial contributions to election campaigns. Ambassadors who are appointed tend to head to appealing countries that are geopolitically significant (such as France or England). That said, there are a lot of political appointee positions way, way,

way below the Ambassador level. Guess what? Anyone can apply for these, so go ahead and throw your hat in the ring! **7**

⋙⟶ *Bricks and mortar*

There are 270 US embassies, consulates and other diplomatic missions throughout the world. We have diplomatic relations with (and embassies in) the vast majority of countries in the world, but not all of them. We don't maintain diplomatic relations with Iran (although the Government of Pakistan represents Iranian interests in the US, and the Swiss represent ours in Tehran), North Korea (we have low-level communication but no third-party government intermediary) and Bhutan (though the diplomatic relationship is informal and cordial, and maintained by the Government of India).

The US also doesn't have formal diplomatic relations with Taiwan even though we do have commercial and cultural relations with them. We don't recognize Taiwan as a sovereign nation because China claims Taiwan as part of Chinese territory, a claim which is rejected by the independent Government of Taiwan (which governs Taiwan as a sovereign nation). Trading with Taiwan without having formal diplomatic relations with them is our way of avoiding diplomatic conflict with China.

In 2015, the US normalized diplomatic relations with Cuba and reopened its Embassy there. Before that, when we didn't have formal diplomatic ties with Cuba, the relationship was maintained through the Swiss Embassy.

In large countries, in addition to the US Embassy in each foreign capital, we also maintain US consulates in other major cities. Consulates are mostly there to be a resource to US citizens living nearby and so that citizens of the host country can apply for visas to the US. Washington, DC plays home to the embassies of 176 foreign countries, and many of those also have consulates in other **8** major US cities.

United States Agency for International Development

THE LEAD AGENCY ON INTERNATIONAL DEVELOP-MENT issues is the US Agency for International Development (USAID). In line with our foreign policy goal, its mission is to "partner to end extreme poverty and promote resilient, democratic societies while advancing our security and prosperity." Development (in case you're wondering!) means assistance to governments, organizations and individuals in other countries to help reduce and alleviate poverty and inequality and improve health, education and employment opportunities. Development supports the goals that the US thinks should be global priorities for creating a peaceful world—such as democracy, human rights, gender equality, free markets and political stability.

President Kennedy created USAID in 1961 with the express intent of countering the influence of the Union of Soviet Socialist Republics (called the USSR or the Soviet Union) during the Cold War. Although the Soviet Union collapsed long ago, development is still a cornerstone of US foreign policy. If this sounds odd, then think about the difference between stable vs. fragile states: people are less likely to join terrorist organizations or gangs, go to war or commit crimes if they are able to provide for their families and have hope in the future. That's why development is a vital foreign policy tool: it helps with our ultimate goal of increased national security because it decreases the possibility of terrorism and other kinds of conflict.

Development aid can also give us diplomatic leverage with some countries (in an 'I'll scratch your back if you scratch mine' sort of way). With other nations, especially those with whom we do not have a strong diplomatic relationship, it's an important foot in the door—creating goodwill and an opportunity for further conversation.

We'll talk more about development in *Chapter 5,* but in a nut-shell: if our foreign policy sets out how we influence the world through a combination of carrots and sticks—then development is a carrot, all the way.

So what does USAID do to achieve its aims? Well, it helps countries to improve things like economic growth and trade, agriculture and food security, health, education, democracy and governance, climate change resilience, water and sanitation and gender equality. Development assistance can be long-term (like helping a developing country create and implement a national education curriculum), or short-term (like training journalists to do investigative reporting). Development can also be in the form of humanitarian assistance, which is a response to natural and manmade disasters, such as providing emergency food aid or temporary housing.

⫸⟶ *Types of staff*

The head of USAID is called the *USAID Administrator.* The Administrator is not a cabinet-level position, so the USAID Administrator reports to the Secretary of State, instead of the President. I often get asked whether USAID is part of the State Department and I think that it's this reporting setup that confuses people. USAID is an independent agency, but it and the State Department coordinate very closely, and there's often discussion about whether the two should be merged.

Take note here of potential career opportunities—USAID has three main types of employees who are US Citizens: Civil Servants, USAID Foreign Service Officers and contractors. It also has some other staff types, such as Foreign Service Limited, fellows, service agreements, etc. As you'd expect, the bulk of USAID staff works abroad. I'm a USAID Foreign Service Officer serving a four-year tour in Armenia.

The head of a USAID Mission in a foreign country is called the *Mission Director,* and the second-in-charge is known as the *Deputy Mission Director.* Recall that the Ambassador is in charge of all non-combatant US Government personnel in that country, so the USAID Mission Director reports to the Ambassador.

⟫⟶ *Bricks and mortar*

After the 1998 bombing of the US Embassies in Nairobi (Kenya) and Dar es Salaam (Tanzania), the State Department started building New Embassy Compounds (NECs), which are more fortified than the old US Embassies. USAID is now usually co-located with other US Government institutions in the NECS. These buildings are typically located on the outskirts of town, instead of downtown where many Embassies used to be. It's safer, but it takes longer to get to meetings!

⟫⟶ *How we work*

USAID carries out development projects through *implementing partners*. For instance, if we identify the need for a country to improve their efforts to fight human trafficking, we would work with an implementer (the International Organization for Migration, for example) to create shelters for people who were trafficked, provide training to the police and border officials and work with the host country government to improve legislation around trafficking. Implementing partners are typically NGOs, but can also be for-profit development companies and international organizations (like the UN). (See *Annex One* for a list of international NGOs.)

In addition to managing projects, USAID Foreign Service Officers spend a lot of time meeting with host country government officials to build relationships and ensure that our projects respond to the country's needs and are implemented smoothly. Even though USAID pays for the projects and they support overarching US foreign policy goals, we always make sure to get host-country support and buy-in and, sometimes, host country governments even directly implement our development projects.

WHERE DOES THE MONEY GO?

Our foreign aid budget covers diplomacy and development (under USAID and State), and the Department of Defense budget includes, well, defense. So when it comes time to dole out the national budget, who do you think gets the most money? Prepare yourself. As of early 2016, over 50 percent of the US Government's annual discretionary budget and almost 20 percent of the non-discretionary budget goes to defense. Whereas the US Government spends only about one percent of the federal budget on foreign aid. 9 According to *The New Yorker*, "The US Government spends less on aid to the world's poor every year than Americans spend on candy." We spend more on defense than the next 10 10 highest-spending countries *combined*, and also spend more money giving ourselves cavities than on helping to alleviate poverty and suffering! Diplomacy and development are essential to creating a more stable and peaceful world—but are we actually putting our money where our mouth is?

Part of the problem here, as many military leaders have articulated, is that we're under-resourcing the civilian (i.e. the State Department and USAID) capacity to prevent or respond to crisis. You know that saying: 'when all you have is a hammer, everything starts looking like a nail'? Well, that's the case when most of our funding goes to DOD. They're asked to 'do it all' which comes at the cost of their war-fighting ability *and* the capacity of other government entities.

Department of Defense

Our armed forces and military installations around the world are run by the Department of Defense. Its three main departments are the Departments of the Army, Navy (which includes the Marines) and the Air Force. DOD is one of the US's oldest government departments—in fact, it dates back to the American Revolution! When I learned this, I remember thinking how rare it is for a country to gain its independence peacefully. That we couldn't do so was a pretty solid reason to establish a defense department—not just during the revolution itself, but also in those fragile first few years as a nation-state.

⇒ *Types of staff*

Today, DOD is our largest government agency. And, not only is it the largest employer in the US, it's actually the largest employer in the whole world! With 3.2 million employees, more people work for the US Department of Defense than any other organization around the globe.

11

DOD employs both soldiers and civilians. There are almost 1.5 million US soldiers on active duty, which means that they can be sent to combat on short notice. There are also over 740,000 civilian personnel working full time for DOD, in non-combat positions, and over 820,000 National Guard (troops to be deployed domestically, should the need arise) and Reserve forces (extra troops on call).

SUPER-SIZE IT PLEASE...

12

China's military comes second in the 'largest global employer' competition (2.3 million employees), followed by Walmart (2.1 million) and McDonald's (1.9 million). Think about that the next time you order a Big Mac!

44

⤳ Bricks and mortar

DOD is headquartered at the Pentagon in Washington DC, and also has a large presence around the US (it's in every state) and abroad (at the many overseas military bases established during WWII and the Cold War). There are more than 450,000 DOD employees overseas at any one time, the majority of which are not involved in active combat. According to the 2015 DOD Base Structure Report, DOD has 587 'sites' overseas. DOD occupies a reported 276,770 buildings **13** throughout the world that cover more than 2.2 billion square feet. Imagine being the one to clean all those floors!

⤳ Organization

DOD calls their overseas operations centers 'Regional Combatant Commands'. There are six worldwide, and they are called: Central Command (CENTCOM) for the Middle East, European Command (EUCOM) for Europe, Northern Command (NORTHCOM) for North America, Southern Command (SOUTHCOM) for South America, Pacific Command (PACOM) for Asia, and Africa Command (AFRICOM) for Africa.

⤳ Role of DOD in foreign policy

It's impossible to fully document the role of the US military across the world in just one book—and in fact, hundreds of books on the subject are out there already. Within the context of *this* book, and your potential future career in international affairs, I'm only going to skim the surface of DOD when it comes to foreign policy.

The Secretary of Defense (the head of DOD) is the President's primary advisor on defense policy, which as we discussed, is an important aspect of our foreign policy's goal. And, of course, defense is considered one of the three pillars of national security.

INTRODUCING: THE INTERAGENCY

By now, you'll have gathered that State, USAID and DOD are all vast and complex organizations doing loads of interesting work around the world. Ever wonder how these three co-ordinate and communicate with each other, let alone with all the other government agencies on the scene? Well, I'll tell you. They rely on what's known as the *interagency*. The interagency is what we call US Government agencies and departments as a collective, and why the NSC was created.

Interagency coordination is important, especially on foreign policy, because no one operates in a vacuum, and most have overlapping goals and activities with the others. Coordination is essential so that what one agency is doing complements what the others are doing, without any over-lap or conflict of effort. In both Washington and embassies abroad, State Department employees are usually in charge of coordinating the interagency on foreign affairs issues.

In a nutshell: DOD isn't just about guns and bombs. In fact, much of DOD's work doesn't involve combat at all. For example, some DOD staff work as defense attachés in US Embassies abroad, advising US Ambassadors on defense policy in relation to the host country. Some help host countries and local communities build infrastructure projects. Others help to train allied countries' armed forces and run joint exercises with them (to practice maneuvers they might use in an actual conflict situation).

Here's another example: my brother works for the National Geospatial-Intelligence Agency (part of DOD and the intelligence community—*hush hush!*), and he was stationed in England for a few years, where he worked on making maps. Some DOD staff work in the Office of the Secretary of Defense setting policy. If you saw them at their desks, they'd seem like your typical office worker—except that they're involved in the nitty-gritty of international relations. And, of course, you don't need to be an international affairs expert or even a national security expert to work for DOD, you could be an accountant or a nurse or technician or logistics expert or human resource specialist or just about anything. Just like any large institution, DOD needs different types of people and different kinds of skills to help it run smoothly. And, just like any large organization, once you get your foot in the door, you can always work your way up!

OTHER FORMS OF COORDINATION

TO COORDINATE ON DIPLOMATIC ISSUES, governments use a broad range of international mechanisms, not just their own agencies and departments. Problems rarely solve themselves, and problems that don't get solved can quickly escalate into conflict, so we've got every incentive to use all the means at our disposal to ensure we all get along. These include:

⇒→ *Multilateral organizations*

When two governments cooperate directly with each other, it's called a *bilateral relationship*. (A bilateral trade deal, for example, is an agreement between two trading partners.) These types of relationships would be maintained by staff from any of the three agencies I've discussed (or other government agencies, where relevant).

Governments also coordinate through what are known as *multilateral organizations*, where three or more parties come together to work on issues that affect each of the members and advance their collective interest. Some multilateral organizations work on a global scale (such as the United Nations), others on a regional level (such as the Organization for African Unity and the League of Arab States). Multilateral organizations are also often called international organizations.

Each multilateral organization has its own unique mission and goals. Some focus on economic, political or security cooperation, others on poverty alleviation. Still others act as global and regional bankers that lend money to governments (such as the World Bank). Others unite producers of key commodities (such as OPEC, the Organization of Petroleum Exporting Countries). The US is a member state (and has historically been a principal funder) of most of the world's international organizations.

Did you know that the European Union (EU) is a good example of a multilateral organization? It was created to secure regional peace by fostering closer economic ties—because history shows that when countries have strong trade relationships, it's less likely they'll go to war with each other. In the case of the EU, that's important, because, before WWII, European countries had a very long history of going to war with one another at the drop of a hat. This might be hard for you to imagine now, seeing as how to us Europe (especially Western Europe) seems like one of the most stable regions in the world. And that peace, in no small part, is due to increased coordination between EU countries. EU citizens don't need passports to travel to other EU countries, and most countries in the EU use a common currency (the Euro). There are currently 28 countries in the EU, although Great Britain recently voted to exit the union, and another eight countries are lined up to join.

Want to learn more about the many multilaterals across the world? Check out *Annex Two* for a pretty darn comprehensive list. Who knows? Maybe you'll want to go work for one of them!

⋙⟶ *International agreements*

Governments also use various forms of international agreements to coordinate on specific issues (which can be bilateral or multilateral, depending on how many countries are involved). In plain English: an agreement means that a bunch of countries get together and make rules that they want everyone to follow (at least, those who sign the agreement). Agreements help us make collective rules for all sorts of issues, including environmental protection, arms control, trade, climate change, disaster management, human rights and nuclear non-proliferation.

When it signs on to an agreement, a government commits to act in accordance with that agreement, or face the consequences agreed upon by the signatories. Different levels of agreements come with varying levels of commitment and consequences. For example, a *treaty* is a contract that formalizes an international agreement under international law. (In other words: break the treaty, break the law.) For the US Government to sign a treaty, it must be ratified (approved) by the US Senate and by the President. There are also *conventions*, which outline how governments feel about important issues covered by international law, but don't necessarily set out a joint commitment on putting that belief into practice. *Accords* are voluntary agreements that can be used instead of treaties or as like a placeholder while governments try to come to an agreement on a treaty.

One example of an international treaty is the Kyoto Protocol, which is a UN agreement on reducing greenhouse gas emissions signed into international law by 192 countries worldwide. The Vice President at the time, Al Gore, signed the agreement, but Congress didn't ratify it because they didn't agree with the agreement. Because of this, we can't be held accountable to the treaty.

The US has a dismal record of not ratifying what would seem to be 'good' treaties. The US, Somalia and South Sudan are the only UN members to have not ratified the UN Convention on the Rights of the Child. South Sudan, which is a brand new country, plans to ratify the treaty as soon as possible—leaving the US in the company of Somalia (a failed state). Ugh.

The US also hasn't ratified the Convention on the Elimination of all Forms of Discrimination against Women, or the Convention on the Rights of Persons with Disabilities. Because the US is such a large, powerful country, it sends the wrong message to the rest of the world when we don't get on board with important issues that affect us all.

Of course, many countries ratify conventions and then don't implement them. And, in fact, most (but not all) US laws are already consistent with the child's rights convention. It just goes to show that every (every!) issue is complicated and, if you're interested, you always have to dig deeper to get the full story.

GLOBAL POWER DYNAMICS

EACH COUNTRY HAS AN EQUAL RIGHT to engage with other countries on the world stage, but not all countries have *equal power* to influence world affairs. That's because the global system is basically a big high-stakes game with no set rules, and there's no one there to make sure that everyone plays fair.

As a result, international power isn't distributed equally between countries. When countries have more power, it's typically on account of having more money or a bigger military. That means they hold a lot of influence over countries with less power, who might value economic support and/or protection. Usually, a country has to be rich to have a big military, but there are some exceptions. North Korea, for example, is a cash-strapped country with a lot of very poor people, but it funnels all of its resources into military spending.

In this section, we'll talk about everyone's favorite word to describe international power relationships: *hegemony.* The term *hegemon* derives from the Latin word for 'lead' or 'power', and is applied to countries that exert control (economic, political or military) over others in a global system. A *hegemonic system* is one in which we have one or more hegemons.

➤ The Cold War

Over the course of history, hegemons have come and gone—including Ancient Greece, Ancient Rome and the Holy Roman Empire. The 19th and early 20th century saw a handful of power players on the global stage (the Napoleonic Empire, the British Empire, the Ottoman Empire and others), wherein no one claimed hegemony over all the others.

All that changed, however, in the aftermath of the two world wars. After World War II, the US became a much more powerful global power, as did the (now former) USSR. The Soviet Union, formed in 1922, was comprised of Russia and countries it subsumed in Europe and Asia. Until its demise in 1991, the USSR was the largest country on earth; still today Russia claims the largest landmass of any single country.

Despite being allies during World War II, the US and the Soviet Union soon became pitted against each other in 'the Cold War', a conflict that shaped geopolitics in the second half of the 20th century. (If you're wondering: 'geopolitics' is how factors such as global geography, economics and demography influence global politics, and especially foreign policy.)

Why was it called the Cold War? Because the US and the USSR never directly fought each other. Instead, they fought 'proxy wars' (battles waged between other countries with financial or military support from the opposing powers). Although many of those proxy wars were large, drawn-out and bloody, the fact that the US and the USSR never directly met on a battlefield is un- doubtedly a good thing. This is in no small part because both sides were busy creating massive stockpiles of nuclear weapons. The only thing keeping either country from using them was the principle of *mutually assured destruction* (with its apt acronym, MAD): whoever pulled the trigger first, even if they succeeded in destroying the other, would also be wiped out in the resulting total global annihilation.

Reading about the Cold War doesn't even come close to living through it (the same as any war, I guess). People of my parents' generation recall practicing crawling under their school desks in the event of a nuclear attack; the witch hunt for communist sympathizers in the US (led by Senator Joseph McCarthy); stockpiling tinned goods in fall-out shelters; James Bond fighting Russian baddies on the silver screen. For most people of my generation, the Cold War was formative in an entirely different way—we didn't grow up under the same cloud of fear, but it was often our first introduction to the concept of geopolitics. And for some of us, it's the reason why we're working in global affairs today.

My friend and State Department Foreign Service Officer, Jennifer Lawson, recalls her Cold War *ah-hah* moment: "The thwacking sound of apricots bouncing down the aisle was unexpected; the plane had suddenly turned sharply somewhere over the Balkans, jettisoning our fruit from the tray tables. I was in high school on my first trip outside the United States. I was ready for an incredible, life-changing experience, but had no idea how incredible, nor how transformative, it would be.

"Through chance, or fate, or just geographic proximity to Washington DC, a representative from UNESCO (the United Nations Educational, Scientific and Cultural Organization) knew my Maryland-based modern dance company, and invited us to represent the United States at the 1985 International Banner of Peace Children's Festival in Sofia, Bulgaria. The company's director must have hypnotized all of our parents to get their permission (and money!) to take us behind the Iron Curtain for ten days.

"The festival was held every three years and was a lot like an Olympic Games for the arts. There were more than 100 countries represented by their most talented (or perhaps best-connected) young artists. There were acrobats from China, dancers from Tanzania, painters from Poland and, inexplicably, one poor figure skater from France with nowhere frozen to show his stuff. For over a week, we rehearsed, attended performances, ate fresh yogurt, drank warm Coca-Cola and frequented a heavily-protected 'disco' with our counterparts. During that trip, I learned that art, youth, hope and goodwill can overcome political differences. My perspective has become more nuanced over the years, but I still believe that shared cultural and educational experiences can create common ground, fostering better communication and deeper understanding."

⫸⟶ *Post-Cold War period*

The Soviet Union disintegrated in 1991, and suddenly the US was left as the only global hegemon. But the Cold War is far from forgotten. In fact, its legacy still resonates across the globe, in some good ways, some less good. Here's my friend, Kevin Grubb, an International Affairs Specialist, and his post-Cold War view of the world: "I'm in a village meeting in a tiny mosque in Southern Kyrgyzstan with about 30 representatives from three villages in two countries. It's bitterly cold outside, and the men (there were no women present) are arguing over the water rights to an irrigation system that straddles the border of their two former-Soviet countries, Kyrgyzstan and Tajikistan. There are just a few bulbs illuminating the mosque, the light is a hazy yellow, but nonetheless, a pleasant surprise that electricity is still running at all this late in the evening. For decades, the Kyrgyz and Tajiks lived mostly peacefully side-by-side in these remote mountain villages, where the border was only a faintly-recognized demarcation, known better in Moscow than here in the isolated Fergana Valley in Central Asia.

"In 1991, when the Soviet Union collapsed, once-shared resources (such as the crucial one of water), became a cause for international concern. The Soviet-built irrigation system serving these three tiny villages crisscrossed the meandering border multiple times along its few miles. The system was in disrepair, but still vital for watering apricot trees, the primary source of income for the villages. By the time the water reached residents in the farthest village, it was just a trickle, not enough for their thirsty apricot groves. Women and children carried heavy buckets of water straight uphill for a third of a mile to water the trees that were the lifeblood of the region.

"One village leader told me: Before 1991, water usage and land was not an issue at all. Then, the USSR falls apart, and there's nowhere to work, and everyone turned to agriculture. Then, the water problems began… The only real work in the village is picking apricots during harvest time.

"Suddenly, ethnic groups that once lived in harmony were fighting over the water, with small pitched battles breaking out, a microcosm of the ethnic tensions and conflicts occurring all over the densely-populated Fergana Valley, which has 14 million people from over 100 ethnic groups. The Kyrgyz accused the Tajiks of stealing the water, while the Tajiks accused the Kyrgyz of using too much water. After several small battles, border conflicts, cattle theft and ongoing tension, a stalemate had taken hold. The meeting at the mosque was called as an attempt to resolve the impasse, agree upon a plan to begin repairing the irrigation system, and conclude a water users' agreement, whereby all parties would be beholden to specific water usage limits.

"So what the hell was a skinny 30-year-old kid from Nebraska doing there, you might ask. Well, funny enough, I was asking myself the same thing. With the help of local government leaders and our fantastic staff, we were mediating the conflict between the two sides, hoping to find an initial shared solution to the deep-seated mistrust. I was working with Mercy Corps (an international humanitarian NGO) as part of a USAID conflict mitigation program in the Fergana Valley, bringing together communities and various ethnic groups to help solve shared problems.

"We didn't solve the water conflict that evening in the mosque. But, a few months later, the two sides would agree on a shared solution to the problem and USAID and Mercy Corps would provide the materials for reconstruction of the irrigation system, while the local communities and government provided the physical and skilled labor."

Kevin's story is a valuable reminder of how, after the fall of the Soviet Union, establishing a new global system wasn't an easy, or straightforward, process. Many former Soviet countries went through long (and sometimes painful) transitions to capitalist economies. Some states endured internal conflict due to the power vacuum. And the fallout didn't end there. The US also needed to adjust to the new world order, and find its place as the last hegemon left standing.

While the US remains the world's only global superpower, its hold on hegemonic power is more tenuous than it was 25 years ago. Now it competes for power with China, Japan, Russia (which is back to being just a single country rather than the epicenter of the entire Soviet Union), and the EU.

One reason why the US is still the main global power is that our economy is a lot bigger than other countries and because the US dollar is the global reserve currency, meaning that our government can borrow almost without consequences (in terms of inflation). As you've probably already figured out, most things in this world come down to money! Having such a large economy means that other countries want to sell their products on the US market, which gives them terrific incentive to keep on friendly terms with the US. Just how big is our economy in relative terms? The facts might make your head spin: in 2015, the US economy was more than one third larger than the world's second largest (China), and our economy was *547 thousand times bigger* than the world's smallest economy (Tuvalu).   **14**

Having the world's largest economy, and lots of allies with large economies, means that the US can spearhead actions against other countries. Sometimes these are military operations, such as the 2001 invasion of Afghanistan. And sometimes, they're diplomatic measures, such as pursuing economic sanctions.

Economic sanctions are restrictions on financial transactions or trade barriers imposed on a country. Sanctions can be unilateral (imposed by one state on another state), or multilateral (when multiple countries impose a sanction, usually through a mechanism like the UN).

For a long time, the US imposed economic sanctions against Iran because of their alleged attempt to develop nuclear weapons. The sanctions meant that Iran couldn't easily sell their oil resources to other countries, which weakened their economy. In this way, sanctions can be a handy diplomatic bargaining chip.

However, they often end up hurting ordinary citizens more than their governments, so they should be used wisely.

Our hegemonic status is also based on the fact that we have the biggest and most powerful military. All of those weapons, military bases, equipment and soldiers come at a cost, though. In 2015, the US spent more on its defense budget than the countries with the next seven highest defense budgets combined. Some would argue that this high rate of defense spending weakens, rather than strengthens, the US's power because the defense budget represents billions of dollars that could be spent on schools and roads back home. On the other hand, others would say that the US is a truly global country, with global interests, and we need a global military to protect those interests abroad—especially in light of increasing threats from non-state actors.

Non-state actors

NATION-STATES ARE NOT THE ONLY PLAYERS on the world stage. Non-state actors are groups of individuals that try to influence domestic or global politics, but that do not operate as part of any recognized government. There are lots of non-state actors, and they don't all have the same goals or methods. Civil society organizations are all non-state actors (e.g. the International Campaign to Ban Landmines or Greenpeace). However, for the purposes of our discussion here, I'm going to focus on the ones with violent motives and methods.

There have always been violent non-state actors on the scene. But recently, their influence and impact have been amplified because improved travel and communication means that they can send people and messages far and wide, and coordinate across national borders with ease. The media visibility enjoyed by non-state actors is also increasing, because improved ease of travel and communication means that, for journalists, a breaking story is rarely out of reach.

One example of a violent non-state actor is Daesh (also called the Islamic State of Iraq and Syria, or ISIS), a militant Islamist organization that has carried out terrorist attacks around the world. Daesh is a group of individuals that operate through a loose means of cooperation throughout the world. It doesn't belong to one nation-state, and this decentralized power structure and membership make it hard to fight through traditional means.

Another example of violent non-state actors are the drug cartels (narco-trafficking organizations) that plague many parts of the world, especially Latin America. These criminal organizations control every aspect of the drug trade: cultivation and production in South America, transit through Central America, and sale in North America. In some parts of Latin America, these drug cartels (through violence and economic power), have more control over the territory and population than the central or local government. The cartels use extreme violence to maintain their grip on power, and are one reason why there are cities in Latin America with some of the highest murder rates in the world.

Non-state actors muddy the global waters because they don't play by the same rules as nation-states. They don't have ambassadors with whom you can engage in diplomatic talks; they don't have economies you can sanction; they don't have respect for the sovereignty of other nations; and they certainly don't abide by the Geneva Convention on Human Rights, which governs how countries should behave in times of war and peace.

Informality is another tricky thing about non-state actors. From the perspective of international law, it's difficult to declare war on an entity that doesn't legally exist; and when governments negotiate with non-state actors, the latter gain a kind of formal legitimacy that only helps their cause.

In a nutshell: fighting non-state baddies is complicated, and that's why the economic, political and social development work we do is so important for creating a more peaceful and stable world. Preventing the rise of violent non-state actors is easier than dismantling them. I firmly believe if ordinary people have enough food to eat, know their voices will be heard in the halls of government and are able to care for their families—they will be less likely to wage war, join a terrorist organization or succumb to the power of illicit organizations. This is, of course, complicated and hard to achieve—and why we need as many engaged global citizens as possible to dismantle the barriers to social and economic justice.

FINAL THOUGHTS

WHILE IT'S IMPORTANT TO HIGHLIGHT the complex and fluid nature of our interactions within the global system, it's also worth saying that we don't always get it right. Nation-states generally try to interact with each other according to a set of norms and rules, but sometimes we still hit bumps in the road. Occasionally, we muck it up *big time*. Rarely (if ever) can a government foresee the full impact of any decision it takes. No one country has a definitive blueprint for how to create stability, prosperity and world peace.

Have you heard the saying *fake it until you make it*? In essence, that's what every country does every day. There are huge global problems to be solved. We don't always know the best way to solve them, but we welcome with open arms the ordinary heroes that show up and try. All of the decisions that are made in the world are made by ordinary people—people just like you.

In *Part Two*, we'll talk in greater depth about some of those global problems. But first: if you love the movie quote 'show me the money'—then the next chapter is your new best friend.

REMEMBER!

- There are 195 countries in the world, and they're (mostly) doing their best to play nicely with each other
- A country's foreign policy defines what it believes, and what it does, in relation to the rest of the world
- The Department of State, the Department of Defense and the US Agency for International Development lead the US National Security Strategy's 3 Ds: defense, diplomacy and development
- International coordination relies on organizations and agreements
- Global power isn't distributed equally
- Global power dynamics are still influenced by the Cold War and its aftermath
- Non-state actors (violent and otherwise) are increasingly playing a role in international affairs.

CHAPTER 4
THE GLOBAL
ECONOMY

THE NUTSHELL...

Money makes the world go round, and no discussion about global politics is complete without mentioning global economics. An understanding of the basic concepts of economics will hold you in good stead, as will understanding the broader context of global trade and economic development. Understanding the anatomy of a financial crisis is also important—because in a globalized world, no one is immune from them.

WHAT KIND OF JOB COULD THIS BE?

Economist for a multilateral organization • Finance manager for a charity • Federal Reserve employee • Risk and compliance analyst for a multinational corporation • Investment banker at a private company • Trade deal negotiator for the US Government

MY LOVE AFFAIR WITH GLOBAL AFFAIRS began in the sixth grade when I wrote a book report on the Amazon rainforest. From that moment, I was hooked on the idea of being an environmental superhero. When I reached high school, I had the opportunity to meet a man named Robert Muller (not to be confused with ex-FBI Director Robert Mueller), who began his own (long and distinguished) career in global affairs in 1948 with an internship at a very new organization—the UN!

He talked about the importance of peace and conflict resolution, something I hadn't even heard about at the time. Nonetheless, a seed was planted in my mind: the best way to help the environment was to help ordinary people—because you can't expect them to 'be green' when they can't even protect their family from poverty, disease or conflict.

After meeting Dr. Muller, I decided to study international affairs in college and pursue it as a career. During my first international affairs class in college, I had to make a presentation on the global economy. I recall that I was utterly mystified at the time. The 18-year-old version of me knew that there were a bunch of countries in the world—but I had never thought about their economies, let alone how all those economies fit together into one big global economy.

What I was about to learn (and why this chapter appears in this book) is that the global economy is a hugely important part of global affairs. Politics is about power, and power is about money. As I've already mentioned, one reason why the US has so much political power is that it has so much economic power.

In this chapter, I'll cover some basic concepts that will serve as a foundation for understanding how economics shapes the global scene. Ready? Let's do it.

ECONOMICS 101

Here's a tough question. What's more valuable: a bucket of water, or a bucket of diamonds? (Don't worry. You can take all the time you want to come up with your answer. I'm not going anywhere.)

What? You say you don't need more time? Think you've got it already? Right. Let's see how you did. The answer is (drum roll please) a bucket of water.

Confused? Maybe I can clear things up by asking another question. What's more *costly:* a bucket of water, or a bucket of diamonds? Are you starting to catch on? If you think that a bucket of diamonds is more costly, you're right.

Why the bizarre quiz? Well, if you're going to hang out at the economists' table, first you need to get your head around the fact that cost and value are *two different things.* Water is invaluable; without it, we cannot survive. Diamonds are really (really!) nice, but if we don't have any, there's little chance we'll die. In other words, water has a higher value and a lower cost, whereas diamonds have a lower value but a higher cost.

The cost for a certain thing (also known as its *price*) changes depending on supply and demand—how much there is of something (called *supply*) and how much someone wants to buy that something, *aka* how much they value it (*demand*).

If someone really, *really*, likes diamonds, then the person selling the diamonds can set a higher price, knowing that the buyer will probably cough up the cash. Prices also go up when the number of people who want to buy diamonds is greater than the number of diamonds available; not everyone is going to end up with one, so to ensure that you get yours, you're more willing to pay a higher price. The price goes up until the number of diamonds people want to buy is equal to the number of diamonds available on the market. Since diamonds are pretty scarce, the price of diamonds is pretty high. This, my friends, is the law of supply and demand in action.

Here's another example: let's say that in your town, the only job that people have is growing strawberries. At harvest time, you all sell your strawberries at the market. One year, after an unusually good summer, you find that everyone in the town has produced twice as many strawberries as they usually do. The trouble is: while the number of available strawberries has gone up, the number of people that come to market has not. So now, every strawberry producer is competing with other strawberry producers to catch the eye of passing strawberry buyers. And to tempt them to buy your strawberries (rather than your neighbor's strawberries) you offer them a lower price. And voilà! Prices fall until the number of strawberries available equals the number of strawberries people want to buy.

All this buying and selling of strawberries and diamonds (and water, and potatoes, and everything else) happens in the *marketplace*. Obviously, water matters more to life than strawberries or diamonds, because water is what we call a *scarce resource*. And the issue of scarce resources is precisely where economics intersects with international affairs. Because simply put, economics is the science of how we distribute scarce resources. Allow me to explain.

Let's imagine for a moment that the only thing that human beings needed to eat to survive was apples. And let's also imagine that the entire planet is covered in apple forests. Everyone can pick all the apples they want, and no one ever goes hungry. In this imaginary world, there are no scarce resources—therefore the people who live there would have no need for economics. They'd just eat apples and lay in the sunshine. It's only when resources are scarce (i.e. there's not enough to go around) that we need to have tricky conversations about precisely how to allocate those resources between people.

* * * * *

THE GLOBAL ECONOMY IS MADE UP OF individual countries' domestic economies, just like the global political system is made up of individual countries. A *domestic economy* is comprised of the mechanisms in the country by which people buy and sell different *goods* (i.e. things we make, such as brooms and buckets) and *services* (i.e. things we do, such as a housecleaning service) These mechanisms could be individual people (including kids with lemonade stands) or businesses. No matter whether those businesses are large or small, local or national, online or bricks-and-mortar—they are all part of the domestic economy.

Every economy is made up of different sectors. The *primary sector* includes natural resource extraction, which is a big part of most domestic economies (even ours). We produce coal, bauxite (used to make aluminum), copper, iron, nickel, gold and silver. This sector also includes agriculture and the fishing industry. The *secondary sector* includes manufacturing. The US manufactures a bunch of stuff including chemicals, transportation equipment, machinery and computer and electronic products.

A country's domestic economy also includes services, which is when someone does something for you in exchange for money, rather than gives something to you in exchange for money. The *service sector* includes lawyers, mechanics, coders, therapists, baristas, hotels, accountants, plumbers and painters.

The total value of all of the goods produced and services provided in a country during a year is what's called its Gross Domestic Product (or GDP), which is a kind of shorthand for the overall value of a country's domestic economy. Here are some large numbers for you: the US's GDP in 2015 was about $18 trillion dollars, which makes up nearly a quarter of the total global economy (about $73 trillion). The next largest economy is China with a GDP at almost $11 trillion dollars.

Of course, the GDP only accounts for officially-recorded economic activity. If you've ever mowed your neighbor's lawn for cash or bought a pirated copy of a DVD, then you've come into contact with the informal economy. All countries have informal economies: mechanisms by which people trade goods and services outside of taxation and regulation (regulations are the rules that keep people safe from things like contaminated meat and fake doctors).

In developing countries, the informal economy can be huge (up to half of all market activity). In India, some estimates say that nearly 70 percent of all workers are in the informal economy. That's a problem because a country that wants to create a thriving domestic economy should make it as easy as possible to start a business, or to close a business if it's not making money. But in some places, starting up a business is very complicated and costly—so it's little wonder that some people opt to stay in the informal economy.

16

That's not to say that the informal sector is all roses and kittens. First off, regulations are there to keep people safe, and we'd really miss them if they didn't exist. Quack doctors and dangerous taxi drivers flourish in informal economies, and people get hurt as a result. Worse still, a subset of the informal sector is the black market that sells illegal goods and services, including: humans (trafficking in persons), drugs, guns, ivory or exotic wildlife, or faux Louis Vuitton bags (okay, that last one isn't so bad—but it's a crime of fashion, no doubt). And because trade on the black market moves across international borders, it's the seedy underbelly of the global economy.

* * * * *

GOVERNMENTS TRY TO CREATE ECONOMIC STABILITY and growth as a way of providing prosperity for its citizens and competing in the global economy. To achieve this, the government needs to provide peace and security, sensible laws and regulation with consistent enforcement, education, health services and basic infrastructure (i.e. ports, roads, electricity). All those things create a positive enabling environment for businesses to thrive. The government also has two tools to regulate the macroeconomic environment: monetary policy and fiscal policy (usually the Central Bank controls the *monetary policy*).

I'll translate: monetary policy is about setting the price of money. *Wait, did you say the price of money?* Yep. You might know it as 'the interest rate'. Here's a really basic (and slightly outlandish) example. Say the Central Bank sets the interest rate at 25 percent. You open a savings account with your bank and deposit $1, and leave it there for a year. You are providing a *good* to the bank (in the form of money that it uses to earn more money, for example by lending it to other bank customers in the form of interest-bearing loans), and in return, the bank will pay you $1.25 at the end of the year. Your dollar is now worth $1.25.

In that example—you'd have made a good return if you saved all of your money in a bank. And if the Central Bank wants to encourage everyone to save money, rather than spend it (because the economy is getting overheated and inflation is rising), it raises the interest rate (so that the best return for your dollar is to put it in a bank and not spend it). If the economy is looking a bit sluggish, and the Central Bank wants to encourage people to go out and spend money, invest and take out loans, then it lowers the interest rate, because then it's less attractive to hoard your cash in a bank account.

The Central Bank is called the Federal Reserve (or the Fed) in the US. The government has oversight over it, but it operates independently. Congress and the President have no say in the decisions it makes, and the Fed doesn't receive any money from the government.

The government, on the other hand, is in charge of *fiscal policy*, which is just a fancy name for 'taxing and spending'. If the economy is sluggish and the government wants to pep things up a bit, it can cut taxes—leaving you with more money every month to go out and spend. It can also increase spending (on things like bridges and highways) that provide jobs (and therefore income for more people to go out and spend) and also benefit the economy in the long-run (by making it easier for people and goods to move about the country). And of course, if the government wants to cool off an overheated economy, it raises taxes and cuts spending.

Something else about the domestic economy: one thing that we debate about a lot (especially in election years!) is the budget deficit. A deficit is when a government spends more money than it collects in taxes. The government can choose to cover the shortfall by borrowing money (which adds to the public debt but keeps things running smoothly), or it can decide to reduce the deficit by cutting the budget. Often a president will try to 'balance the budget'—meaning to bring taxes and spending into line. This is obviously quite a complicated and politically-charged issue!

Economic development

WE USUALLY JUDGE HOW SOPHISTICATED (developed) an economy is by looking at the mix of things that it produces. The US, and other industrialized countries, went through an industrial revolution over 200 years ago (in the late 1700s and early 1800s). This means that our economy used to be mostly based on agriculture and small businesses, but with the advent of new manufacturing technologies, the economy grew and transformed to one more focused on the production of goods. Since that time, many other countries have taken the same path towards development: by shifting from agriculture to manufacturing (usually for export, especially in the case of Latin America's development trajectory).

In a lot of ways, the US economy is now evolving *beyond* a reliance on manufacturing, as the service sector grows in size and importance. Our service sector includes financial services, entertainment, hospitality, retail, health, information technology and higher education. Our evolution to a service economy is also because operational costs for businesses (i.e. wages, rent, compliance with regulations, etc.) are higher in the US than in developing countries, and it's easier to cover those costs if you're involved in high-value services rather than low-value manufacturing. Accordingly, US companies have moved the production of goods to developing countries where they're cheaper to produce.

Many countries' economies are still based on the extraction and sale of natural resources, which isn't a particularly effective way of developing an economy because you don't benefit from the added value derived from turning raw materials into finished products (which you can charge more for). To add value to natural resources, they need to be made into something, which is what we call the production of goods (e.g. turning extracted metals into microchips, or crude oil into refined oil).

A second problem with economies being reliant on natural resources (like oil or diamonds) is that the wealth can be captured by a small group of elites. (Be on the lookout for an explanation of the natural resource curse later in the book.) This challenge is not an inevitable one: oil-rich Norway distributes its oil wealth to all citizens, which gives us a good model for how it can be done. The final problem for extractive economies is this: the potential for growth is limited by the finite nature of those natural resources. What happens when they run out?

NATIONAL ECONOMIES WITHIN THE GLOBAL ECONOMY

WE LIVE IN AN INTERCONNECTED WORLD, which is why national economies interact with one another in the global economy—primarily through global trade.

Global trade is based on the laws of supply and demand on a global scale. When a country's domestic economy can't produce something that its people want, a country will import those goods and services from another country. For example, people in the US like fresh produce during winter months, but most of our farmers can't produce year-round crops. That's why the US imports produce from warm countries that can grow food all year long, or from countries in the southern hemisphere where the seasons are opposite to ours. Imported produce usually doesn't taste as good as the same food grown nearby because it has a lot further to travel between the farm and our table (we call this 'food miles') and sometimes it needs to be frozen or otherwise messed with until it reaches our grocery stores. On the other hand, it's absolutely thrilling to get a juicy peach in the middle of winter. Nice one, global trade!

So just how big a deal is global trade? Well, the International Labor Organization used data available from 40 countries to estimate that more than *one in five* jobs worldwide is linked to global supply chains—that is, jobs that contribute to the production of goods and services that are either consumed or further processed in other countries.

As you might expect, not all trading relationships are the same. Some countries import (buy) more from other countries than they export (sell) to that country. This imbalance is called a trade deficit (or a trade surplus, if it's the other way around).

The US regularly runs a trade deficit, meaning that we import more than we export. The US's global trade deficit hovers around $500 billion. There are varying perspectives on the size of the trade deficit—ranging from those who think it is not a big deal to those who find it alarming. High domestic production costs are 17

DOLLARS AND SENSE

Most global financial transactions use the US Dollar as the trading currency—it's kind of like a 'universal' currency (another sign of our status as a hegemon). Some countries like Ecuador, East Timor and El Salvador even use the US Dollar as their domestic currency. But most countries have their own currency: Japan uses the Yen, Mexico the Peso, and South Africa the Rand. Within the EU, 19 out of 28 member countries use the Euro.

one of the leading causes of the deficit, so it makes more economic sense to import cheaper products from other countries. And indeed, there's nothing to say that a country actually *needs* to produce everything it wants to buy. In theory, importing more basic goods means that your domestic companies are free to produce more complex goods and services.

But really, what's the big deal about trade? We want stuff, we buy stuff. Does it actually matter where we buy it from? Remember when we talked about the price of money, and how it actually can change? Well, things get tricky when those dollars start crossing national borders.

If lots of countries around the world are using dollars to trade—that means that significant amounts of our currency are actually being held abroad. For example, when the US imports a lot of products from China, it means that China now holds lots of *foreign exchange* (the currency of another country) in the form of US dollars.

This, in and of itself, is not necessarily a problem. But, if China were to decide to sell off its entire pile of dollars at once, it would *lower the price* of the dollar because there would be more of them available on the currency market. That's because the rules

GLOBAL-WHAT-IZATION?

Globalization is the interconnection among people, companies and governments from different countries. International trade and investment have been key drivers of globalization, as has the spread of technology. There are heated debates about whether globalization is a good thing. For sure, it's changing life for everyone on the planet. There are no easy answers, but one thing we do know is this: globalization is here to stay. We can't pull up the drawbridge, but we *can* work to make the system fairer for everyone.

of supply and demand apply both to strawberries and money. And when I say lower the price—I mean *relative to other currencies*, which is what we call the *exchange rate*. If the price of the dollar falls, we need more dollars to buy a product from another country. (Remember how I said that we import much more than we export?) When I say 'we', I'm not just talking about you and me as individuals. I'm also talking about companies and multinational corporations.

These days, multinational corporations (MNCs) make up a lot of the buying and selling (trade) within the global economy. MNCs are based in several countries and often produce products across multiple countries. For example, the company that made your shirt could have designed it in its headquarters in Vermont, bought cotton from India, sent it to a factory in Cambodia to turn it into fabric, then sent it on to another facility in the Philippines to sew it together. (If you're fascinated by all of this, pick up a copy of *Stuff: The Secret Lives of Everyday Things* by John C. Ryan and Alan Durning; it traces the production and distribution of ordinary consumer goods, from design to doorstep. Definitely worth a read!)

Because the dynamics of global trade have an enormous impact on the size of our wallets, governments take different approaches to shaping their trading relationships with the rest of the world. (Here's where economics and politics collide, big time.) A *protectionist approach* is like raising the drawbridge against imports—either by limiting the number of goods you'll import or by putting tariffs on imports to increase the price of those goods relative to ones that are produced domestically. A *free trade approach*, on the other hand, means having less restricted, more open markets where goods and services can flow freely and cheaply across borders. A government can also opt for a mixed approach, where it protects a few key industries.

Proponents of free trade claim that protectionist policies distort an economy and will ultimately weaken it. They also view free trade as an effective means of reducing conflict between nation-states. Also, they argue that it's hard to stop thanks to technology making communications instant and global transportation accessible.

There are pros and cons to global trade. A few of the pros are that there is more diversity in a country's domestic market and products are often cheaper because there is more competition, which could also improve the quality of products. Some people argue it helps alleviate poverty and brings higher standards of living to developing countries. However, others point out that these benefits often go to corporations and those that were already wealthy, leading to greater income inequality in developing countries. Global trade also has the potential to weaken domestic production because there is too much competition from foreign products. This is particularly the case for developing countries that don't have as much money to invest in domestic production, thus often producing inferior or more expensive goods than imported products.

HOW DOES GLOBAL TRADE WORK?

THE GLOBAL ECONOMY IS BASED on the buying and selling of goods and services between countries, which is what we call global trade. So how does this all work in practice? Let's find out!

⤳ *Trade agreements*

For global trade to work, countries first have to agree whether (and what) they'll trade with each other. This is why the global economy is governed by various kinds of policies, regulations and agreements. A *trade agreement* establishes the terms by which countries trade with one another. There are bilateral trade agreements (between two countries), and multilateral trade agreements (between three or more countries). They outline the types (if any) of barriers: tariffs, quotas or other restrictions that will be placed on the trade between countries. Trade agreements also cover what benefits countries will receive from trading with one another (like tax breaks). The US has free trade agreements (which do away with trade barriers altogether) with 20 countries, including both bilateral and multilateral trade agreements. And while the US has some kind of trade agreement with 52 countries, China is now the world's largest trade partner with a whopping 124 countries!

Acknowledging that trade is an essential part of development, the US Government has trade preference programs that are intended to help developing countries. One example of a US trade program designed to promote economic growth in the developing world is the Generalized System of Preferences, which provides preferential duty-free entry for up to 4,800 products from 129 designated beneficiary countries and territories. The African Growth and Opportunity Act is another example that enhances market access and offers trade incentives for Sub-Saharan African countries.

In the US, the Office of the United States Trade Representative (or USTR, which is housed in the Executive Branch) is in charge of developing, coordinating and implementing US trade policy. The head of this office is the US Trade Representative, which is a cabinet-level position that advises the President and negotiates trade agreements on the US's behalf. If you find international trade interesting, you should apply to work in the Office of the USTR, or another US Government agency that works on trade issues (there are a lot of them!). 18

The World Trade Organization (WTO) is the world's primary trade organization. Its members are national governments, and they use the WTO to resolve trade problems that they have with each other (all WTO members are legally obliged to follow its rules and regulations). While I was living in Tajikistan, they were granted WTO membership, which was a big deal for them.

Annex Two has some more information about the WTO for your reading pleasure.

⫸⟶ *Investments*

If you spend money in the US (on gas, movie tickets, clothes, etc.), you are automatically a part of the global economy, even if you're not aware of it. That said, you could be *even more engaged* with the world economy by investing in foreign companies. Many stock portfolios or money markets are comprised of MNCs (Apple, for example). That means that, if you have an investment portfolio, you're most likely already investing in the global economy.

Most big international companies are MNCs, and they have offices and/or factories in countries different than their countries of origin. If you're interested in the global economy, working for an MNC is another global affairs career option.

Financial markets are a big part of the composition of the global economy. These include stock markets, bond markets, currency markets, derivatives markets, commodity markets, money markets, futures markets, insurance markets and foreign exchange markets.

Foreign direct investment (FDI) is another form of investing that is part of the global economy. FDI is where a person or

IT'S A FAIR TRADE...

Fair Trade is an important part of any trade discussion, especially when that trade is between developed and developing countries. Fair Trade is focused on fair prices being paid to producers to create greater equity in international trade and to promote sustainable development. Many organizations are working on this important issue, including the World Fair Trade Organization, which is a global network of organizations representing the Fair Trade supply chain. Add Fair Trade to your list of important topics to learn more about!

organization has a controlling stake in a business enterprise that is based in another country. According to the White House's FDI report, the US has been the world's largest recipient of FDI since 2006. According to the report: during the 2006–2012 period there was an inflow of $1.5 trillion dollars of FDI into the US—$166 billion in 2012 alone. A lot of the FDI in the US is in the manufacturing sector—pharmaceuticals, petroleum and coal products. Eighty percent of the FDI in the US comes from Japan, Canada, Australia and Europe. In 2016, the Chinese invested over $45 billion in US companies. To imagine how this intersects with our political relationships with these places—consider what would happen if those investors all decided to sell their shares of all those companies at once (hint: go back to the principle of supply and demand…).

SOMETIMES THINGS FALL APART…

BECAUSE NATIONAL ECONOMIES INTERACT with one another within the global economy, what happens in one country will invariably have ripple (or domino!) effects in the others. No country is immune; even isolationist countries such as North Korea still have trading partners—China being North Korea's largest. Because China's national economy is plugged into the global economy, global economic waves eventually wash up on North Korea's shore.

You might recall that in 2008, the collapse of the US housing market triggered a global financial meltdown. Because we are the world's largest economy, what happens in Vegas never stays in Vegas (so to speak). Most countries have some economic relationship with the US, so what began as *our* crisis spilled over into most other countries' economies.

The global economy was in a recession from 2008–2012, and is slowly recovering from this downturn. Part of the recovery came from an economic package that the US Government prepared to help bail out the banks involved when the housing bubble burst, and to invest in infrastructure projects and other activities that would funnel money back into the US economy.

Another example of a global economic crisis was one that spread throughout Asia in the late 1990s. This crisis mostly affected Thailand, South Korea and Indonesia, but had ripple effects throughout the region. It was called the *Asian flu*, and it started because Thailand pegged its currency to the US dollar, but it didn't have the foreign exchange to support this, and the country essentially went bankrupt. This led to a domino effect that weakened currencies and devalued markets throughout Asia. Foreign investors, who until that point had been pouring money into the region, were suddenly skittish about investing in developing economies—which pinched other developing countries in the wallet, and also led to an 'anti-globalization' movement in the US and elsewhere.

Obviously, I've only really scratched the surface of the global economy. It's interesting stuff though, and there is a lot of information out there if you're curious to learn more.

20

For now, remember: everything is connected. Politics and economics are related. The food you can afford to put on your table, and the food that a rural woman in Paraguay can afford to put on her table, are related. When a country is rocked by an economic crisis (of its own making or otherwise), price increases usually show up in food and fuel bills and hit poor and vulnerable people the hardest. If you're only just barely getting by (which for many people means trying to live on two dollars a day), then even the smallest increase in prices is going to absolutely devastate your ability to feed your family, keep them healthy, and keep a roof over your head.

REMEMBER!

- Politics and money are closely entwined, which means the global economy is an important part of global affairs
- Supply means 'how many strawberries are there?' whereas demand means 'how many people want to buy strawberries?'
- The global economy is made up of lots of different domestic economies trading with one another
- Global trade is about the laws of supply and demand on a global scale
- A trade agreement establishes the terms by which countries trade with one another
- Foreign direct investment is when a company (or individual) invests in a business based in another country
- The integration of the global economy means that economic crises spread fast across the globe.

Chapter 5
International
development

———•••———•—•———•••———

The nutshell...
International development was born in the ashes of World War II. Since then, our approach to development has evolved considerably. Today, the UN's Sustainable Development Goals frame our global efforts to create social justice, which we achieve through tailored programs that reflect local needs, include local stakeholders, and build local community capacity to diagnose and tackle local challenges.

What kind of job could this be?
Grants officer at a foundation • Project manager at an NGO • Communications specialist with the US Government • Program assistant at private development company • Fundraising officer for a charity organization

———•••———•—•———•••———

GLOBAL POVERTY SUCKS. We can all agree on that, right? So, what is the world community doing about the problem? *International development* is an attempt to improve people's well-being by alleviating poverty and inequality and improving health, education and job opportunities. International development goes by many names, depending on whom you're talking to: you'll hear people say *humanitarian development, global development*, or just *development*.

Whatever it's called, it means assistance in the form of money, skills and training (medical training, police investigative training, etc.) and/or stuff (like medical equipment, school books or fertilizer). It can originate *from* governments, non-governmental organizations, multilateral organizations or private foundations and can be sent *to* governments, organizations and even individual people in developing countries.

Development typically focuses on long-term goals (poverty reduction, gender equality), but also includes *humanitarian assistance*, which is a short-term, rapid response to a crisis (such as an earthquake or refugees fleeing a war zone). There are also cases of continued humanitarian assistance in ongoing crises, such as in Syria and South Sudan. Humanitarian aid supports peoples' basic needs (such as shelter, food, water and medical services) to save lives during a crisis situation. Humanitarian aid workers are the storm chasers of the development world.

CURRENT DEVELOPMENT EFFORTS

MANY DEVELOPMENT ORGANIZATIONS around the world are working together towards a commonly agreed set of development goals. The idea of global coordination of our development efforts started with the 2000 launch of the Millennium Development Goals (MDGs). The goals of this 15-year plan were to: 1) eradicate extreme hunger and poverty, 2) achieve universal primary education, 3) promote gender equality and empower women, 4) reduce child mortality, 5) improve maternal health, 6) combat HIV/AIDS, malaria and other diseases, 7) ensure environmental sustainability, and 8) develop a global partnership for development. Each goal was accompanied by a detailed list of targets, and different development organizations worked on various pieces of the poverty puzzle.

Since then, we've made progress in achieving the goals—and we even met our target of reducing extreme poverty rates by half five years ahead of the 2015 deadline! Other goals, however, we didn't meet. To build on the work that had been done, and the momentum for positive change that we created, the UN created 17 new common goals called the *Sustainable Development Goals* (SDGs), which frame many development efforts today.

This might sound to you like a case of 'moving the goalposts', but the fact is: development is complicated. It takes time, and it takes a lot of money. It also means tackling a lot of different challenges within society at once. It's not as simple as just providing more jobs. First of all, you can't create jobs out of thin air, as any politician will tell you. Jobs depend on lots of other factors. You need to improve the education system to create a more skilled population to fill those jobs. You need improved health care so that kids don't miss school and workers are healthy enough to work. You need a well-functioning government that isn't corrupt, to have an economy that helps businesses thrive rather than cripples them through embezzlement, bribes and favoritism. You need a stable economy to attract local and foreign investment. You need infrastructure, worker safety regulations… the list goes on and on and on. This is why the development sector is so diverse, and why this book covers so many aspects of the development agenda. One of them might turn out to be the thing you're most passionate about!

A BRIEF HISTORY OF DEVELOPMENT

GLOBAL DEVELOPMENT HAS ITS ROOTS in the late 1940s, following World War II. Western Europe had been devastated by the war; infrastructure lay in ruins after heavy bombing, and national economies had been crippled by a lack of security, trade, able-bodied workers and access to markets.

On the other hand, the US economy was actually strengthened by the end of the war and accounted for 50 percent of the world's GDP after WWII. That meant that the US was in the best position to rebuild the countries of Western Europe, and that's exactly what we did, through something called the Marshall Plan (named after then-Secretary of State, George Marshall).

In many ways, the Marshall Plan was the birth of international development. And, it was one of the US's shining moments— the very idea of dedicating financial resources to rebuild nations (some that you had just defeated in war) was unprecedented. Seeing the success of the Marshall Plan, developed countries (many from Western Europe, the initial recipients of international development!) started using a similar approach to assist other nations in need. The birth of international development also corresponded with the birth of many new countries, as 36 countries in Asia and Africa gained their independence between 1945 and 1960!

23

Over the past 70 years, our approach to development has evolved. Some of this is in response to the changing environment in developing countries, but mostly it's a case of development theory catching up with practice. We learn from our mistakes, and we try to do it better the next time.

In the 1940s and 1950s, as I mentioned, the US implemented the Marshall Plan, and the international community created the UN, the World Bank and the International Monetary Fund (IMF).

In the 1960s, development assistance had a big focus on large-scale industrial projects with funding going directly to developing country governments (which, very often, turned out to be quite corrupt).

In the 1970s, we moved away from large-scale industrial projects, and towards rural agricultural development and the provision of social services, including housing and literacy. A lot of development assistance through this point was in the form of loans taken from the International Financial Institutions (IFIs). What's more, it was during the seventies, after the UN's First World Conference on Women in Mexico City in 1975, that women and development started as an essential part of the theoretical and practical approach to development.

In the 1980s, IFIs raised interest rates, which led to the explosion of developing countries' aid debt. Another change in this decade was that a lot of assistance moved away from poverty alleviation and toward helping developing country governments adopt their own free-market policies (in the belief that the market was the answer to the poverty problem).

The 1990s saw a shift toward promoting democracy—the gold standard of governance systems. One reason for this was the fact that our previous decades of development assistance appeared to be making only a very slight dent in global poverty rates. The conventional wisdom of the day held that focusing development on democracy and governance would be a good way to help countries create the foundation for development (recognizing that the quality of development outcomes hinged on whether the government was stealing development aid for itself, or not). The relationship between economic growth and democratic reform is vast and fascinating, and I urge you to dig into it if you're interested.

24

The dawn of the 2000s saw, for the first time, a coordinated effort between development experts to target specific development goals through the MDGs. The MDGs also elevated the focus on *sustainable* development. Sustainable development is about creating lasting long-term change, rather than creating impact that is limited to the life of a particular development project.

LOCAL IS BEAUTIFUL...

As you explore development theory and practice, you'll notice that local ownership, local solutions and local leadership are essential. Your in-country partners are best-placed to identify the challenges in their own lives, and design development programs to meet those challenges. The host-country government, civil society, private sector and citizens are the best development resource that any country has. You must engage your local resources to best support them in achieving positive development outcomes. Remember, we're not there to 'fix' local communities; we're there to collaborate with local partners to create lasting, sustainable change.

We wanted to turn vicious cycles into virtuous ones, and make sure that we weren't creating 'aid dependency'.

Sustainability relies on our ability to tailor our development efforts to the needs of a particular country, and avoid the 'cookie-cutter approaches' we had used in the past. We also started thinking more about developing the capacity of local organizations to design and implement their own development projects, rather than parachuting in experts from abroad. After all, local communities have all the expertise they need to tackle the challenges they face—our job is to support them to do so, and fill in the skill/funding gaps as needed.

These days, the private sector is increasingly getting more involved in development. Many NGOs, USAID and local governments have joint projects with private-sector companies. It's an awesome way for the private sector to do corporate social responsibility and to improve the lives of people living in countries where they extract resources, have factories and sell their products. What's more, it makes strategic sense for those companies to get involved in local community development, because their businesses won't exist in the long-run if they destroy the community and environment they work in. Innovation is another new arrival on the development sector agenda. As you might expect, that means using creative, out-of-the-box thinking and technology to improve the effectiveness of development aid.

You might be asking: if we were so successful in rebuilding post-war Europe, why has the 'new wave' of development in the global south proved so much more complicated? Good question. Remember how we talked about how colonial powers were generally more interested in extracting natural resources from their colonies than helping them develop their capacity? This, in fact, made a huge difference to the future development trajectory of the newly-independent countries (most of which were in the global south), and that particular ghost is still rattling its chains today.

Development through the Marshall Plan wasn't starting from scratch. Europe had previously had robust economies and reliable, well-functioning infrastructure. It also had a well-educated workforce, so the human capital was ready to go back to the jobs that they already had been doing before the war and required minimal training. My point is: it's great that developed countries were inspired by the Marshall Plan to start providing assistance to other nations through international development. But when it comes to less developed countries, no one knew just how complicated it would be, or how long it would take.

IT'S COMPLICATED…

POVERTY IS COMPLEX; development is even more complex. The success of even the most well-designed development initiative is beholden to a multitude of external factors that are completely out of our control, including global power dynamics, local power dynamics, gender inequality, greed, corruption, institutional racism, tribal conflicts, and even the weather. You could fill a swimming pool with all the books written about all of the factors that complicate our development efforts (many of these are worth a read, and you can find a list of some of them in *Annex Three*), so I'm not even going to try to crack that egg. However, in that great big swimming pool of complicating factors, several particular challenges tend to float up to the top a lot—and so a few are worth mentioning here.

≫➤ *No silver bullet*

Perhaps our biggest challenge is that when it comes to solving the problem of global poverty, there simply is no silver bullet. With a silver bullet, you could kill a werewolf, but that sort of magic doesn't exist in development. (But look on the bright side: neither do werewolves!)

There's no *one cure* for global poverty, no *one thing* we can do to make it all better. Each developing country is different from the next, and we need to create unique solutions to meet those unique challenges. We are lucky that bright, motivated and passionate people are showing up to solve those challenges, but it's not like we have a blueprint that we can hand them when they walk in the door. I truly believe that we are doing the best that we can to make the world a better place for everyone that lives in it, but sometimes I just want to know, *really know*, that we are doing the right thing. But there's no scientific approach, set equation or proven way to help a country develop. The devil is in the details.

For example, take the so-called Newly Industrialized Countries (NICs), which include South Africa and South Korea. They've both recently made the jump from developing to developed, but not in the same way. And, it's highly unlikely that you could've replicated South Korea's development approach in South Africa.

And, of course (of course!), those development success stories were in no small part due to one or more global factors (even coincidences) that were completely outside of anyone's control. For example, you can argue that 'development' alone didn't help the NICs develop, but rather preferential trade agreements or large deposits of well-managed and valuable natural resources. In fact, places like Hong Kong and Taiwan (tiny nations with no land) rode the wave of high-tech development, rather than resource extraction and manufacturing—which they only did because they had well-educated and highly-skilled workforces. Countries with lots of land and a low worker skill base (think: Mali) can't follow the same development trajectory.

⫸⟶ *Sometimes things go wrong*

For the past two decades, development professionals have been committed to 'do no harm,' which means ensuring that whatever development project or initiative is undertaken, it makes things better rather than worse. This might seem obvious to you now, but it wasn't always the norm in our industry. Mary B. Anderson first articulated the 'do no harm' principle in 1993, based on her extensive research about development projects that actually made situations worse for poor and vulnerable people.

I remember, in grad school, hearing about a development project that went horribly wrong, because the designers hadn't thought through the potential negative impacts. The project gave rural women seeds to plant and instructions on how to care for their crop. They then sold their vegetables at the market and had money to buy their children food and pay school fees. Sounds great, right?

But come harvest time, there was also an increase in domestic violence in the community. As it turned out, the women's husbands wanted the money that their wives were making through the development project and resorted to violence to get it. Had the project designers thought about 'doing no harm' by changing the relative economic power of women within established gender dynamics, they might have provided training for the men on how to respect their wives as household decision-makers, or they could have provided the men with similar agricultural inputs.

Today, an important part of the project planning process is to understand the dynamics of the context that you're working in (culturally, economically, politically, etc.), identify possible negative outcomes, and create a plan to mitigate them. (Yet another reason why cookie-cutter approaches to development don't work!) Designing programs in collaboration with local communities is a great way to ensure that you understand and respect the local context.

⫸⟶ *Developing country debt*

Let's go back to the seventies a moment. Not to the bad hairstyles, but to our approach to development. Free-market thinking was all the rage, and we gave developing countries lots of aid in the form of loans. Fast forward to today—and most developing countries' governments are utterly crippled by the fact that they owe a lot of money to IFIs. So what went wrong in between?

SOMETIMES THINGS GO RIGHT...

Development isn't always about identifying what's wrong and fixing it. Some approaches identify what's working well, and helps the community do more of that thing. An example of this is 'appreciative inquiry', which is a model that seeks to engage stakeholders in self-determined change.

There's also the 'positive dissonance' approach, which identifies success stories, and figures out what they're doing right. For example, instead of studying why children in a village are malnourished, we'd identify the ones that are unusually healthy. Then, we'd pick apart the parent's cooking habits to see what contributed to that success—and help other villagers to replicate that approach to cooking. Focusing on solutions, rather than problems, can work really well!

First off, let's talk about who is attending this particular party. The IFIs in question include the World Bank, the International Monetary Fund and the European Investment Bank. Most IFIs were created after WWII to help with Europe's reconstruction. When it comes to their dealings with developing countries, the IFIs' stated intention is to assist countries to develop by loaning them financial resources (money!) and by providing advice on how to better run their economies. Getting the money is contingent on the developing country government adhering to that advice (rules around fiscal policy).

Here's where things get complicated. All governments have at least a little corruption—and a lot of governments have much, much more than a little. Many dictators who rose to power immediately after independence (sometimes violently) took out massive IFI loans in the name of boosting their country's economies, and then funneled significant amounts of the loans directly into their personal bank accounts, leaving the government to cover the bill when it came due. Or, if the money was invested in the country, the funds were often given to a company owned by one of the dictator's cronies, which meant that there was little to no oversight of whether that company did a good job, or indeed did the job at all.

So, these developing countries now owe the IFIs billions of dollars, with having little to show for it (in the form of schools built, doctors trained, etc.). In many cases, even if the dictators was overthrown (or died in office) the loan agreement still stands. Worse still, because of interest rate spikes, the outstanding amounts have only gotten larger over time. Today, as a result, these countries need to use a large part of their earnings (from state-owned enterprises, taxes, etc.) on loan repayments rather than investing in their country's development.

Some people argue that the IFIs should forgive all of the developing country debt because the IFIs were the ones who entered into financial relationships with people that they certainly had to have known were corrupt. But it's more than an ethical argument.

The practical fact remains that if a developing country government were giving less of its money away in loan repayments, and had more of its own resources to invest in improving its economy, it would be more in control of its destiny, and less reliant on development aid. Others argue that if an official government representative took the loan, then the loan should stand. If countries can default on their debts without warning, then IFIs will be less likely to lend to poor countries in the future, the theory goes.

Developing country debt is an issue you'll hear about a lot as you learn more about global development and international relations. That's because money and power are constant bedfellows. Economics and politics—they go hand in hand at a local, national and global level.

Throughout your development career, you'll frequently be confronted by people who think that development doesn't really work, that countries actually need more investment in trade and commerce, that development creates a relationship of economic dependence without improving living conditions or alleviating poverty. (Google 'development aid effectiveness' for more on this.)

To all those critics, I say this: I know what I've seen. I've seen people whose lives have been improved because of development efforts: a young mother in Indonesia who was taught how to cook nutritious food for her child; a forensic science lab in Guatemala helping to determine the identity of the remains in a mass grave from the country's civil war; a tuberculosis clinic in Tajikistan providing treatment to patients; a microfinance collective in Mali enabling women to provide for their families; a hospital in Northern Nigeria providing life-saving surgeries.

Seeing these people's lives possibly saved, and definitely improved, by development efforts, I don't spend too much time contemplating whether development 'works' or not. The questions worth asking are: *What's working best and how can we get development to work better?* In fact, lots of brilliant people (like you!) around the world are putting their brains to these very questions, every day.

In *Part Two*, we're going to dive into the detail of what poverty means, and what you can do about it. And, as you're about to learn, poverty is not just a lack of money. Poverty is a lack of access. A lack of access to income, but also a lack of access to health services, education, gender equality, rule of law, physical security, banking services and a healthy environment.

By now, I hope you're starting to appreciate: everything is connected. And maybe, just maybe, you'll start to get an idea of where you belong in this complex and fascinating web of human endeavor and progress towards social justice.

REMEMBER!

- International development is an attempt to improve people's wellbeing by reducing and alleviating poverty and inequality and improving health, education and job opportunities
- The UN's Sustainable Development Goals frame our global effort to improve 17 different areas of human development
- The Marshall Plan was the birth of international development
- Development is continuously learning, evolving and adapting to be as effective as possible
- When it comes to solving the problem of global poverty, there is no silver bullet
- 'Do no harm' means designing development projects that make things better, rather than worse
- Many developing countries' governments are burdened by their debt to international financial institutions.

PART TWO

GLOBAL ISSUES

CHAPTER 6
POVERTY

THE NUTSHELL...

To understand development, you need to understand poverty: what it really is, and different ways of thinking about how it manifests itself in the world. This includes absolute, relative and multi-dimensional poverty, as well as income inequality at home and abroad.

WHAT KIND OF JOB COULD THIS BE?

Researcher at a think tank • Economist at a multilateral development bank • Monitoring and evaluation expert for a social impact investor • Communications strategist for a global anti-poverty campaign • Value chain specialist for an NGO

THE WORLD IS FACING AN ENORMOUS RANGE of social justice challenges—from the environment to health, education, malnutrition and more. Some of those challenges get a lot of attention from the media, others less so. But the one thing they all have in common is: they are symptoms of a larger problem, and *poverty* lies at the heart of them all. This is especially true when it comes to conflict.

If people were free from poverty, they wouldn't be tempted by alternative (read: violent) methods of supporting their families. If resources were abundant, we wouldn't need to create artificial social divisions (between religions, class, caste, gender, etc.) to describe winners and losers regarding how those resources are allocated across society.

Without poverty, we'd never have witnessed the Arab Spring, sparked by a Tunisian street vendor who set himself on fire to protest the confiscation of his wares and harassment by municipal officials. This one man, this one poor man trying to earn enough money to feed his family, catalyzed a series of uprisings spanning many Middle Eastern countries, including a protracted and bloody civil war in Syria.

And without the poverty that pushed one man to fight the government that sparked an uprising that led to that civil war, we wouldn't be witnessing millions of people from impoverished and conflict-affected countries pouring into Europe and beyond. It's easy to read about the refugee crisis in the news from the comfort of our homes, but it's harder to fully understand the utter desperation that makes someone flee their country. Somali-British poet Warsan Shire nailed it in her poem 'Home': *No one puts their children in a boat unless the water is safer than the land.*

So let's talk about poverty. If I asked you to define it, you might say that it's when a person doesn't have money. That's a pretty good place to start. If we're talking about poverty in terms of money: over 900 million people get by with only two bucks per day. Put another way: if the world were made up of only 100 people, 13 of them would be extremely poor.

Now think about all the things that you and your parents spend money on every day. It really adds up! In fact, it's an interesting experiment to calculate how much money you spend on food, rent, transportation, school fees, health care, clothing, utilities, household goods, etc., versus how much you earn in an average day. I'll bet that you'll find that only having a few dollars to spend every day just won't cut it! It would take you two days just to save up enough money to buy a Big Mac, and over a month to save up for that cool new shirt you wanted at the mall (during which time you wouldn't have any money to eat).

But for people living in poverty, it has nothing to do with not being able to buy the latest on-trend accessory or gadget. It's about not being able to afford the bare minimum they need for survival, starting with food and water. If you double the current population of the US, that's the same as the number of people in the world without access to clean water (who suffer disease and

28 death as a result). If you doubled the populations of *both* the US and Mexico, that's the number of people without enough food to eat. Poor nutrition causes three million children (more than the total population of Chicago) to die from hunger-related causes

29 each year.

Think of all of the things that make your house so comfortable. Maybe it's your bed, your room, your pillows, your hot shower, your computer, smartphone, video games, microwave, couch, or your fridge full of food. For much of the world's population, these are unimaginable luxuries. They sleep on the floor or a thin mat, they sleep in the same room as the rest of their family, and they don't have electricity or running water.

30 Think about this too: one in three people in the world lacks access to a toilet. It's easy for us to take for granted a clean and working toilet, but for two and a half billion people in the world, it's an unaffordable luxury. That means they have to find other places to go to the bathroom. Beyond the social unpleasantness of having to go to the bathroom outside, there are other issues at play. For example, it makes girls and women more susceptible to sexual violence because they're vulnerable when they're outside going to the bathroom. It also creates a lot of health problems because fecal matter (the brown stuff) gets into food and water supplies, and there's nowhere to wash your hands afterwards.

DIFFERENT TYPES OF POVERTY

WHILE LIVING BELOW THE POVERTY LINE is difficult for all the reasons I've just described (and so many more), that experience will, of course, vary from country to country. That's where different definitions of poverty come in.

Absolute poverty represents the minimal amount necessary to just barely get by (i.e. food, clothing, health care and shelter). The World Bank has set the absolute poverty measure at $1.90 a day; this measure is the same no matter what country you're in, and it doesn't change very frequently. We use the concept of absolute poverty to compare poverty between different countries (e.g. how many poor people in India vs. China). The global poverty line used to be set at a $1, then $1.25 and now, because of increases globally in the cost of living, it's now $1.90.

Relative poverty, on the other hand, is useful for comparing poverty within a country. Relative poverty describes how well you're doing in relation to the average standard of living in the country. For example, you might say that people in a particular region or city typically live on less than 40 percent of average income in the country. Relative poverty is important for looking at how wealth is spread within a country. For example, you might have a small number of people within a country living in absolute poverty, but a high number of people living in relative poverty. Both are important ways of thinking about poverty, as you're about to find out.

Development is about creating *inclusive growth*, meaning there is a reduction in absolute poverty thanks to economic growth, and an increase in the income of the poorest 20 percent of the population at a rate equal to, or even faster than, the rest of the country (read: there's more focus on the poorest of the poor). Countries where the economy is largely based on natural resource extraction, such as in many developing countries, tend not to have inclusive growth (although really, it's a challenge for every country in the world).

We see this in the growing gap between the 'haves' and the 'have-nots'. Rich people are getting richer while poor people are getting poorer. Oxfam's 2016 report 'Even it Up: Time to End Extreme Inequality' presents the startling truth about the state of global inequality, namely that the world's richest 8 people have as much wealth as the poorest *3.6 billion people*. Put it another way: if all those poor people wanted a bigger bank account than *just one* of those richest people, then you'd need over 58 million names on the account.

The Oxfam report makes for uncomfortable reading: "the gap between rich and poor is reaching new extremes. The richest one percent has now accumulated more wealth than the rest of the world put together… Although the number of people living in extreme poverty halved between 1990 and 2010, the average annual income of the poorest 10 percent has risen by less than $3-a-year in the past quarter of a century. That equates to an increase in individuals' daily income of less than a single cent a year. Had inequality within countries not grown between 1990 and 2010, an extra 200 million people would have escaped poverty… One of the other key trends behind rising inequality… is the falling share of national income going to workers in almost all developed and most developing countries and a widening gap between pay at the top and the bottom of the income scale. The majority of low-paid workers around the world are women. By contrast, the already wealthy have benefited from a rate of return on capital via interest payments, dividends, etc., that has been consistently higher than the rate of economic growth. This advantage has been compounded by the use of tax havens, which are perhaps the most glaring example set out in the report of how the rules of the economic game have been rewritten in a manner that has supercharged the ability of the rich and powerful to entrench their wealth… Globally, it is estimated that a total of $7.6 trillion of individuals' wealth sits offshore. If tax were paid on the income that this wealth generates, an extra $190 billion would be available to governments every year."

While measuring absolute and relative poverty is useful, it's also important to remember that poverty is more than just a lack of money. For example, income growth among poor rural people in India has been strong in recent years, yet child malnutrition rates remain stubbornly high (in fact one of the highest in the world). If we were only thinking about income poverty, we'd say that India was doing pretty well. But are those poor people really better off than they were before if malnutrition is still so widespread?

Increasingly, we're starting to talk about *multi-dimensional poverty*: meaning being poor in health, education, political voice, empowerment, decent work and physical safety. This more nuanced thinking around poverty is driving our current work in the development sector, and it's why the SDGs cover so many dimensions of human life.

We've also come up with ways of measuring non-income poverty. For example, the *Global Multidimensional Poverty Index* (as defined and tracked by the Oxford Poverty and Human Development Initiative and the UN Development Program) looks at poverty across three dimensions (health, education and living standards) and ten indicators (child mortality, nutrition, years of schooling, school attendance rates, cooking fuel, toilet, water, electricity, floor materials and physical assets).

Global poverty (income and otherwise) manifests itself in different ways. In fact, it manifests itself in all the issues that we're going to talk about in the rest of *Part Two*. Be warned: it's not an exhaustive list. However, these are some of the most pressing development challenges facing the world today, and all are areas that governments need to invest in so that their citizens can live healthy, productive and secure lives.

Nor is it possible to say which of these issues is a 'higher priority' than the others. Some people say that the priority should be health—because a country can't develop if its citizens are dying or sick all of the time. Others say education—because you need education to get a good job and become economically productive. Whereas other people say it's economic growth—because it doesn't matter how much education you have if you live in a country with a weak economy: there won't be opportunities to put your knowledge to use.

To me (as a democracy and governance specialist), it all starts with the rule of law and good governance, because you need good leadership to create stability and to have a government that's willing and able to invest in its own education system, health care and economy. But, of course, all of these areas are intertwined and necessary for truly sustainable development to occur. The rest of the chapters in this part will talk about the different faces of poverty and development.

THE POVERTY NEXT DOOR

POVERTY IS EVERYWHERE. It's true that most of my examples of 'what poverty looks like' come from overseas. There's a reason for this—the poverty picture you find in a developing country is much starker than you would find at home.

But listen carefully: poverty exists in the US too. Being the richest country in the world doesn't mean that *everyone* is well-off. In fact, there's more poverty in the US than you might expect. The US Census Bureau calculates our national poverty line by creating an income figure (a threshold) based on who is in a family (how many people and if they're of working age or not). If the family's income is below this threshold, everyone in the family is considered to be living below the poverty line.

In 2015, the poverty line for a family of four was set at $24,250 annually—which is about $16 per day per family member for paying for everything (food, rent, heath care, etc.).

So how do we stack up? You won't like the answer. In 2015, one in eight people was living in poverty in the US. Poverty rates among children are worse—if you're under the age of 18, you have a one in five chance of being poor. Children growing up

33

in poor neighborhoods are at higher risk of health problems, teenage pregnancy, dropping out of school and other social and economic problems, compared with children living in more affluent communities.

Worse, there are probably a lot of people living *just above* the poverty line, who are still struggling but not 'officially poor'. Also, the cost of living is different in different cities, so it's imperfect for describing poverty conditions—but it's still a place to start when trying to determine how many of your fellow Americans are living in poverty.

Here's why all of this is important. First, if you want to become an ordinary hero tackling the problem of poverty abroad, I don't ever want you to fall prey to the mindset that the 'US is perfect and it's our job to fix the rest of the world.' We've got problems at home too, and I would urge you to approach problems abroad with as much humility as you do courage. Secondly, maybe one day you will turn your time and talents towards solving the domestic poverty crisis. (And when you do, drop me a line, so that I can delete this section from the next edition of the book!)

THE JOY OF STATISTICS...

I've splattered statistics all over this book, so I want to say a quick word about them—because they're slippery beasts!

Most developing countries don't have sophisticated data collection systems to keep track of, for example, how many people have tuberculosis, how many students are enrolled in school, or how many people are living on/under $1.90 a day. Development organizations help with data collection, but it's not just a matter of someone going out and counting people—you have to know where to look. For example, there might be people in a rural village with tuberculosis who aren't getting treated, and so can't be counted.

Another challenge is that sometimes data questions are personal, hard to ask, or culturally understood in ways we don't expect. For example, in some cultures, domestic violence is so common that it's accepted as 'normal'. So when a woman is asked if she suffers from domestic violence, she is more likely to say 'no', because she understands what's acceptable/not acceptable in a different way than was intended. In other places, you can't ask how many children a man has—you need to ask how many children live in the home (because it's generally understood that the man has children scattered across different homes that the wife doesn't know about).

Data also needs to be sliced and diced by sex, wealth brackets, rural/urban, ethnicity, religious affiliation, sexual orientation, etc. This helps us understand how development outcomes differ between various groups in society.

Another challenge in statistics is keeping up with the pace of change in the data so that it's as relevant as possible. This is expensive! It takes money to hire people to undertake surveys, collect data and synthesize that data. With the internet, we have access to a wealth of information, but I think that we sometimes take for granted how hard it is to get that information and how quickly it can be out of date. So that's one reason why data is often prefaced with 'an estimated' or 'roughly'.

Finally, data can tell you *what* is happening, but it can't tell you *why*. For that, you need to do follow-up interviews to explore the trends that your data reveals.

Does all this talk about data make your mind go all tingly? If so, you may be looking at a future as a monitoring and evaluation (M&E) expert. M&E is fundamental to good development. It helps us understand what is happening as a result of the work that we do.

REMEMBER!

- Poverty alleviation is the key to creating a prosperous, stable world for everyone
- The global absolute poverty line is $1.90 per day, and helps compare poverty rates across countries
- Relative poverty looks at how poor a person is compared to the average standard of living in their country
- Poverty is more than a lack of money: it's a lack of health, education, political voice, empowerment, decent work and physical safety
- Income inequality has skyrocketed: the world's richest eight people have as much as the poorest 3.6 billion people
- One out of every eight Americans (and one in five American kids) lives in poverty.

Chapter 7
Health

The nutshell...

Healthcare challenges in developing countries have a huge impact on the success of our development efforts. Current global health justice issues include infectious diseases (such as HIV/AIDS and tuberculosis), maternal health and child health (such as entirely preventable ailments like diarrhea, malnutrition, maternal mortality and family planning).

What kind of job could this be?

Nutrition analyst for an NGO • Medical volunteer for a multilateral organization • Epidemiologist for the US Government • Malaria advisor for a public health organization • Water and sanitation expert for a development company

IT CAN BE HARD TO BE HEALTHY if you live in a developing country. Sometimes there aren't enough doctors and nurses to treat you when you're ill—or public education around how to avoid getting ill in the first place. The health workers you do have are often poorly trained or poorly paid. Your local clinic or hospital might not have the equipment and medicine it needs to help you get better. Your local ambulance might be out of service or non-existent. You might not have health insurance, making going to the doctor unaffordable in the first place.

These are some of the common ailments plaguing healthcare systems in most developing countries, although beyond that it's hard to generalize. In some countries, you can access adequate health care if you're lucky enough to live in the capital. Other places, good health care is readily available—but only if you can afford it. And there are still other places where you have to go abroad to receive good health care.

The ripple effects of a poor healthcare system are huge. People get sick more often and stay sick longer, which means they can't work or attend school. If a kid is sick, a parent needs to miss work to care for the child.

A lot of people in the US are lucky to have jobs where they have a certain number of 'sick days' (paid time off when they're at home sick). When you don't, or when you're self-employed or working in the informal sector: if you don't work, you don't earn. An estimated one in three people in the US doesn't get sick days, so they either have to come to work sick or lose out on earnings.

In developing countries, this figure is much higher—not least because so many people work in the informal sector. But even when it comes to formal employment (at a registered business), few countries have labor laws that guarantee the right to paid sick leave.

For almost one billion people around the world living in poverty, a sudden illness is a big deal. It's not just a matter of lost income—you might not have money to buy medicine. Here, I'm not just referring to everyday medicine, like cough syrup or decongestants, which can help take the edge off a common malady. I'm talking about the stuff that can make the difference between life and death, such as rehydration salts for children suffering from diarrhea, or antibiotics for pneumonia.

When I moved to DC after two years in Tajikistan, I was so grateful for the amazing health care we could access. In Tajikistan, a US nurse and a Tajik nurse served Embassy staff for routine matters. However, I knew that if anyone in my family got seriously sick or injured, we'd have to be flown abroad for more advanced medical care—and you'd just hope that this wasn't too much of an emergency because there were so few flights out of Dushanbe! I know that I'm lucky just to have had that option. Most Tajiks can't hop on a plane every time they have something worse than a cold.

It's estimated that poor health costs the US economy $576 billion per year (in other words, more than the entire GDP of Belgium)—and that's in a country where a lot of people have access to decent health care!

In poor countries, the bigger worry is that people are more likely to die earlier. There are 20 countries in the world (all in Sub-Saharan Africa) where the life expectancy is less than 60 years old. That means that an average person in one of those countries will celebrate anywhere between *20 and 30 fewer birthdays* than the average person in the US will. This is a direct reflection of the poor state of health care in these countries. More people die for all sorts of reasons, many of which are common things in the US that don't even frighten us because they are so easily handled, like diarrhea, childbirth or pneumonia.

People in poor countries also die of things that used to be a big problem in the US, but that we've since eradicated. Polio used to be a huge problem globally, but now it only occurs regularly in Pakistan, Nigeria and Afghanistan. Typhoid fever affects over 21 million people a year, but only 6,000 of them are American (and most of those cases are acquired while traveling abroad).

Measles, one of the world's most contagious diseases, is a leading cause of death of children—killing 16 children every hour (400 per day). It's heartbreaking to think that a safe and effective vaccine exists that could save millions of children around the world if only they had access to it. (Think of this the next time

34

you hear about the recent measles outbreak in the US – the first one in over a decade – because parents are *choosing* not to vaccinate their children.)

INFECTIOUS DISEASES

INFECTIOUS DISEASES LOVE PLACES with poor sanitation and weak health systems. When I say 'infectious', I mean diseases that spread through human-to-human contact, through bites from insects or animals, through contaminated water or food, or through organisms in the environment (think: parasites and other really gross things).

Some infectious diseases, like measles and chickenpox, can be tackled with vaccines. Others (such as pneumonia) can be controlled by frequent and thorough hand washing. The most common infectious disease in the US is influenza (the flu). Luckily, many people in the US can get a flu shot—about 60 percent of kids and 40 percent of adults do so annually.

We also learn basic hygiene rules at home and in school (such as washing our hands often and covering our mouths when we sneeze) that reduce the spread of the flu. Still, the flu kills almost 57,000 people in the US every year. Next time you wash your hands with soap and water—remember how important it is (and how lucky you are to have access to those things!).

Infectious diseases cause 16 percent of deaths globally (mostly in developing countries), are the leading cause of death in children and adolescents, and one of the leading causes in adults. The sad thing is: infectious diseases can be tackled through vaccines, better sanitation, safe sex, mosquito netting and other easy-to-use things. (Unless of course you're watching one of those doomsday thriller movies in which some man-made infectious disease threatens to wipe out the entire globe, but then Tom Cruise or Will Smith saves the day with seconds to go on the clock.)

Infectious diseases (especially those spread by human contact) are particularly brutal on already-weak economies. Poor

35

WORSE THAN A VAMPIRE...

36 Nearly half of the world's population is at risk of malaria: men, women and children. Malaria is a life-threatening disease that most people associate with mosquitoes because infected mosquitoes transmit the parasites that cause malaria. Sub-Saharan Africa is home to 90 percent of the world's malaria cases, and 92 percent of malaria deaths. In 2015, there were

37 about 212 million malaria cases.

Malaria is not inevitable (although it's a huge problem in 91 countries around the world); it can be cured and even prevented by avoiding mosquito bites. While traveling in a malaria-prone area, you can take malaria prevention tablets, but this isn't a realistic option for people living in developing countries.

One way to drastically reduce transmission is through insecticide-treated bed nets. It's estimated that using these can reduce malaria transmissions by as much as 90 percent. Notably, the rate of new cases of the disease fell by 21 percent globally between 2010 and 2015, and malaria mortality rates fell by 29 percent, and by 35 percent for children under five! However, that same year, roughly 438,000 people died from malaria, and 69 percent of these were children under

38 five (because they are particularly vulnerable to the disease).

healthcare systems quickly become overloaded, and business grinds to a halt when sick workers die, and healthy workers don't show up to work to avoid falling prey themselves.

An *epidemic* is what we call very high rates of infection across a large geographic area. During the 2014 Ebola epidemic in West

39 Africa (which claimed over 11,000 lives) the already-fragile economies of Liberia, Guinea and Sierra Leone almost collapsed. All three countries now have no Ebola cases (though one or two

cases keep popping up every now and then), but only after over a year of international effort, and hundreds of millions of dollars from over 30 countries.

The casualty list doesn't end there: West Africa as a whole felt the effects of the epidemic in those three countries. It cost the region millions, if not billions, in lost revenue because of a sharp decline in trade, closed international borders, canceled flights, reduced foreign investment and decreased tourism. For a corner of the world that already has incredibly high rates of poverty, Ebola was a costly epidemic.   **40**

Outbreaks of infectious disease are all the more alarming because we live in such an interconnected world. In 2014, for example, a few cases of Ebola hopped a plane with nurses from the US and UK who went out to volunteer in West Africa—which might have been enough to see outbreaks in those countries, had they not been quickly diagnosed and treated.

≫⟶ *HIV/AIDS*

HIV/AIDS is the world's most notorious infectious disease.   **41** It's now classified as a *pandemic*—which is what we call an epidemic that's gone global. HIV is spread through bodily fluids and (in the US) most new infections are from unsafe sex or sharing drug needles with an infected person. It can also be spread from an infected mother to her child during pregnancy, childbirth or breastfeeding. At the time of writing, there are 2.6 million children infected with HIV/AIDS in the world (a number that also describes the total population of Chicago).

There is no cure for HIV, but with the right treatment and care, an HIV-positive individual can manage the disease without it developing into AIDS. But many in the global south don't have access to the necessary medication (which is called antiretroviral therapy,   **42** or ART). Since HIV/AIDS was first discovered in the 1980s, it has claimed the lives of 34 million people worldwide. Today, almost 37 million people worldwide are living with HIV, although nearly half of those cases are undiagnosed (meaning that the individual isn't aware of having it, and is potentially engaging in risky behavior that can infect others). While new infection rates still hover around two million people per year, the good news is that in the last 15 years, infection rates have fallen by a third, and AIDS-related deaths have fallen by a quarter.

43 For developing countries, however, the news is a bit less reassuring. There were over one million AIDS-related deaths globally in 2015. HIV/AIDS spreads more quickly, and has higher fatality rates, in developing countries because poor people can't access affordable treatment (due to a nasty trifecta of smaller stocks of medicine, fewer doctors to prescribe that medicine and no money to afford the medicine anyway). Even when drug companies agree to lower their prices in developing countries, the cost can still be too much of a burden for those living in absolute poverty.

Worse still, national health ministries in the global south aren't often leading the charge regarding HIV/AIDS prevention—especially education about how it is spread. Without the information they need to stay safe, poor people are particularly at risk.

Predictably, infection risk isn't spread equally over society. Girls and women are much more likely than men to contract HIV, because of the biology of sexual intercourse, and because of the structural drivers that increase girls' HIV risk (poverty, gender inequality, sexual violence and poor education). Globally, young women (aged 15–24), are twice as likely to be infected with HIV than young men of the same age, and it's the leading cause of death for women between 15 and 44 years old. The majority of these deaths occur in Sub-Saharan Africa—which is also where you'll find the most cases of people living with HIV (almost 26 million), and 70 percent of new infections globally.

People in developing countries are also more likely to die from HIV/AIDS because of other health factors. Many are malnourished, which further weakens their immune system and makes them more susceptible to contracting other diseases (such as pneumonia) that could kill them.

So: if you were put in charge of a new global ministry of health tomorrow, one of your first priorities should be to make HIV/AIDS treatment, education and prevention a reality.

My friend Janell Wright is part of this fight. Today, she's a Public Health Specialist with the Centers for Disease Control. Reflecting on the journey she took to get there, she notes: "after graduating from college, I decided to take a year to turn my passion for public health into my vocation by working in HIV/AIDS clinics in Ecuador, Malawi and Guatemala. In 2005, when I was in Guatemala, HIV testing and counseling services were available in other parts of the country, but not yet where I was in the north. While I was in Ecuador and Malawi, I had seen the benefits of preventing HIV infections and connecting HIV-infected patients with local clinics to receive counseling and testing services. That's why I wanted to help establish the first comprehensive counseling and testing site in a rural hospital in the town of Flores, Guatemala.

"The very real need for public health services was made even clearer to me when I saw my second patient. She was 16, pregnant and, unexpectedly, tested positive for HIV. I was angry, frustrated and at a loss about how to help her—because the closest lab for treatment and further testing was over six hours away by bus. As she walked out of the clinic that day, my anger crystallized my desire to champion access to health services among the poor and marginalized populations of the world. So I decided to pursue a master's degree in public health at the University of North Carolina at Chapel Hill to gain the tools I needed to work in health policy and advocate for the people in developing economies around the world that were in desperate need of health care.

"Because healthcare services are expensive, they can be neglected by governments, donors and communities and treated as a low priority in light of other economic issues. This is a travesty, because lack of access to basic health care ultimately destroys communities, families and children who suffer and die from ailments and diseases that could be systematically prevented. Based on my experience, I know that without health care the people who will suffer the most in developing countries are often the poor, women, children and grassroots laborers. Health care is crucial to breaking the cycle of poverty and disease that blights and destroys their lives.

"After my studies, I wanted to explore managing programs serving marginalized and vulnerable populations, so I pursued a fellowship through the Association of Schools and Programs of Public Health called the Allan Rosenfield Global Health Fellowship with the US Centers for Disease Control and Prevention Office (CDC) in Vietnam. After my two-year fellowship, I stayed on to lead health system strengthening programs as a contractor for a year and a half. During that time I realized how much I enjoyed leading teams to develop and implement HIV/AIDS programs among vulnerable populations. This led me to apply for a position in the CDC's Central Asia regional office in Kazakhstan to lead the HIV/AIDS programming. This regional program is responsible for the post-Soviet Central Asian countries of Kazakhstan, Kyrgyzstan, Tajikistan, Uzbekistan and Turkmenistan focusing on prevention, care and treatment of populations affected by HIV/AIDS."

⇛⟶ *Tuberculosis*

Tuberculosis (TB) is the stuff of nightmares. You might be shocked to learn that roughly a *third* of the world's population has latent TB (which means they're carrying the bacteria, but they're not sick and they can't infect others). The scariest thing about TB is that you don't have to be intimate with someone to catch it. You don't even have to come into physical contact with them. It's transmitted through the air, so if someone nearby has TB and coughs or sneezes on you, you can contract it. You only have to inhale a few of the infected germs to become infected yourself.

Every year, TB kills about 1.5 million people (mostly in low- and middle-income countries. There's a stigma around TB, and even though it can be treated, most people don't know that treatment exists, or don't want to be tested for it.

For those that do seek medical help, the treatment can be expensive and drawn-out. TB patients need to go to their local clinic every day to receive the medicine—at least for the first few months.

This might seem like a pain, but it's to ensure that the patient actually takes the TB medicine. That's because it only works if the patient completes the cycle—and if they don't not only will they not be cured, they can develop a drug-resistant form of TB. This isn't just a theoretical risk: there is now multi-drug resistant TB (that's resistant to several common TB drugs) and even extensively drug-resistant TB (that's resistant to an even longer list of drugs). Drug-resistant TB is far more expensive and challenging to treat than regular TB—so we don't want that cat getting out of the bag any more than it already has.

TB is very rare in the US (only 3.8 people in every 100,000 contract it), but it's more widespread in other parts of the world (for example, in Tajikistan, the rate is 128 per 100,000). Part of the problem with TB in Tajikistan is the fact that so many people (especially men) migrate to other countries (mostly Russia) for work because jobs are scarce in Tajikistan (due to its weak economy). If someone learns they have TB after they've migrated, they don't seek treatment because they know that it will get them sent back home. So, they keep working: getting sicker and sicker, and infecting others as they do.

The good news is that there has been a global effort to reduce the spread of TB and it has been really effective. Even though TB is still a major killer around the world, the death rate has been reduced thanks to improved diagnosis and treatment: between 2000–2015, an estimated 49 million TB-related deaths were prevented.

MATERNAL AND CHILD HEALTH

DIARRHEA, NEONATAL INFECTION, PREMATURE BIRTH. These conditions are all easily preventable and/or treatable, but developing countries don't have the resources, skilled healthcare workers, informed individuals and infrastructure needed to make sure this is the case. As a result, most of the six million kids that die every year die from things that shouldn't have killed them in the first place. The scale of this heartbreak is impossible to measure.

Make no mistake about it: this is a problem of poverty. Every day, 16,000 children under the age of five die from preventable causes. That's one child every 20 minutes, killed by something that wouldn't kill someone living in a wealthy country. To put it another way: an Ethiopian child is *30 times more likely* to die before their fifth birthday than a child in Western Europe.

And perhaps what's most heartbreaking is that it wouldn't take a massive investment to make a huge difference to the problem. Half of these deaths are caused by malnutrition and a lack of safe water and sanitation. In fact, lack of clean drinking water is a major culprit in these preventable deaths. An estimated 1.5 million people, mostly children, die every year from water-borne diseases (such as diarrhea) due to a lack of clean drinking water.

⫸⟶ *Diarrhea*

We've all had an episode of diarrhea, usually due to a stomach bug or eating food after it has gone bad. Usually, the worst that happens is that you spend a few days in bed binge-watching *Game of Thrones*.

But in developing countries, diarrhea can be a death sentence—especially for children under five, who are fragile and vulnerable to dehydration and malnutrition. Mortality can be significantly reduced just by giving children and babies oral rehydration salts and zinc along with continued breastfeeding and/or fluid intake. It's a simple remedy, if parents know about it and can afford the treatment.

In the US, unsafe drinking water is the exception, not the norm. Even if we prefer fancy bottled water, it's a relative luxury that our tap water has been treated to clean it and ensure that it's potable (safe to drink).

In most developing countries, the majority of people don't have running water in their homes, so they get their drinking water from public taps, wells, rivers, or lakes—none of which have been treated. Not to mention that collecting that water every day is hugely time-consuming and sometimes dangerous for women (who are usually the ones who have to go get water and are at risk of sexual assault). The UN estimates that women in Sub-Saharan Africa spend *40 billion hours* per year collecting water—equivalent to a year's worth of labor by the *entire work-force* of France.

Even when people in developing countries do have running water, the water most likely hasn't been treated to be drinkable. Dirty drinking water can have all sorts of bacteria in it that can hurt your stomach and cause diarrhea. (Travel tip: when you live or travel in a developing country, brush your teeth using bottled water, and avoid ice cubes in your drinks!)

⟫⟶ *Malnutrition*

A lot of children in developing countries are malnourished, which means they don't eat enough nutritious food. There are various degrees of malnutrition: stunting, wasting and being underweight, as well as being overweight and obesity. Three million under-fives die every year from hunger. Children that are malnourished are more vulnerable to diseases, find school more difficult, and will earn less as an adult compared to their healthier peers. The right nutrition during the first 1,000 days **44** (from conception to a child's second birthday) is essential for **45** protecting a child's ability to grow, learn and thrive—all of which have a lasting effect on a country's health and prosperity.

Millions of people around the world are still subsistence farmers (and most of them live in developing countries). If you're a subsistence farmer, you only grow enough food to feed yourself and your family, and you often can only grow staple crops (e.g. corn, beans, wheat, sorghum) that don't give you a diversified diet. A family can even have enough to eat of a staple crop but still be malnourished, if they don't have a diversified diet.

The crop yield that a subsistence farmer can produce depends on a lot of things, like how much land they have, as well as how many seeds, pesticides and fertilizers they can afford. It also depends on things they can't control, like floods and pests. If they're lucky, they will have some extra crops left over to sell for cash or trade for other types of food, fuel and other essentials (such as cooking oil). This typically doesn't leave much money to buy anything like medicine or mosquito nets.

The children of subsistence farmers are particularly vulnerable to malnutrition. That's because if the crop fails, the family won't have enough food to feed itself, or cash to buy different food. When that happens, everyone eats less often, and less nutritious food, which leads to malnourishment.

⋙⟶ *Women's health*

It's scary to be a woman in much of the world, and one of the big reasons is because of the low level of attention and investment in women's health. It's important to recognize that health threats impact men and women differently.

Some of this is down to biology: it's easier for women to contract HIV than it is for men. In some countries, it comes down to cultural norms: poor families spend more on their sons' health than on their daughters', so treatable conditions such as TB, malaria and dengue fever more often turn deadly for girls. Girls are also often fed less, so are more prone to malnutrition.

46
47

The food thing is particularly troubling. In some countries, women eat after everyone else has finished, and don't have the same access to nutritious food like dairy, fruits and meat as their male relatives. In South Asia (Afghanistan, India, Pakistan, Bangladesh, Nepal and Bhutan), the death rate due to nutritional deficiencies for women between 15–19 was *three times greater* than that of males in 2010.   **48**

⇶⟶ *Maternal mortality*

As if all that wasn't enough, women have to grapple with an even bigger threat to their health and lives: childbirth. Maternal mortality is when a woman dies either from pregnancy, from giving birth or from complications after delivery. Every 90 seconds, a woman dies from pregnancy and childbirth related issues. That's 830 women every day. You could fill *two* jumbo jets with 830 women. Even more heartbreaking: most of these deaths are preventable because 99 percent of maternal mortality cases occur in developing countries where you'll find weak healthcare systems and low levels of investment in women's health issues.   **49**

Where there's maternal mortality: there's also neonatal, infant and child mortality. All of it is caused by poor nutrition, infection, lack of knowledge of simple life-saving practices, lack of awareness of risk factors, post-partum hemorrhage and hypertension. Another big factor is a lack of skilled birth attendants: globally, approximately one in four babies are delivered by someone with absolutely no medical training. If you're in Africa and South-East Asia, this percentage jumps to 60 percent. I've had two babies,   **50** and I can attest to the fact that you really, *really* want someone there with you who knows what they're doing and can help you if you run into complications. Lack of access to emergency interventions, like a caesarean operation if the labor is obstructed, can be a death sentence to both the baby and the mother.

Studies also show that when a mother dies, her children are more likely to die and, if they survive, are at a greater risk of poverty and neglect. Even when a woman does survive childbirth,   **51** other complications can occur during labor and delivery without good health care.

Obstetric fistula is one of these terrible complications that can happen when there is an obstructed labor that is allowed to last too long. There's no way to sugar coat this: obstetric fistula is when a hole is created between the vagina and the rectum or bladder, so the woman leaks urine or feces all the time. Every year, somewhere between 50,000 and 100,000 women are affected by obstetric fistula, and there are approximately two million women in Asia and Sub-Saharan Africa living with the shame and suffering it brings.

52

Fistula can be fixed by an operation, but most women who suffer from it don't have access to the medical resources needed. It's also easy to *prevent*, by delaying the age of a first pregnancy, stopping harmful traditional practices like female genital mutilation, and improving access to prenatal care. Without prevention or an operation, fistula can become a death sentence. If a woman's husband is not willing to live with her in that condition, then she can be cast out and shunned. The husband can keep the children if he chooses, or let his wife take them (although poor health would likely prevent the woman from being able to provide for her children).

⟫⟶ *Family planning*

Family planning is another important part of women's access to health care. The lack of access to contraceptives (because they are unavailable, she doesn't know about them, or her husband won't allow them) means that a woman cannot control her fertility. This means that many women in the world are pregnant a lot more often than they would themselves choose to be.

Family planning means deciding when and how many children a couple wants. It protects the health of women and children, strengthens reproductive rights, improves economic women's opportunities, reduces poverty, decreases unsafe abortions, mitigates the impact of population dynamics and reduces the transmission of HIV/AIDS.

53

If that weren't enough, greater access to family planning information and services could help reduce maternal deaths by 30 percent annually; save the lives of 1.4 million children under the age of five every year; save $7 for every $1 invested, and most amazingly of all, achieve all 17 SDGs by the year 2030! This makes me wonder why the heck development experts aren't doubling down on family planning interventions!

REMEMBER!

- Challenges facing health care in developing countries include lack of trained medical professionals, lack of access, insufficient medicine supply and lack of information
- Infectious diseases are contagious diseases that spread through human-to-human contact, through bites from insects or animals, through contaminated water or food, or through organisms in the environment
- Infectious diseases include malaria, HIV/AIDS, pneumonia, TB, measles and influenza
- Clean drinking water is vital for good health
- Malnourishment means not having access to enough nutritious food
- Maternal mortality is one of the leading causes of death for women and is preventable
- Family planning is when a couple decides how many children they want, and when.

CHAPTER 8
EDUCATION

THE NUTSHELL...

Millions of children around the world do not attend school, even though education is the cornerstone of development. The *youth bulge* in many developing countries only compounds this problem. We also need to pay attention to girls' school enrollment—because it's lower than for boys and there are huge potential payoffs for investing in girls' education that we're not tapping into!

WHAT KIND OF JOB COULD THIS BE?

Education officer for the US Government • Teacher • Girls' education specialist for an NGO • Curriculum developer for an education consulting company • Literacy expert for a multilateral international organization

SOME PEOPLE LOVE SCHOOL, SOME PEOPLE HATE IT.

I loved school, but there were definitely times that I faked a stomach ache just to get out of going. What I didn't know at the time was just how lucky I was. I didn't know that millions of children around the world want to go to school, but can't.

Children are kept away from school for all sorts of reasons: perhaps there's no school nearby. Perhaps there's a school, but the only teacher moved away for a better-paying job in the city, or the parents don't recognize the economic payoff in educating their kids. Perhaps the road between the village and the school is unsafe due to political instability, or because the bridge washed out in last year's flood and hasn't been rebuilt. Perhaps the latest outbreak of Ebola means that the school has shut down for the year to limit cross-infections. Maybe a child's parents need him to work on the family farm. Perhaps her parents can only afford to send her brothers to school, what with needing to buy uniforms, pencils, paper and books. Perhaps they can afford to send the girls, but they can't afford to buy sanitary products, and so the girls have to miss a week of class every month, and they fall behind in their schoolwork as a result. Or—perhaps local cultural norms don't look kindly on educating girls in the first place.

Yet this we know: education unlocks a better future, for everyone. This isn't just some hokey trope that teachers and parents reel out to get you to do your homework; the statistics will knock your socks off. Here's what the US Department of Education has to say on the matter: "College graduates with a bachelor's degree typically earn 66 percent more than those with only a high school diploma, and are also far less likely to face unemployment. Over the course of a lifetime, the average worker with a bachelor's degree will earn approximately $1 million more than a worker without a postsecondary education. By 2020, an estimated two-thirds of job openings will require postsecondary education or training." For developing countries, the figures differ, but the principle remains the same. School is where it's at.

Taking attendance

OUR GOVERNMENT PROVIDES FREE EDUCATION to every student from kindergarten through high school (this is also true of most developed countries). The majority of US students (81 percent, in fact) graduate from high school in the US (and those that don't find it a lot harder to get a stable job with a decent wage). Almost 40 percent of people in the US hold at least a two-year college degree.

The picture in the global south, however, isn't nearly so rosy. Let's start with the good news: 91 percent of primary (elementary) age children are enrolled in school around the world. However, that 9 percent that isn't in school translates into *59 million kids*.

Once we get to secondary school, the numbers drop further. Globally, 83 percent of 13–15 year-olds (lower secondary school age) are in school. This might not seem too bad on the face of things, but when you combine all the kids that dropped out of lower secondary school with those that never even made it to primary school—we've got a whopping *120 million kids* out of school. That's a big number, so let's put it into perspective. If the entire population of the US were below the age of 15, then over a third of us wouldn't be in school.

The bad news doesn't end there. Many kids stop going to school after 15 or 16 years old, which isn't really considered 'dropping out' because they've already had loads of schooling compared to their peers that left school sooner (or never attended), and sometimes that's the upper limit of what their school can offer them.

As you might expect, the situation varies by individual region and or country. Sub-Saharan Africa (made up of nearly 50 different nation-states) has the lowest school attendance rates in the world. For example, in Niger, only 22 percent of lower secondary school age kids are in school. South Asia has a low rate of lower secondary school attendance too—in India alone,

16 million kids aren't in school (that's twice the entire population of New York City).

You might have noticed that I've been focusing on numbers of kids in school, without talking about whether kids in school actually get a quality education. There's a good reason for that. Because most US students stay in school through high school graduation, the dialogue about school and school reform in the US is centered on the quality of education, rather than how many kids show up.

In contrast, the debate around education in developing countries has to initially be focused more on attendance than substance. The quality of teaching definitely deserves our attention, but there's no point talking about quality until we sort out the *quantity* issue. If you're a developing country, the consequences of having far too few students in school are startling, so simply getting more kids sitting at school desks has got to be the first battle that we fight.

YOUTH BULGE

ONE REASON WHY IT'S IMPORTANT FOR CHILDREN to attend school is that, particularly in developing countries, they're the fastest growing segment of the population. If you're between the ages of 10–24, there's a 90 percent chance you live in a less developed country, and most likely you'd be living in the Middle East and Africa. Countries in Sub-Saharan Africa, in particular, have very young populations: with over 70 percent of the region's population aged below 30. When a large percentage of the population is young, it's called a *youth bulge*. This mostly happens in developing countries where the birthrate is high (this is linked to poverty) and where people have shorter life expectancies (this is also related to poverty). More babies, fewer old people? Youth bulge!

There are different ways of looking at a youth bulge. If they have the access to education and jobs that they need, youth can

54

be an untapped resource with the potential to drive innovation and social progress. If they don't, they turn into the human equivalent of a ticking time bomb. I'm not being melodramatic here: when young people have little money, little education, little prospect of finding a job, and little hope for the future —they're effectively locked out of society.

When they don't go to school (and can't find work as a result), many of these young people (often young men, since women are more likely to work inside the home) look for other ways of belonging, and other ways of securing themselves a better future. What this looks like in practice depends on the country, but the menu of options in developing nations broadly includes joining gangs, rebel groups, militias or jihadist groups. Not good.

On the other hand, if a country can invest in their youth, keep them in school and ensure that youth unemployment doesn't get too high, those young people can be an excellent resource for a country. Today's youth in school are tomorrow's workforce, and they can drive economic development if given the right tools.

GIRLS' EDUCATION

ON THE SUBJECT OF OPPORTUNITY: in many developing countries, parents are often more likely to send boys to school than girls. Today, there are about 3 million fewer girls than boys in primary school, and around 66 million girls denied access to education altogether. The majority of girls out of school live in Sub-Saharan Africa and South Asia. This disparity is even worse in secondary school; for example in Chad (in Central Africa), girls' enrollment is less than half of that of boys.

That's why girls' education is so high on the development agenda, and why it receives more airtime in this book than boys' education. By and large, it's the combination of crushing poverty and crushing sexism that keeps girls away from school in developing countries. Parents are more likely to invest in their boys' future than their girls', especially in those places where women still do not fully participate in the formal economy. Globally, 77 percent of men participate in the labor market compared to only 50 percent of women, but as you know by now: global averages mask regional differences. **56**

In the Middle East and North Africa, only 22 percent of women participate in the labor market and only 31 percent in South Asia. When you look at specific countries, it dips even lower. Only 14 percent in Syria, 15 percent in Iraq and 16 percent in Afghanistan, West Bank and Gaza and Jordan.

If your girl won't be able to earn much when she grows up, there's little point in educating her, right? Of course, a woman's inability to make money is not just a cause of her lack of education, but a result of it. So culturally, it stops being a statistical trend and turns into a self-fulfilling prophecy.

Another reason that parents neglect their daughter's education is that it's just not a good return on investment—at least not for them. In many places, a grown boy is expected to stay nearby and care for the parents when they are older, whereas a girl gets married off (sometimes through an arranged marriage) and goes to live with her husband and in-laws (this is called *patrilocality*). But patrilocality means that even when a young girl is still living at home, she's not really seen as 'one of the family'.

⫸→ School can be a risky place for girls

Those girls fortunate enough to go to school face another horrific risk: as potential victims of sexual harassment and assault. It starts in the morning as they travel to school by foot, bus or taxi—often over long distances. Because they undertake the journey without an adult, they're vulnerable until the moment they arrive at school.

In fact, at the school gates, girl students just swap one risk for another as they contend with the potential for sexual violence from other students or even the teacher. An estimated 246 million school children (mostly girls) are harassed and abused **57** in and around school every year. That's like saying that if the US were populated only by children, then three out of every four Americans would be sexually assaulted or abused every year. Girls can view using the school bathroom as a threatening ordeal—in fact, one in four girls globally say that they *never* feel comfortable using their school latrine. Most schools in developing countries don't have indoor plumbing, so students have to use outhouses or pit latrines. Using the bathroom is a time when girls are targeted for assault.

Solving this problem isn't just a matter of passing tougher laws. Cultural gender norms, beliefs and practices are what lead to the power imbalances that make girls particularly vulnerable to violence, especially sexual assault, at school.

⋙→ A monthly challenge

The hassle for girls doesn't end there. If a girl is allowed to stay in school until she reaches puberty, she may have to stay home from school every month while she has her period. In many developing countries, disposable sanitary products are too expensive for lots of girls and women, so they have to use rags, leaves, newspapers or even mud, which can cause infection and be really hard to dispose of and replace at school. In India, only 12 percent of women use sanitary pads, and 23 percent of girls drop out of school after they start menstruating. An estimated one in ten African girls skip school during menstruation—for example, in Kenya, girls miss an average of almost five days of school every month because of their periods. Oft times, schools don't offer a place for girls to change their sanitary menstrual materials—a monthly reality for 83 percent of girls in Burkina Faso and 77 percent in Niger.

⋙→ A substantial payoff

Investing in a girl's education is not only good for her—a girl with just one extra year of education can earn *20 percent more* as an adult. When you add up all these potential individual

58

59

earnings across an entire economy, the wider impacts are astounding. For example, India's GDP would increase by an estimated *$5.5 billion dollars annually* if they enrolled just *one percent* more girls in secondary school. Educated mothers are also more than twice as likely to send their own children to school.

Educating girls isn't just smart money. It also has an enormous impact on their health, and the health of their future children. Consider this: a child born to a literate mother is 50 percent more likely to survive past the age of five. Girls who have received at least eight years of education are four times less likely to be married off as children—meaning you can stem the tide of both child abuse and maternal mortality (because childbirth is one of the leading causes of death for girls aged 15–19).

That's why educating girls is a great way of reducing population growth—because girls will get married later and start having babies later and a woman who has been educated tends to have fewer children and further apart, which means that she can invest more resources in the health and education of each individual child.

Better yet, girls who have even a little education are less likely to experience intimate partner violence. And because women are *experiencing* less intimate partner violence, their children are *witnessing* less violence, which means that you're reducing the culture of violence and are on the road to making violence a cultural exception, rather than a cultural norm. And that, my friends, is what we call 'intergenerational impact'.

WHAT'S WORSE THAN STUDYING FOR MID-TERMS?

SO WHAT HAPPENS TO KIDS that don't go to school, or drop out before they're 13? Well, a lot of them are expected to earn money or work in the home. In fact, there are 168 million children (aged 5–14) around the world working, and missing some or all of school (roughly double the population of Germany). Half of them work in hazardous conditions (defined as work that harms their health, safety or morals).

The good news is that there has been focused attention, resources and partnerships among governments, multilateral organizations, civil society and the private sector to end child labor. This means that, since 2000, the number of child laborers has fallen from 246 million. That's great, of course, but we still have a lot of work to do—because even one child laborer is one too many, let alone nearly 170 million.

YOU DO ACTUALLY USE IT WHEN YOU GROW UP

WHEN KIDS MISS SCHOOL TO GO TO WORK EARLY, they effectively miss out on their childhood. Skipping school also means that they miss out on an important part of their adulthood, too—because not being able to read, write or do

NO HOME, NO SCHOOL...

Homelessness is a huge barrier to getting an education. Around the world, an estimated 100 million children live on the street. The exact number is hard to pinpoint because it's nearly impossible to take a census on this portion of the population. Many of these kids are orphans; others have run away from abusive homes or simply need to fend for themselves if their parents are too poor. For these children, without outside help, going to school is simply not an option.

Fortunately, lots of NGOs are laser-focused on this problem. We've got a long way to go before we achieve 100 percent school attendance; but if you're passionate about this issue, maybe you could join the ranks of those fighting for the cause!

math makes nearly everything they need to do in a day a million times more difficult.

For example, if a poor person turns to agriculture to make a living—math helps them calculate how much seed to buy, how to set prices and keep track of profits. Math helps them calculate whether they're actually getting a better deal for buying in bulk. Math helps them make the right change for a customer when they're selling goods at a market. Reading helps farmers make sense of the instructions on the packet of fertilizer, helps them make sense of crop reports or a newspaper article on new government farming subsidies.

Reading also helps parents to give the right amount of medicine to their children when they're ill. Education helps people read maps, understand their legal rights, take out a loan, compare interest rates on savings accounts, decide which local political party to vote for, and so on. For poor and vulnerable people— being locked out of education means being locked out of life.

So what's the scale of the problem? Globally, literacy rates are pretty decent: 86 percent overall, with 90 percent of men and 83 percent of women able to read. But as with all statistics, global averages just aren't that useful because they mask poor performers. UNESCO data, for example, put overall literacy rates in Niger at 19 percent. Of course, that's a *national average*. When you drill down into the detail, you find out that men in Niger are the lucky ones: 27 percent of them can read, as opposed to 11 percent of women. For those of you keeping track, that's a 16-point difference in literacy rates between men and women. UNESCO puts Yemen's literacy divide at 30 points between men and women, with Liberia, Mozambique, Afghanistan, Pakistan, the Central African Republic and Senegal all above 25 points.

The stories about how low educational attainment affects people are heartbreaking. Missing out on school severely limits a poor child's chance of having a better future, and a life where they can make the best choices for their family.

At a national level, moreover, having a poorly-educated workforce creates a huge drag on the economy. When workers can't fill highly-skilled positions; when entrepreneurs aren't financially literate enough to get a loan to launch a new business; when half the potential talent in the adult population needs to stay at home to look after the children rather than contributing to creating national wealth—everyone loses out, plain and simple.

Education is the cornerstone of economic development, health and stability in developing countries. Children are the future, and the best hope for every nation to create a peaceful, stable society. To realize this potential, resources need to be directed toward education—both quantity and quality.

REMEMBER!

- Education is the cornerstone of economic development, health and stability in developing countries
- Millions of children around the world do not attend school
- A youth bulge is when a large percentage of the population is young, which is common in developing countries
- Girls' school enrollment is lower than for boys, and there are substantial payoffs for investing in girls' education
- Children miss school when they're forced to work, when their parents can't afford school fees. Girls who make it to school often miss school during their period or drop out when they hit puberty.

CHAPTER 9
WORK

THE NUTSHELL...

Work is an important part of economic growth—and creating opportunities for *decent* work is even more important. The work question echoes through debates around economic labor migration, living wages, the complexity of employment in developing countries and the barriers to female employment, all of which affect the potential of an economy to grow sustainably.

WHAT KIND OF JOB COULD THIS BE?

Labor and working conditions expert for the US Government • Ethical fashion advocate • Livelihood security manager for an NGO • Child labor expert for a fair trade organization • Ministry of Labor advisor • Union organizer

TO EARN MONEY, people in developing countries need access to work. In the ideal scenario, they'd also have access to *decent work*: jobs with rights, social protections and a voice in decision-making. We know that most people in developing countries do not have these things, and can't get them overnight—but we try to move them along the continuum from 'work' towards 'decent work'. That's because people can be healthy, well-governed and well-educated, but if there is no decent work, then the end goal of economic development will always be out of reach.

The International Labor Organization estimates that in parts of the developing world, 90 percent or more of workers don't have stable jobs. This means that they're either working in the informal economy (more on that soon), in unpaid family jobs, or in the formal economy as day laborers, on short-term contracts or other unstable hiring arrangements. Job instability means income instability—and unpredictable cash flows mean that it's harder for poor people to plan, save money and cover emergency expenses (in the case of illness or accident, for example).

Unemployment rates in developing countries are typically quite high. Why? The biggest cause is low levels of economic growth—which means there are simply not enough jobs to go around. It's also harder for poor people to access information about available jobs, and they might not have the skills needed for the jobs they do find. Also, potential employers are sometimes reluctant to hire people, because the local law makes it hard to fire an employee if it's not working out. (It's a textbook case of legislation designed to protect workers creating perverse incentives for businesses that end up hurting workers—ouch!)

In the US, we have a pretty well-structured labor (work) force that our government regulates. This means that laborers (all of us working fools!) have certain rights that the government protects (like our working conditions, compensation benefits, minimum wage and overtime pay). The government also deducts part of our salary to fund social security—our old-age safety net. Some workers form unions to further protect and advocate for their rights—and our right to organize is guaranteed by law. Nice one!

While most Americans have a pretty good shot at finding

decent work, labor issues still aren't perfect here. For example, the minimum wage is still not a *living wage*, and women are still paid less than men for doing the same job. Moreover, the salary gap within companies (between the top job and the workers), which we use as a kind of shorthand for wage inequality, is widening at a worrying rate. Yet still, with these (and other) problems, the labor situation in the US is drastically better than in developing countries.

A HISTORY OF LABOR IN THE US...

During the industrial revolution in the early 1800s, labor rights were terrible in the US. There was no minimum wage, no minimum working age or enforced time off (*aka* weekends). People often worked in dark, cramped, or unsanitary conditions, and weren't allowed to organize to improve things for themselves.

Starting around 1866, labor unions began forming in the US; these created a 'collective voice' to demand better working conditions. Around the same time, the US also started passing labor laws that further protected laborers and created legal precedence for worker's rights. Today, the US Department of Labor manages more than 180 federal statutes related to labor issues.

We now have a minimum wage, regulations for workplace safety and even regulations for workers compensation (in case you get hurt on the job). Some states also require work permits with parents' permission for teenagers to work under a certain age. Even for adults, there is an established 40-hour workweek—so if you're paid hourly, you get paid time and a half if you work more than 40 hours a week. (I've often wondered why the people advocating for a shorter workweek didn't aim for 30 hours instead of 40!)

DECENT WORK

HIGH UNEMPLOYMENT RATES in developing countries tell us that people are having trouble finding work. But it's harder, from a distance, to discern whether they're finding *decent* work. The issue of decent work deserves our attention, and I suspect that you've already come into contact with this issue without knowing it.

Have you ever noticed that t-shirts made in Bangladesh, India and Cambodia are always cheaper than ones made in the US? One of the reasons we import so much of the stuff we buy is that it's cheaper to produce elsewhere. Part of this is due to a lower cost of living in places like Bangladesh (i.e. the cost of

AT A MINIMUM, A LIVING WAGE...

The minimum wage represents the lowest amount that an employer is legally obliged to pay you per hour. A 'living wage', on the other hand, represents a level of income where you can actually support yourself and your family. This means getting paid enough where you can pay rent, buy food, go to the doctor, etc. Nothing extravagant, just the basics.

In the US, we have a set federal minimum wage of $7.25 an hour. It is good that we have a set minimum wage and, at the same time, this amount is too low to provide for a decent standard of living. Those who like a low minimum wage argue that a higher one would reduce business growth (especially for small businesses).

On the other hand, people who argue for a living wage feel that people should get paid at least enough to provide for themselves and their families and that businesses are being subsidized by federal programs that support poor families that just can't get by on the minimum wage.

housing, food, fuel). But it's also because workers are paid far, far less in developing countries than in developed countries (not just in absolute terms, but also relative to the cost of living).

In fact, the people making our very affordable latest fashion trends barely earn enough money to properly care for themselves and their families. That's because in many countries, even if there is a legally-mandated minimum wage in the formal sector, it's far below a living wage. This is because it is kept artificially low to compete with neighboring countries to attract investment—it's a 'race to the bottom'. How's that t-shirt looking to you now?

It gets worse. It's easy to keep the price of a t-shirt low if the company isn't legally required to spend money on ensuring the health and safety of its workers. Or, where labor standards might exist, sometimes the government is too weak to actually enforce them, so companies can pay their employees low wages, expect them to work really long hours, and to work in terrible conditions. (If this issue makes your skin crawl… you might be looking at a future career in the ethical fashion industry!)

Around the world, there are about 170 million children who are forced to work because their families are poor, or because they don't have parents to provide for them. These kids also work (instead of going to school) because there aren't laws to protect them from being forced to work (or if there are laws, they aren't enforced). They might have to work in mines, garbage dumps, the family farm, or in factories.

In fact, the US Department of Labor has compiled a list of 130 products from 70 countries made by forced labor, child labor, or both. Common, everyday products. Products that might be in your shopping basket. Products such as bananas, beans, blueberries, brazil nuts, chestnuts, broccoli, cashews, chili peppers, citrus fruits, cloves, cocoa, coconuts, coffee, corn, cotton, cucumbers, cumin, eggplants, fish, flowers, garlic, grapes, green beans, hazelnuts, lobsters, melons, olives, onions, palm oil, peanuts, pineapples, poultry, pulses, rice, rubber, sesame, shellfish, shrimp, strawberries, sugarcane, sunflowers, tea, timber,

61   tomatoes, vanilla, wheat… should I go on? (Top tip: Buying Fair Trade certified products is a good way of ensuring that kids

62   haven't made the stuff in your shopping basket.)

INFORMAL WORK

LABOR LAWS ONLY APPLY IN THE FORMAL SECTOR (hint: that's the part of the domestic economy that is regulated by the government). However, all countries have an informal sector that isn't regulated, taxed or monitored by the government. For workers, that all adds up to a lack of stability and even safety.

Outside of agriculture, informal employment accounts for at least half of all employment in most developing countries. In South Asia, it accounts for 82 percent of total non-farm employment; in Sub-Saharan Africa, 66 percent; in East and Southeast Asia, 65 percent. Even (or especially!) agriculture isn't stable—in developing countries, it's usually a family business. The success of the farm is at the mercy of weather, pests or gluts in the market, and time off work for sickness means no income that day.

What drives people to the informal economy, rather than trying to find formal employment? Well, there's no easy answer to that. In many cases, it's just easier. Sometimes people don't have the skills they need to apply for an available job. Other times there are just too few formal jobs available because people are isolated from markets, and there's a lack of infrastructure (such as the roads and bridges that connect the places where people make things with the places that people sell things).

If you need a loan to start a formal business, you might be out of luck. You might find it hard to find a bank that will give you a tiny loan (or will lend to someone without credit history and collateral). It's also a question of there being too much red tape (requirements) that stop people from starting a formal business.

Running the gauntlet of the paperwork, permissions, approvals and fees required to set up a business might be too difficult.

In a highly-efficient economy, businesses should be able to open and fold easily. But the reality of developing countries is usually far from that. In fact, the World Bank conducts an annual 'Ease of Doing Business' survey, which tracks a number of key indicators including: time and costs of starting a new business, ease of dealing with construction permits to build new facilities or buy existing ones, getting electricity/water connected, getting credit at a bank, regulations protecting investors and business that go bankrupt, the tax burden (in terms of cost and filing time), and how easy it is to hire, fire and trade across borders. The two things that slow down the creation of new businesses the most are onerous regulations and corruption. Regulations, of course, **63** are a delicate balancing act. Too few, and workers suffer. Too many, and businesses suffer.

Informal employment is sometimes also the *only* option for poor people because a company might not want to hire someone who is illiterate, innumerate, or who lives in a remote location. However, informal employment also tends to consist of low-skilled, low-wage work. Here, I'm talking about people with roadside food stands, people selling bottles of water and souvenirs to tourists, men driving tuk-tuks, women selling baskets and handicrafts in the market, and waste pickers at the landfill.

Often this work is done for cash in hand, which means that the person is vulnerable to theft in their home or when traveling to market. And very often, this type of work doesn't involve any prospects of growth, because the potential for innovation (doing more with the same amount of resources) is limited.

REMITTANCES

THERE ARE OVER 250 MILLION MIGRANTS in the world, and the vast majority of these are not refugees, but *economic migrants*. Economic migrants are people (usually sons and **64** husbands) who go abroad looking for paid work. These migrants, in turn, send money back home in the form of remittances (like sending money via Western Union); these remittances play a major role in supplementing the family income. In 2016, formal remittances to developing countries totaled $429 billion (we can't track informal remittances that people carry across borders, but no doubt it's at least that amount again).

While I lived in Tajikistan, I once heard that an estimated two million Tajiks were working abroad, mostly in Russia and Kazakhstan. No one knows the exact number, but even that estimate is astounding, considering that Tajikistan's population is only about eight million! Tajikistan is the most remittance-dependent country in the world—in 2013, remittances accounted for nearly half of its GDP! (It has since decreased a bit, but only because of economic downturns in the countries where Tajiks migrate to work, not because of increased economic opportunity or decent work in Tajikistan.)

Just think of the infrastructure you need to make remittances work. First, the worker abroad needs access to a bank account. The family back home needs access to a bank account. Those two banks need to be able to send and accept international transfers in a way that is cheap and reliable. And if you happen to live in a developing country, you can't take any of those things for granted. The number of people in the world without a bank account is falling, but still hovers around the 2 billion mark, which works out to be about four in every ten people that are unbanked. (If you're interested in learning more about banking for the poor, read up on financial inclusion, microfinance and mobile money.)

Of course, these days, the internet reduces some of the reliance on commercial and microfinance banks for remittances—there are many e-transfer services like Western Union or Money Gram that help people get money to their loved ones. All you need is an identification, which honestly can be just as challenging to get as a bank account for many people around the world (but that's a whole other discussion)!

VOTE WITH YOUR WALLET

YOU CAN INFLUENCE WORKING CONDITIONS in developing countries every day from the comfort of your own home, long before you embark on your exciting career in global affairs. Here's a quick reminder of why.

If your clothes are cheap, you need to ask yourself how good the working conditions were in the factory where they were made. All too often, the people who make our clothes in developing countries work long hours with little pay in terrible conditions. Most of the money you're paying for your clothes goes into the pockets of the company that manufactured it, or the store where you're buying it, not the person (usually a woman) who made it. And while there's increasing public pressure on companies not to use 'sweatshop' labor, there's no actual law that forces companies to comply with ethical standards. Of course, many factories do treat their workers well, abide by international standards and pay living wages—these are the ones you want to support.

However many factories (not just in the garment industry but also car parts, electronics, etc.) treat their employees awfully. For the workers, it's a textbook 'rock vs. hard place' dilemma. The pay may be a pittance, the working conditions awful, they might have zero job protection, sick leave or vacation days—but it's better than working elsewhere, and definitely better than nothing when they have mouths to feed.

When factories with awful working conditions are discovered, and public pressure is brought to bear on the company—closing them down can feel like the right thing to do, but can actually cause massive amounts of disruption for the workers involved, who need to go find new work. That's why it's better to work *with* the factories to increase wages, improve working conditions and ensure workers' rights, rather than to put them out of business entirely.

Why can factories get away with keeping wages so low in the first place? Supply and demand, my friend. The supply of unskilled workers far outstrips the number of factories jobs available—so factories can set the price of labor (i.e. wages) quite low. Because there are so many people lining up to fill each job opening, it also means that a factory can set high productivity targets (e.g. how many aprons you can sew per hour), and fire anyone who doesn't measure up. Remember the race to the bottom?

So if high supplies of unskilled labor are keeping wages low—where are all these workers coming from? The reality of economic life in most developing countries is that huge numbers of people are moving from rural areas (i.e. the country) to urban areas (i.e. cities, where the factories are). In the past 40 years, the urban population of developing countries has grown more than 320 percent. It's estimated that there will be almost two billion new urban residents in the next 20 years and that, by 2030, developing countries will have more people living in urban than rural areas. Over 90 percent of urban growth is in developing countries, where we see roughly 70 million new urban residents every year. (You gotta ask yourself who's left in rural areas to do the farming…)

Across the globe, millions and millions of people are migrating to cities to find work. Often their families collect money to help pay for them to get to the city, and expect them to send money back home to support the rest of the household (internal remittances).

Many rural people arriving in a city don't have the money to afford decent housing, which is why urban slums are swelling. Slums are large areas in cities where poor people live in poorly-constructed housing (often made out of found material like pallets and tin), with no or little clean water, electricity, schools, or medical care—and lots of crime.

Despite living and working in terrible conditions, this person needs to find work in order send money back home. But they might not even have enough money to buy nutritious food for

WORK

their immediate family, to find decent housing, or send their kids to school—so the vicious cycle of poverty continues.

If we want to really make a difference in developing countries and really help alleviate poverty, we need to start demanding that factories workers receive a living wage and have improved or quality working conditions.

A study on factory labor revealed that doubling factory workers' salaries (giving them a living wage) would create only a two percent increase in retail prices, whereas most consumers would be willing to pay up to almost 30 percent more if they knew that the item that they were buying was produced under good conditions. For a ten-dollar H&M shirt, we're talking about an additional 20 cents to help make the world a better place. This seems like a no-brainer to me!

It also makes you think that when Big Business says that increasing the wages of factory workers is bad for business, it's just bogus. Companies would still reap their profits, and retail outlets would still make money. The fact is: most consumers in the US would happily pay a few extra bucks to know that their clothes weren't being made in terrible conditions. I know I would!

If a factory worker starts getting paid better, she can invest in her family. If she has more money, she can buy school clothes and pay the school fees for her children, so now her children get an education and can obtain better jobs when they grow up, which means they have better educated and healthier children. If the factory worker starts getting paid better, then it means that she can pay to take her kids to the health clinic when they get sick. Not only is her whole family healthier, but this means that more of her children survive. (Remember that almost six million children die every year before their fifth birthday.)

What can you do to help? Well, it's partly about voting with your dollars, and partly about lobbying companies to pay their laborers higher wages. There are quite a number of organizations focused on this very issue—search online for 'lobby against

139

sweatshops' to find out how you can get involved. The increasing public pressure on this issue is really working.

Throughout the nineties, lobbying and protests against Nike for its relationship with sweatshops put a huge dent in both its image and sales. In response, Nike established a business code of conduct, including safety regulations, a minimum wage and a 60-hour work week at all of its factories (and if that still seems like too many hours, imagine what that says about how long the working hours are in other factories). Nike also started auditing and monitoring its factories, and publishes its findings as part of its corporate social responsibility report. The wages and working conditions in Nike's factories increased dramatically as a result of sustained pressure from activists and consumers—this is a great example of the power that consumers have to create positive change in other countries.

By holding companies responsible for ethical practices, we can help improve the working conditions of millions of people. As the old saying goes: vote with your wallet!

CHICKEN AND THE EGG

WOMEN'S LACK OF ACCESS to economic opportunity is a 'chicken vs. egg' scenario; women aren't allowed to work because they're seen as less valuable, and they are monetarily less valuable because they're not allowed to work. Solving this problem means attacking it on two fronts at once: structural and cultural. Structurally, access to education and land ownership would give women a huge boost toward economic opportunity.

⇒ Access to credit

Another factor affecting women's economic opportunity is a lack of access to credit and other financial services (such as savings and insurance). This affects their ability to create and run micro, small and medium-size enterprises, which are the backbone of the economy in most developing economies.

Lack of access to the financial sector is a reflection of gender inequality, and just one of the many hurdles women have to jump over to enter the formal sector or grow their business. If they can't, it means that women have to stay in the informal sector with all of the uncertainty and risks that come with being there.

You might be thinking: isn't the informal sector better than no paid work? And I'd say: yes, but nothing beats formal employment for reducing poverty and improving health, education and equality. Not to mention the benefit to the development of the country that formal employment brings in additional revenues from taxes.

In the past 30 years, women have enjoyed increased access to small amounts of finance with the advent of microfinance—a development tool that provides impoverished women with 'micro' loans, often without collateral requirements. But we're a long way from universal financial inclusion—and lots of women are still locked out of the formal banking sector.

⋙━━➔ *Women's work*

Jobs that have been traditionally considered to be 'women's work' (such as teaching) are poorly paid, in line with their lower perceived status. And get this: the feminization of a sector (when women enter an occupation in large numbers) can actually cause average wages in that sector to *decrease*. This **65** is linked to the devaluing of work done by women.

To top it all off, much of the work that women do is unpaid or in the informal sector—neither of which count as formal work. Women also rack up unpaid contributions to the household—housework, cooking, caring for children, laundry, caring for elders, etc.

Even though many fewer women are in the formal labor force, **66** women 'work' more hours than men. It's estimated that men work about 7 hours and 47 minutes per day (1.5 hours of which is unpaid), whereas women 'work' 8 hours and 39 minutes per day (4 hours and 47 minutes of which is unpaid).

Overall, the estimated annual value of unpaid work by women is (a mere) *$10 trillion dollars*, which is roughly equivalent to half the GDP of the US. Sadly, however, the economic value of women's labor is officially invisible, because unpaid or informal work simply doesn't appear in national and global financial accounting.

Even when women are paid for their work, they are consistently paid less than men. It's estimated that, throughout the world, women earn 60 to 75 percent of men's wages. And, of course, global averages don't tell us much. In the US, for example, women overall earn 80 percent of men's wages. But Asian

67

69

YOU MAKE THE CALL...

The call center industry in India is a great example of how improving economic opportunity for women can have wider positive impacts. The results of a recent experiment there showed that female employment not only improves the economic opportunity for the working women, but that it can also improve gender equality for women who aren't in formal work.

The experiment increased the recruitment of female call center employees in randomly chosen villages for three years. In the villages that had increased recruitment, there were significant gains in schooling and nutritional levels of girls ages 5–15.

68

These improvements were seen both in the families where women had paying jobs and also in the ones where no woman had paid employment. This reflects the fact that all families were able to see an increased value in girls and women because of the call center employment. The parents were able to see that an investment in their girl children paid off like it did for their boy children.

American women earn 85 percent of men's wages whereas Latina and Hispanic women only earn 54 percent, African American women only 63 percent and White non-Hispanic women earn 75 percent.

Scanning the rest of the world shows things are better off in some places more than in others. In the Middle East and North Africa, women earn as much as 40 less than men and in South **70**
Asia, around 33 percent. On the other hand, in parts of Europe, **71**
the wage gap is only 6–10 percent. There is no country in the world where women earn more than men, and the smallest wage gap is New Zealand, where women make 94.5 percent of what men do. **72**

⋙⟶ No ladder to climb

When women do try to enter the formal labor sector, it can be challenging to get jobs or promotions. According to the World Economic Forum's 2016 *Global Gender Gap Report*, **73**
women are held back by a number of challenges. These include an unconscious bias against women, lack of work-life balance, lack of female role models, lack of qualified incoming talent, and lack of confidence and aspirations.

So much of what reinforces these factors is gender inequality and patriarchal norms, which are when males hold primary authority and power. This is also true for the legal barriers women face. The World Bank's Women, Business and the Law research has shown that legal gender differences significantly decrease female labor force participation and undermine GDP growth.

Getting women into the workplace is smart money. Some estimate that eliminating barriers discriminating against women working in certain occupations could increase labor productivity by as much as 25 percent in some economies, simply by increasing women's labor force participation. **74**

For example, in Armenia, where I'm living now, it is culturally acceptable for women to attend college, but then often times, once they graduate, they're expected to get married, have babies and stay home. This is a huge missed opportunity for Armenia's

75   economy. The World Bank estimates that, in Armenia, as much as 14 percent of potential GDP is lost annually due to unequal opportunities for women to participate in employment and entrepreneurship. This is a country whose GDP is $10.5 billion (not

76   trillion; *billion*) and with a gross national income per capita of $3,880. That 14 percent, or $1.5 billion, could sure do some wonders to the wallet of the average Armenian.

Globally, around 82 percent of men participate in the formal

77   labor force, compared with only 56 percent of women. Statistical analysis has revealed that in the Middle East and North Africa, there is a 27 percent income loss due to gender gaps in the labor

78   market. In South Asia, it's 19 percent; in Latin America, it's 14 percent. Even in Europe, there is a 15 percent loss, which means that income per capita could be increased by 15 percent if gender inequality was substantially reduced.

There is good news, of course. Around the world, women have made small strides toward equality in labor force participation and pay. That's not to say that we don't still have work to do. It'll take another 170 years for women to receive equal pay

79   as men, and until that happens, men's predominance in economic activities consolidates their political and educational privileges, and the cycle continues.

REMEMBER!

- Decent work is a job that has rights and social protections (around pay and safety)
- Economic migration and remittances play a significant role in the global economy and in development
- A living wage is not the same as the minimum wage. The latter is a legal threshold, the former is what someone actually needs to get by (and is usually more than the minimum wage)
- Many people in developing countries work in the informal economy, which isn't regulated, taxed or monitored by the government
- Factory workers in developing countries often work in unsafe conditions, with little pay and few benefits
- Women experience structural and cultural barriers to joining the labor market, which is a drag on the overall economy.

CHAPTER 10
FOOD SECURITY

THE NUTSHELL...
Farming is vital to the economies of most developing countries. Yet farmers the world over face huge challenges, including land reform (which can cause conflict), and women are often at a disadvantage. As a result, food insecurity is high on the development agenda.

WHAT KIND OF JOB COULD THIS BE?
Agronomist for a food security advocacy organization • Food security project manager for an NGO • Demographer at a private company • Agriculture specialist for the US Government • Food security and gender expert for a multilateral organization

I'LL BE HONEST: when I was young, I didn't think about the hard reality of farming all that often. Living in the city, my view of agriculture was fairly narrow. Food was just that stuff that you bought at the grocery store (but good luck buying decent peaches in winter). I was aware of some of the big debates in agriculture—such as the value of organic farming, fears over genetically modified crops, farmer subsidies, competition from imported foods, and whether Monsanto (a huge agriculture company) really was evil or not.

Aside from that (and eating whatever was on my plate), my life was completely divorced from the reality of growing food in the ground and getting it to market. I think I'm right in saying that this is something that most people in the US can relate to: food comes from the store, not the farm.

In the rest of the world, it's an entirely different story. Most people's lives are intimately intertwined with agriculture. Farming is how one third of the world's economically-active population makes its living. So let's look at some of the key challenges facing the world's farmers today.

But first, let's get a picture in our heads of who we are talking about. When I say 'farmer', I'm not talking about people on those huge farms in the Midwest that stretch out as far as the eye can see. The ones who produce loads and sell most of what they grow (and use that money to buy food at the store for their table). Nope. I'm talking about subsistence farmers.

Most people involved in agriculture, particularly in sub-Saharan Africa, are subsistence farmers. Subsistence farmers usually grow only enough to feed their families, without extra food for selling or trading. This means that they eat the same one or two staple items every day. *Every day.*

Being a subsistence farmer is like saying: 'I grow rice and potatoes, so every day I am going to have rice and potatoes, and that's it. And, if I am really lucky on very special occasions, I will get to have some meat and green vegetables.'

Most Americans usually don't eat the same one or two things every day, unless you're a college student living off of Top Ramen (that's another story altogether). For subsistence farmers, eating the same thing every day all day means they don't have a diverse diet. It also means that if the crop fails (due to floods or drought), they go hungry that season. So, beyond it being a boring diet, it's not nutritious. And in many instances, it's not even enough to survive on.

LAND RIGHTS

LAND IS ONE OF THE MOST VALUABLE RESOURCES in the world (as the old saying goes: they're not making any more of it). Agricultural reform focuses on the use of land: specifically, who owns it, and who gets to use it. Access to land and land rights are essential to help alleviate poverty and suffering because even if you've only got a little land, you can start growing food (or raising animals) to feed your family and sell at market. However: land is also a complex issue, one that people often fight wars over.

In Guatemala (where I worked for a few years), the democratically-elected president was overthrown in a coup in the 1950s, which led to a civil war that spanned three decades and killed hundreds of thousands of poor and indigenous Guatemalans. The US backed the coup, claiming that the sitting president, Jacobo Árbenz Guzmán, was a Communist (remember, this was during the Cold War) because he was trying to undertake agrarian land reform.

Part of the reform was a proposal to buy some of the unused land held by the American-owned United Fruit Company (now Chiquita) and to redistribute it to poor and indigenous Guatemalans so that they could grow their own food and be less malnourished. So, along comes the coup, and any idea of pro-poor agrarian reform goes out the window. End of story.

Or not. Sixty years later, Guatemala still has staggering levels of malnutrition: nearly half of all children in Guatemala suffer from chronic malnutrition.

This is just one example of why land is such a hot-button issue. Ordinary people need land to grow food and survive, yet massive political and economic forces have a vested stake in the land they need. When these two sides clash, ordinary people seldom win.

Let's go back to our typical subsistence farmer for a moment. Of the more than 570 million farms in the world, more than 90 percent are run by an individual or rely primarily on family labor. This means that there are over 500 million small, family-run farms. These small farms produce more than 80 percent of the world's food.

The problem is: in most developing countries, land ownership is a tricky thing. Particularly in rural areas, people don't have deeds to the land they live on, and it's not uncommon for many generations of the same family to live on and work a parcel of land over which they have no formal, legal control. Sometimes land ownership is informally recognized within a community but could be challenged legally in a court of law. Where a country does have a formal land registration system, sometimes only men are legally allowed to own land.

If a woman can't own or inherit land, she can get kicked off her land when her husband dies (or leaves her) and be suddenly unable to provide for her children. Nor can the woman put up her land as collateral to get a loan for (for example) fertilizer or machinery that would improve her agricultural yield.

The scale of this problem is immense! Women account for 43 percent of the farm labor in developing countries but own only 10–20 percent of farmland. Just imagine the dent that we could put in global malnutrition levels if we empowered all of these women to be the most productive farmers they could be.

Luckily, we don't have to imagine. We know! Studies have shown that, if women farmers had similar access to the sorts of resources that male farmers have, they could reduce the number of undernourished people in the world by up to 150 million by increasing their agricultural yields by up to 30 percent. If I had to choose between more hungry people and fewer hungry people, I'd choose fewer hungry people every time!

80

Food security

FOOD SECURITY MEANS HAVING RELIABLE ACCESS to enough affordable and nutritious food (like vegetables, protein, etc.). Persistent food insecurity is a huge problem all over the world. Globally, almost 800 million people are chronically hungry, which means that they don't have enough food to lead a healthy active life (that's about one in nine people in the world). Of the world's children, one in four is stunted, which means that, as a result of long-term malnutrition, their little bodies fail to develop fully. In developing countries, this rate is as high as one in three. Chronic hunger isn't about short-term emergencies, like the aftermath of an earthquake or flooding. In fact, less than eight percent of people suffering from chronic hunger are in emergency situations. Rather, it's about a long-term suffering due to poverty, instability and underdevelopment.

For example, in Sub-Saharan Africa, years of instability (due to wars, coups, droughts, natural disasters, etc.) have wreaked havoc on the continent's food security. Forty years ago, Sub-Saharan African exported more food than it imported, but today it imports most of its food, including a lot of its grain—its main food staple. Sub-Saharan Africa suffers from declining soil fertility, land degradation, high agricultural input prices, the AIDS epidemic and other crises, which all affect its food production capacity. As a result, an estimated one in every four people in Sub-Saharan Africa is undernourished.

Bottom line: food is important, and I hope that the world finds the political and practical will to tackle this issue—because the impact of hunger is horrific. Hungry kids can't pay attention in school. Malnutrition kills three million children every year. Malnutrition causes half of all deaths in under-fives. What's more: *we can solve this problem.*

According to the World Food Program (the food assistance branch of the UN and the pre-eminent global food security organization), it would only take $3.2 billion each year to adequately feed the 66 million hungry school-age children living around the world. Three billion dollars might seem like a lot until you learn that the US's annual defense budget is about 600 billion dollars.

Speaking of the US, don't think for a moment that hunger is something that only happens 'over there'. An estimated 14 percent of US households face food insecurity, which means almost *eight million kids* in the US don't have regular access to nutritious food.

83

I can't even begin to justify why so many children face hunger and under-nutrition in a country as wealthy as the US. We're also facing an obesity epidemic as never before, which is something we see in developing countries as well. It's called the double burden: malnutrition *and* obesity, often in the same household. A child that is malnourished from the beginning has a greater propensity to be obese later in life and/or suffer from other chronic illnesses.

The crazy thing is that *there is enough food in the world*. Seriously. We just need to make sure it gets into the hands of people that need it. There is no reason for anyone to go hungry, ever. Not at home, and not abroad. According to the World Food Program, there is enough food in the world for every single person to have the nourishment needed to live a healthy and productive life. Yet still, we have chronically malnourished and hungry people: mostly women, children and those living in rural communities. What's the roadblock?

Even if a person can't grow enough food for themselves and their family, there is, in theory, enough food out there if they had the access (i.e. money and ability) to buy it. That's true at a national level as well: not every country is 'food self-sufficient', and most countries import one or more essential foodstuffs. The problem arises when people (and governments, such as those in Sub-Saharan Africa, Asia and Latin America) are too poor to buy or import food. Even when outfits like the UN want to donate food, poor infrastructure (and/or corruption) means that the food doesn't always reach those who need it most. Worse, there are parts of many countries or regions that are 'no-go' zones, even for humanitarian workers. That means that the people in need in these unstable or war-torn areas cannot access humanitarian food assistance.

One thing that can improve access to food is agricultural reform. A lot of donors work on food security, including the US Government (through its initiative called Feed the Future, designed to reduce global hunger and increase food security). Working with host country governments, the US (primarily through USAID) helps farmers increase their agricultural productivity, boost harvests and incomes of rural smallholder farmers, improves agricultural research and development, and fosters **84** policy environments that enable private investment.

REMEMBER!
- Most people's lives in the world are closely linked to farming
- Subsistence farmers grow enough to (hopefully) feed their families, usually without extra food for trading
- Agricultural reform focuses on the use of land: who owns it, and who gets to use it
- Food security means having reliable access to nutritious food
- Food insecurity can be lethal, cause chronic illness, and lower a person's IQ and future earning power
- There is enough food in the world, but not enough access for everyone.

OFF THE BEATEN PATH...

Working in development takes you far outside large cities and towns in developing countries (especially when you're working on rural agriculture projects!). In my time, I've traveled to some really remote villages in this world!

In 2009, while in Mali, and I went to a village a little north of Timbuktu. To get there, we drove for several hours from Bamako (the capital) to Timbuktu. From there we drove through a desert (where our car got stuck in the sand) for an hour to get to a river. At the river, we got in little canoe-like boats and headed upriver for half an hour. Finally, we arrived at the village! That might sound like a crazy journey, but comparatively speaking, that village wasn't even considered all that 'isolated', because it was on a river.

In your globe-trotting career, you might very well head to some really remote villages that aren't connected by any roads, or connected by roads that are impassable during the rainy season.

Want some travel tips? Always carry water, hand sanitizer and tissues for toilet paper. And when traveling for hours on the bumpy roads, the best way to avoid getting a sore neck is to let your neck go limp, so your head rolls around. Trust me, it works!

CHAPTER 11
DEMOCRACY AND
GOVERNANCE

THE NUTSHELL...

International development only works in the context of a functioning and stable state. We can build all the schools, hospitals and village wells we like, but if the government is corrupt and doesn't respond to the needs of its citizens, our development efforts are ultimately doomed to fail. That's why we also work on things like rule of law, good governance, elections, human rights, civil society and the media.

WHAT KIND OF JOB COULD THIS BE?

Democracy, rights and governance officer for a human rights organization • Citizen security advisor for an international organization • Civil society capacity building expert at a development company • Elections and political transitions officer for a multilateral organization • Judicial advisor for an NGO

STABLE, FUNCTIONING GOVERNMENTS provide an essential backdrop to all of our international development work. Our efforts depend on local communities having a strong sense of ownership over the future of a country, which is only possible when they trust that the government has their best interests at heart—as evidenced by strong rule of law, free and fair elections, low levels of corruption, a respect for human rights and a healthy civil society and media.

It's only in recent decades that development efforts have started investing more heavily in good governance. Our big 'ah-hah' moment on the importance of governance and democracy followed on the heels of decades of development efforts that failed to create more prosperous, stable countries. Many still had high levels of corruption, weak rule of law and civil society, and a scant regard for the rights and voice of its citizenry. (Were I to be cynical, I'd mention that this focus on good governance broadly coincided with the end of the Cold War, when the US and the Soviet Union stopped stacking their sides of the battlefield by propping up corrupt dictators in developing countries. But who's counting?)

Now, in full disclosure, I'm a democracy and governance expert, so I'm biased when it comes to its importance to development. But surely we can agree that throwing resources and money at corrupt dictators seems like a bad idea—whereas helping to foster governments that represent their citizens and use state resources for the good of their country seems like, well… a much better idea?

Certainly, development efforts are inherently worthwhile because they help save lives, alleviate suffering and create meaningful change in individual's lives. But they cannot create widespread, long-term, sustainable change without government buy-in and support. Why's that? Well, first: in a corrupt country, we can't guarantee that all of our aid dollars are actually reaching the intended recipients (or whether the president's cronies are siphoning off funds meant to build the new hydroelectric dam). Second: poor governance undermines the work we do on the ground (for example, why bother training journalists if the government clamps down on press freedom?). Finally: we need buy-in from the government, civil society and local communities so that they take the reins on our efforts (whether it's running the new hospital or managing the new school) when the development project is over.

In a nutshell, governance is where the 'rubber hits the road', because it intersects with all other aspects of development. The impact of all other development sectors will be stronger and more sustainable if there is citizen and government buy-in.

What's more, we tackle the question of democracy and governance from both sides of the spectrum. We engage with citizens to help them demand better, more responsive and accountable government. We also work with governments to help them supply more transparency, human rights and rule of law. When they finally meet in the middle? That's called good governance.

THE RULE OF LAW

ON MY MORNING COMMUTE IN TAJIKISTAN (I worked at the US Embassy there for two years), I'd typically see traffic police standing by the side of the road, waving random drivers down (even though they weren't breaking any rules). This never happened to me because of my diplomatic plates— but if you got waved down, you were supposed to pull over, give the officer a small bribe, and be on your merry way. The bribes weren't massive, usually only a couple of bucks—which doesn't sound like much until you consider that the average monthly salary is about $120.

Meanwhile, however, all around the officers, drivers were speeding, passing on the left (i.e. pulling out into oncoming traffic!) and making turns from the far lane. Drivers were reckless, aggressive and breaking every traffic law in Tajikistan, but they didn't get pulled over because there is very weak rule of law in the country.

In fact, it seemed like you were more likely to get pulled over for *not* breaking the law!

Rule of law, as you've learned, means that *everyone* in a country follows the law, no matter who they are. This includes ordinary people, police officers, politicians, civil servants, and even the prime minister or president; *no one* is above the law. The law is the same for rich people as it is for poor people. (Granted, if you're rich, you can hire a better lawyer, but you cannot outright buy your freedom.)

We have very healthy rule of law in the US (despite the odd hiccup). There's a lot about our rule of law that you probably take for granted: our well-functioning judicial system, our well-trained and equipped police force, the relatively low levels of violence throughout the country. Rule of law means that citizens understand their responsibilities (what is expected of them), and their rights (what to expect from their government).

A simple, practical example of the rule of law in the US is that drivers stop at red lights, and go at green lights. If someone runs a red light and a police officer (or camera) sees it, the driver will get a ticket and have to pay a fine for running the red light. If they don't think they were breaking the law, they can appear in court to contest their ticket. And, if they don't pay their fine, they will get additional penalties and eventually have to serve jail time. That's because breaking the law has clear and consistent consequences.

This might all seem a bit obvious, but in practice, there are so many steps that have to be taken for someone (in this example the driver who ran a red light) to be held responsible for breaking the law. You need functioning traffic signals in the first place. You need well-established traffic laws, and the driver has to understand these laws. You need enough police officers patrolling, or there has to be good enough infrastructure that there are traffic cameras at intersections.

The police officer who stops the driver has to be trained well enough to know the traffic laws, and paid well enough to give the driver a ticket instead of asking for a bribe to overlook the violation. There also has to be a culture within the police force that discourages corruption even if the police receive sufficient pay. (When a culture of corruption exists, the higher-ups at the police force will demand bribes from their staff, which will put pressure on the police officers to demand bribes from citizens so they can afford to pay the bribes they 'owe' to their bosses.)

To create an incentive for our hypothetical bad driver to pay the fine: there have to be well-known and well-understood repercussions for not paying, and the driver needs to believe that they will face them (i.e. receiving jail time for failure to pay). There also has to be a process in place for collecting fines that is easy enough that the driver will do it (i.e. just mailing it in rather than having to go to the police station in person to pay the fine).

To contest a ticket (when you feel you've been wrongly charged), you have to know your rights as a citizen. We receive a lot of civic education in the US, which means we have a pretty good grip on our rights and responsibilities as citizens. This information can be shared formally (in school) or more informally (through the media, religious organizations, the government and other members of the community).

Civic education is an important part of rule of law because it creates a culture of lawfulness in which citizens and government have entered into a pact where they will both follow the laws and society will function within these confines. Our government operates in line with a clear set of rules and regulations, and these are clearly communicated to citizens. Curious about what these are? There are lots of resources on the internet describing our laws, legal codes, regulations, etc. Seriously, you have no excuse for being in the dark about your civic rights and responsibilities!

Let's go back to our example for a moment. To contest the ticket, the driver not only needs to know their rights, but there also has to be a process in place for contesting tickets. This means there has to be a functioning judicial system, including a courthouse, a judge, lawyers, police officers, stenographers, guards and so on. Not to mention that the people working in the judicial system should be well-trained (i.e. you're not in front of a judge that bought their diploma online for five bucks) and free from corruption. A functioning judicial system is also necessary if the driver doesn't pay their fine and has to be taken to jail.

Bottom line: even though stopping at a red light seems like a pretty common sense thing to most drivers—it's also an excellent example of how complicated rule of law is and how important it is to the smooth functioning of a country. Pretty awesome, isn't it?

We are lucky to have such good rule of law in the US. There is still crime and murder in the US, but a well-functioning judicial system makes it less enticing to commit a crime. In Guatemala, for example, there is 98 percent impunity for murder, which means that only 2 percent of the people who commit murder go to jail. It is any wonder that Guatemala has one of the highest murder rates in the world?

Speaking of which: a high impunity rate is one reason why extrajudicial killings are synonymous with 'justice' in some developing countries. Extrajudicial killing is when someone is murdered for a crime that they committed (or are assumed to have committed), or in retaliation against a crime that someone else committed. A well-functioning judicial system protects innocent people too. In some developing countries, women are raped as a form of justice for a crime their brothers committed, or sons are murdered for a crime their fathers committed. In other words: never take rule of law for granted. It could save your bacon one day.

* * * * *

MY FRIEND DAVID RUBINO talks about his own work on rule of law with the American Bar Association Rule of Law Initiative (ABA-ROLI). He's currently its Country Director for Tajikistan, but his first encounter with the organization was when he went to volunteer for ABA-ROLI in Azerbaijan. He recalls: "When I arrived in Azerbaijan, the Women's Bar Association (WBA) consisted of eight female lawyers with no real plan for their organization. They were clear on their goals, but not how to get there. Part of the problem was a cultural one. There were two competing 'camps' in the WBA: the older generation, and the younger generation. Due to their culture's unique hierarchical dynamics, these groups rarely saw eye-to-eye. I started by identifying the common ground, racking up some quick wins, and in doing so building the trust we needed to tackle more divisive issues. And sure enough, once we did, we started growing. Soon there were 20 members. Then 50. Then 100.

"I trained them in grant writing, budgeting and the art of networking. Their ranks continued to grow. When the numbers hit three hundred, it was time for me to call in some backup. Help arrived in the form of a 73-year-old attorney named Barbara from the US. Barbara's progressive mindset won over the younger members, while her age and seniority earned her respect from the old guard.

"In addition to being a professional network, the WBA wanted to act as the legal guardians of women's rights in Azerbaijan. They secured grant funding to take on issues such as such as domestic violence, early marriage, human trafficking and workplace discrimination. I loved meeting the women that the WBA had helped and hearing their stories. I met a number of domestic violence victims served by the organization, including a young woman who the WBA helped to extract from a forced marriage. By then, the WBA was a 400-strong force for justice in the country. And, by helping to empower them, I felt as if their victories were mine.

"The program grew so successful that we received a visit from the then-Secretary of State, Hillary Clinton, and US Ambassador for Global Women's Issues, Melanne Verveer, during their scheduled trip to Azerbaijan. During the meeting, I sat proudly as the WBA members highlighted their successes and detailed the many challenges they had overcome. It was an honor that they thoroughly deserved, and a moment that I will not soon forget."

GOOD GOVERNANCE

A WELL-RUN GOVERNMENT PROVIDES for the needs of its people. All of its people. And the idea of *good governance* is really just that: a government that does a good job at doing its job.

Part of a government's job is to provide regulations, policies and laws for its citizens to follow in order to create an orderly, safe society (hello rule of law!). Governments are also supposed to provide services (schools, police stations, fire stations, hospitals, waste disposal) and infrastructure (roads, bridges, sewage removal, electricity).

For a government to be able to do a good job doing its job, the government needs adequate resources, both financial and human. A government needs educated, well-trained individuals to work for it and help run it. It also needs enough money to build and maintain infrastructure. And to have all of this, there has to be minimal corruption, lest state resources start finding their way into offshore bank accounts.

No country is immune to corruption, but some are less immune than others. In some places, the 'president' has complete control over the economy and exploits it for their own benefit. Worse still: no matter where it starts, corruption tends to trickle down until you get to the point where everyone functions using some sort of corruption as a practical and cultural reality.

Transparency is key to tackling corruption because the more transparent a government is, the harder it is for it to be corrupt. Transparency refers to how open government decision-making processes are (for example whether members of the public can attend Congressional committee meetings or official notes from meetings are made public). Transparency also means that the government's budget is recorded and available for public scrutiny. And it means that the government is held accountable by 'watchdog' institutions within the government—like the US Government Accountability Office, and the House Committee on Oversight and Government Reform. US Government departments and agencies also have their own internal accountability mechanisms, which are called the Inspector General's Office. Many civil society organizations and think tanks also play the role of external government watchdog, which complements the government's own watchdog bodies.

Lowering corruption isn't just good for government—it's good for business too! Less corruption means the government has more resources to invest in things that help economies flourish (like roads to connect rural areas to markets, or building the schools needed to have a highly-skilled workforce). It creates an appealing investment environment for the private sector: companies are more likely to invest in a country with a strong rule of law, fair taxation and stable regulation. On the other hand, a weak private sector results in fewer jobs and economic opportunities—which means that citizens will go abroad to find work, turn to the informal market (in turn creating less taxable income), use black market economic opportunities, turn to crime, or become dependent on charity. See how it all fits together?

That having been said, corruption is a really, really tough nut to crack. Even though everyone wins in a society free of corruption, the people benefitting from corruption are the people that need to be convinced to stop doing it—and they have no incentive to stop since they think they'll lose out by doing so.

ELECTIONS

FREE AND FAIR ELECTIONS are a fundamental requirement of any democracy. Democracy is considered the ideal form of government because it involves more accountability for results.

No one is saying that democracy is perfect. Indeed, as Winston Churchill once observed: "Democracy is the worst form of government except for all those other forms that have been tried." And, considering the alternatives, democratic governments do a pretty decent job providing for their citizens (social services, infrastructure, security, etc.). Otherwise, they'd be voted out of office in favor of a government that the people think might do a better job.

In the US, because we have such a well-run country, government representatives are usually elected based on their policies (economic, social, foreign, etc.) instead of their personal connections, their largesse in handing out bribes for votes, or blatant voter manipulation.

The point of having elections is so that citizens can choose who will represent them in government to manage the country's affairs. Elections are one of the most visible and participatory parts of the democracy and governance sector. It's where we see stuff happening. We see candidates out on the campaign trail giving speeches, we see debates going on in the run-up to the elections, and we see voters going to polling stations to cast their votes. Elections represent the intersection between politicians and voters.

An election is considered 'free and fair' if there is no ballot stuffing (i.e. fake votes being counted), no bribery, no use of fear or intimidation to get people to vote, and a viable opposition party. In a lot of countries, there is at least a little bribery or ballot stuffing or intimidation, but if it's not too widespread, then the election results are still considered legit.

In very corrupt countries, the president (i.e. dictator) can essentially steal an election by lying about how many votes they've received, and they don't care if it's seen as 'free and fair' or not. (What's amusing to me is that they still go through the theater of having an election in the first place, since they obviously know the results in advance…)

Election monitoring means that independent observers go around to polling stations and support the national election commission to make sure that the election process follows national and international electoral standards. There are always domestic observers, but it's common for diplomats from foreign embassies and staff from NGOs and multinational organizations to supply election monitors as well.

Election monitoring is most common in developing countries where electoral corruption is prevalent. One reason for this is that donors provide foreign assistance for democracy and governance projects—and are therefore invested in monitoring the elections to ensure that they are free and fair (to make sure that their investments in strengthening democracy are paying off).

Election monitoring is also more widespread in developing countries because there are not as many mechanisms in place to ensure free and fair elections. This is because the voter registration process might not be very rigorous, vote-buying might be commonplace, or the officials and volunteers running the elections might be corrupt or poorly-trained. There's also more of a possibility of candidates ignoring national elections rules (e.g. how much you can spend on campaigns, or where campaign financing comes from), and there's more of a possibility of opposition candidates not having equal exposure to citizens (e.g. the ruling party might dominate state-run television with its own campaigning and not give anyone else airtime).

I have done presidential election monitoring in Guatemala and Tajikistan. Guatemala is (to say the least) an imperfect democracy. Large numbers of its high-ranking politicians have been accused of genocide or other human rights abuses during the 30-year civil war. Other politicians have been named as members of narco-trafficking organizations or other illicit organizations. The president who won the Guatemalan election that I monitored in 2011 had been accused of human rights abuses during the civil war, and was subsequently kicked out of office during his term (along with his Vice President) on corruption charges. But all in all, the elections that I monitored were considered to be generally free and fair because there were minimal voter intimidation and ballot fraud.

In contrast, during the elections that I monitored in Tajikistan in 2013, there was no doubt that they were *definitely not* free and fair. The president, Emomali Rahmon (who had grabbed power after the fall of the Soviet Union) won around 87 percent of the vote, and wouldn't let the main opposition representative run in the elections. So, even though they had elections, no one would dare accuse Tajikistan of being a democracy!

In the US, we have two main political parties: Democrats and Republicans. There are other smaller political parties, like the Green Party, and candidates can run as Independents, but everyone knows that there are really only two parties that have any power. It might be nice if there were more political parties in the US to give voters a broader spectrum to choose from. But, because there are two main parties, we're pretty clear on what both stand for. Democrats are more socially and fiscally liberal, whereas Republicans are more socially and fiscally conservative.

In countries with scores of political parties (when I lived in Guatemala, there were more than fifteen political parties!), you don't necessarily know what a political party stands for. In fact, a political party is often just a vehicle for an individual candidate's agenda. This sort of situation means that the candidate isn't necessarily required to their campaign promises because they don't have a big party machine keeping them accountable.

POLITICAL REPRESENTATION (OR LACK THEREOF)

WOMEN'S LACK OF REPRESENTATION in the halls of government is yet another vicious cycle regarding gender inequality. Gender inequality runs through every level of government (local and national) and affects the policies and regulations that inform and reinforce societal gender inequality. Betty Reardon said it well: "Women's economic and social rights have continued to be denied, some argue, because their legal and political rights are severely restricted, limiting their power to make policy decisions affecting economic and social matters. Consequently, women are caught in a vicious

circle—they are poor because they are underrepresented...
[and] underrepresented because they are poor."

Let's start with a simple headcount. As of the time of writing in 2017, there are only 22 female heads of state out of a total of 195 countries. This means that despite making up 50 percent of the population, women only make up about 11 percent of heads of state. Is this just a case of 'change comes slowly?' Maybe; maybe not. In the nineties, there were 35 female heads of state, so by all appearances, we're losing ground.

Worse, this lack of representation trickles all the way down the whole political apparatus. Women aren't represented in lower levels of government either: from cabinet members (i.e. ministers or heads of departments), congresswomen, governors, mayors and city council representatives. Even when a woman is appointed as a minister, it's often as the minister of culture or education (considered 'female' spheres). Women are rarely appointed as the minister of economy, foreign affairs, defense or justice.

One effort to increase women's representation in government is the use of quotas. A quota is a legal mandate to guarantee that women will be a designated percentage of political representatives. There are roughly 45 countries in the world that have electoral quotas for female politicians enshrined in law. There are arguments on both sides as to whether electoral quotas help increase women's representation in government and reduce gender inequality.

The bottom line is: women will have a stronger, more equal, voice in society when we achieve more gender equality in political representation.

HUMAN RIGHTS

AFTER THE ATROCITIES OF WWII, the nations of the world committed to protecting human rights by creating the United Nations Universal Declaration of Human Rights. This declaration articulates the right to life, the prohibition of slavery, freedom of movement, freedom of association, thought, conscience and religion—as well as a number of social, economic and cultural rights. Human rights are rights that should belong to every single human being on earth.

Much like the broader democracy and governance agenda, the development sector's focus on human rights has only gained serious traction in the last few decades. Today, we recognize that human rights are a fundamental part of development— because our efforts to improve the lives and livelihoods of poor and vulnerable people are not as meaningful if those individuals are suffering from persecution from the state, or from other members of society.

In many ways, talking about universal human rights is our way of ensuring that a person is not persecuted for being a member of a socially excluded group. Socially-excluded groups include (but are not limited to): women, poor people, minorities (ethnic, tribal, religious, etc.), LGBTQ individuals and people with disabilities.

Human rights apply to everyone: marginalized or not. Rich white Protestant men are afforded the same protection of their human rights as poor rural Sikh women. That protection is supposed to be guaranteed by your government if it is a signatory of the Declaration. Moreover, that protection of your human rights doesn't hinge upon whether you agree with your government. In countries that have dictatorships, like North Korea, citizens don't enjoy human rights. They must do exactly what the government says, and when they say it. They cannot say anything bad about the government in the media or probably even to one another because the government has spies among the general population.

We have good protection of our human rights in the US. And I really do believe that we're on the right side of history. No one should be treated poorly just because they have a disability, are gay, a minority or a woman. The world is made up of a multitude of types of people, and no one type is better than another. That's all human rights is—it's the protection of people's differences.

Sadly, however, human rights abuses are all too common throughout the world. Here, I'm talking about thingS like ethnic cleansing; imprisonment without due process; treating women like slaves; persecuting LGBTQ people; or extrajudiciously arresting, torturing or murdering opposition politicians and activists.

Even though the world has declared its commitment to human rights, we've still got work to do to ensure that everyone enjoys the same access to human rights. Notably, those countries in the world with strong democracies and strong economies tend to have strong human rights records—which makes me believe that as a country develops, its human rights will also improve.

In the meantime, we can support civil society and governments in their efforts to protect human rights in lots of ways. One of these is to support the national human rights ombudsman, which is a position that many countries have. The role of the human rights ombudsman, and other national human rights defenders, is to respond to human rights abuse cases, advocate for victims, and strengthen legal frameworks to prevent *future* violations of human rights.

It's also vital to build the capacity of the human rights protection community (made up of community and watchdog organizations, lawyers, journalists and others) so that they can more effectively monitor, prevent and report on cases of human rights abuses. Often countries need to improve (or create), their anti-discrimination laws—yet even where laws exist, they may not be sufficiently enforced to prevent cases of abuse. Improving the legal framework is one thing, enforcing it is a whole other can of worms—not only for human rights but also for many types of legislative reforms.

Part of the effective implementation of human rights laws is educating everyone (and I mean *everyone:* judges, police, students, parents, government officials, teachers, etc.) that these laws exist. Then we train folks like the national human rights defenders, human rights ombudsmen, human rights NGOs, judges and police about how to respond to human rights abuses. Laws need to be enforced by clear and consistent consequences— this is true whether you're talking about running a red light or committing a hate crime.

There are also some outstanding organizations – local and international NGOs, and multilateral organizations – working on human rights. A lot of times, these human rights organizations are on the front line of protecting individuals' rights and freedoms—whether at the police station, in a trafficking shelter, on the floor of parliament or in direct protest action. Many of these organizations are founded by individuals with a passion for human rights issues, or who have been directly affected by a human rights abuse. We help them build on their passion and create an effective organization by training them on how to raise funds, engage constituents, publicize their efforts, etc.

One way that the US Government supports other countries on the human rights issue is by publishing a national-level *Human Rights Report;* this report is released annually in every country by the US Embassy. It is kind of like a 'human rights report card'. The reports advance human rights by presenting the facts gathered from in-country interviews, data and analysis. These facts help local human rights activists, journalists, scholars and government bodies raise awareness on the issues. Check out the State   92
Department Human Rights Reports to learn more about individual countries.

If we do all these things and do them well, then we're improving both the *supply* and the *demand* for human rights.

My friend Jennifer Lawson works on these issues as part of her role at the Department of State. She says: "Selecting and preparing local students, artists and professionals to visit the United States on a specialized exchange program are among my very favorite activities in this job. When these participants return to their home countries, we consider them 'alumni' of US Government exchange programs, and I love coordinating with them to

HUMAN TRAFFICKING

Think that the global slave trade is over? Think again. Trafficking in persons (TIP) is the modern-day version of slavery. It impacts women, men and children in every country around the world. The two main categories of TIP are for labor (domestic work, agriculture, construction, manufacturing) or sexual exploitation. Victims are forced to work or perform sexual acts against their will with no freedom to leave or compensation.

Victims are kidnapped and sold, or tricked. Migrant workers and indigenous people are particularly vulnerable. As you might imagine, it's tough to determine exact statistics on trafficking, because it all takes place 'underground'.

The most reliable source is the International Labor Organization (ILO), the UN's agency focused on promoting social justice, human rights and labor rights. According to ILO estimates, there are nearly 21 million victims of forced labor currently scattered across the globe. A little more than half of these are women and girls. The countries with the highest rates of forced laborers are India, Pakistan, Bangladesh, China and Uzbekistan.

Why does this happen? Because it's big business. Forced labor generates roughly $150 billion in illegal profits every year. However, even that much money can't justify such an abhorrent practice, and increasingly this issue is getting international attention. Governments, civil society, private sector and citizens all have a role in reducing TIP, and education is essential for everyone: for those at risk, and for those trying to eradicate this practice forever. The State Department has a Counter-Trafficking in Persons office; its annual report on the global state of human trafficking makes for harrowing reading.

promote our shared interests, such as strengthening education, human rights and democracy in their communities.

"I am proud to have selected Guatemalan social workers, lawyers and other professionals who we sent on a tailored tour of the United States to learn about how we counter trafficking in persons. They returned to Guatemala and, within months, opened a shelter specifically for victims of modern-day slavery.

"Another time, the director of an LGBTQ film festival in Ecuador met in the United States with grassroots organizers and artists advocating for the rights of diverse sexual and gender communities. He came back to grow his own festival into one of the most popular cultural events in the city, with our own US Ambassador delivering opening remarks in support of LGBTQ rights to cheers from the crowd.

"During the first two years of President Obama's Mandela Washington Fellowship for Young African Leaders Initiative, 42 young Zambian civil servants, entrepreneurs and non-profit leaders have studied at US universities for the summer, and then listened to President Obama speak at a town hall meeting in Washington, DC. These vibrant trailblazers returned to Zambia to reduce the incidence of child marriage, increase efforts to protect wildlife and conserve the environment, and many, many other impressive and exhausting feats."

CIVIL SOCIETY

CIVIL SOCIETY IS THE BRIDGE between citizens and their government. Having a robust civil society to amplify the voices of ordinary individual and groups within public discourse is aboslutely vital to ensuring that the government meets the needs of all of its citizens, not a small group of them. An independent media also plays an important role: as watchdog, early warning system and information provider. Together, civil society and the media are the hallmarks of a well-functioning state, because they help people engage with their government and with one another. For that reason, civil society and the media are high on the 'global development agenda'.

Civil society is an important means of providing services to beneficiaries (such as providing shelters for victims of domestic violence), representing marginalized portions of the population (such as indigenous groups, or persons with disabilities) and it also serves as a government watchdog and advisor (e.g. holding government accountable to established anti-corruption legislation, working with the government to improve domestic violence laws, mobilizing citizens to respond to cases of corruption, or advising the government on how to improve environmental regulations).

In many ways, civil society is almost like the non-governmental fourth branch of the government, because its role is ultimately to check and balance the power of the state over the citizenry. This is because it gives citizens a mouthpiece to communicate with their government as a collective unit. If there is something you care about, you can be sure that there is advocacy group out there that you can join.

Civil society organizations (CSOs) are typically founded by people who are passionate about a particular social injustice and motivated to do something about it. For example, in Armenia, a woman named Mira Antonyan launched the Armenian Association of Social Workers in 2004 to introduce the concept of social workers to the country, and to improve the well-being of individuals and communities as a result.

In 2007, Dilbar Khalilova saw the need for vulnerable members of her community in Tajikistan to get a leg up. That led her to start an organization called Fidokor, which provides training and services to vulnerable populations in her local Khatlon region. The Myrna Mack Foundation fights for human rights in Guatemala; it was launched in 1993 by Helen Mack in honor of her sister who was murdered during the Guatemalan civil war. Today, the Foundation is hugely active in defending people against human rights abuses.

Like I said, civil society groups grow in the fertile soil of passion and dedication. You certainly don't have to start your own CSO, there are plenty out there that you can join in your community or in another country to help bring positive change to people's lives. And they are playing a vital role in reducing global poverty and inequality.

Where countries have a weak civil society, people have fewer opportunities to organize in ways that speak to their interests and identities, voices their opinions, and advocate for their needs. This is one reason why less 'open' governments (such as dictatorships or pseudo-dictatorships) aren't fans of civil society—they feel threatened by any mechanism that helps citizens organize around a common cause, and fear that citizens will use CSOs to demand the rights that they aren't receiving.

One way that development efforts support civil society is through helping CSOs navigate complicated legal regulations established by their governments. Where government wants to clamp down on civil society, it passes draconian laws to make it really challenging for CSOs to operate. For example, the government can make it mandatory for a CSO to register as a legal organization, but then make it incredibly complicated and expensive to complete the registration.

A government can also make it tough for a CSO to *keep* their registration. In Tajikistan, one of the government's tactics was to revoke registration if a CSO moved offices without officially notifying the government within a certain period of time. The government would also send officials to CSO offices to see if they could catch them not following any of the complex regulations (like how many people are allowed to protest at any one time, whether foreigners are allowed to join the protests, and whether the organization accepts funding from foreign sources).

Development efforts also support civil society through capacity-building initiatives. Capacity building is exactly what it sounds like: building the capacity (skills) of an institution. For

CSOs, this could mean giving them training on fundraising, budgeting or reporting.

Why do they need this? Because USAID and other donors historically have given money to US-based or international organizations that are run by Westerners, who in turn gave that money as sub-grants to local CSOs in return for running a part of the development project.

More recently, we've started giving development assistance funding directly to local CSOs. Not only does this enable the local CSOs to grow, develop and become more sustainable, but it also means a lot more of the development funds go directly to the beneficiaries because of lower overhead costs. The downside is that local CSOs need to be trained up quickly on how to manage complex projects and budgets on their own. That's where capacity-building comes in!

The upsides, of course, are clear. It costs less for USAID to hire a local CSO than an international organization because international organizations have higher operational costs (offices, staff salaries, etc.). But the US Congress (who sets USAID's budget every year) is very interested in knowing where US funding goes and how it is spent, so the local CSOs have to be taught how to correctly monitor and report their spending. Other donors (such as the EU, the Brits, the Germans, the Japanese, etc.) also have their set reporting requirements and regulations that require local CSOs to have the ability to record, monitor and report on their finances and outcomes—so really, everyone benefits from ensuring that CSOs are organizational management ninjas!

THE MEDIA

A FREE AND INDEPENDENT MEDIA is the healthiest soil in which to nurture and grow a country's civil society. While *both* the media and civil society work to hold the government to account, their ultimate objectives can differ. Civil society organizations exist to advocate for the needs and interests of their members. Media outlets educate citizens by reporting stories about the government, but they also make money by selling newspapers, magazines, subscriptions, etc.

Civil society organizations provide the media with the content that they can use to achieve that objective (i.e. stories to print), while at the same time increasing visibility for their own issues within the public discourse. For this relationship to work, the interests of both parties must be aligned.

For example, when it comes to reporting on social injustices, the media is usually better at covering short-term crises (like earthquakes and civil wars) than long-term slow-burn injustices (like an ongoing famine in South Sudan). In that case, it's up to the CSOs to lobby media outlets to help their story gain visibility in the press.

Worse, in some countries, again like North Korea, the government doesn't allow any independent media. The only news available to people is from state-run news outlets. This includes news through television, radio, newspapers and even the internet (because the government blocks websites that they don't agree with). So the only news people hear is the news that the government wants them to hear. It's hard to imagine this reality coming from the US because we have such an overabundance of news sources!

In some countries, journalists are thrown in jail, or even murdered, for publishing stories that are critical of the government. This shows the power of the press. Dictators feel threatened by a free press because, much like CSOs, it serves as a watchdog of the government and as a mechanism for citizens to express their opinions and needs. Freedom of the press is essential to development because it helps people to understand the real situation in their country and, accordingly, to be able to advocate for themselves.

Here's one final bit of 'food for thought': media is changing. A lot. And fast. In the past decade, we've seen the rise of social media, citizen journalists and online bloggers. Advances in technology, and access to that technology, have democratized not just access to information, but have thrown open the question of *who gets to make the news*. Here I'm talking about ordinary citizens reporting to the world via Facebook from cities under siege, BBC journalists interviewing factory workers using WhatsApp, marginalized groups that leverage the power of social media to ensure that their story is heard far and wide. It's as simple as this: today, anyone with a smartphone can be a journalist.

This is one reason why it is so important to train journalists on how to do proper reporting. With so many people being able to 'report' on the news, it's important that there are media outlets with reporting based on verifiable facts. This is also where *investigative journalism* comes in handy: which is about going deeper into an issue than just daily reporting, to talk about not just *what's* happening, but *why*. Another important question raised by this onslaught of new 'citizen-reporters' is media literacy, which is the ability of the reader to access, analyze and evaluate the mountain of 'news' coming their way.

Of course, more news doesn't always equal better news; it's difficult to know just how to sift through the mountain of information available on any given issue; and no one has really figured out what this all means for traditional journalism—especially when it comes to social media being used as a source of news. No answers yet, but plenty of interesting questions!

REMEMBER!

- Stable, functioning governments are vital for sustainable development
- Rule of law means that everyone follows established laws, no matter who they are
- Good governance is a government that does a good job at doing its job
- Free and fair elections are a must for democracy because they are how citizens choose who will represent them
- Gender inequality runs through every level of government
- Human rights are rights that should belong to everyone
- Trafficking in persons, when people are forced into labor or sexual exploitation, is a problem all over the world
- Civil society and the media help citizens engage with their government and with one another.

Chapter 12
Humanitarian
assistance

—————•—————

The nutshell...

Humanitarian assistance is an immediate response to crisis situations caused by natural or man-made disasters. There is a close link between humanitarian assistance and development, because poor and vulnerable communities are hit the hardest when disaster strikes. Disaster also impacts the sustainability and viability of our development efforts.

What kind of job could this be?

Security and humanitarian access coordinator for an international organization • Humanitarian policy advisor for the US Government • Protection and advocacy manager with a human rights watchdog organization • Civilian liaison officer in the armed forces • Emergency nutrition coordinator for an NGO

—————•—————

GLOBAL DEVELOPMENT IS DESIGNED TO create long-term, sustainable change (poverty alleviation, improved access to quality healthcare and education, improved governance, etc.). When disasters strike (such as earthquakes, floods, famines or wars), we use humanitarian assistance to support the basic needs of communities within a very short-term time frame. At least: that's the theory, but disaster situations can last longer than we expect them to. Sometimes people's homes are destroyed by an earthquake, or there is ongoing fighting in their community. For example, Bethlehem's Deheishe refugee camp has been in operation since 1949.

Humanitarian relief includes basic emergency provisions such as food, water, shelter, healthcare, clothing—the stuff that people need to survive from day to day. When the crisis abates and the situation is stable enough for reconstruction to begin, our humanitarian assistance transitions back into development aid. At that point, you'll see displaced populations returning to their communities, buildings and other infrastructure being rebuilt, and people trying to go back to their normal lives. There's no clear line to mark where disaster assistance stops and development starts, and sometimes the two operate alongside each other until a situation stabilizes.

Disaster situations are terrible, to put it mildly. Many, many people are killed during humanitarian crises; homes and lives are destroyed. The after-effects are also terrible because they impede (and often reverse) years of development efforts. Take for example the 2010 earthquake in Haiti—it killed over 300,000 people, injured just as many, displaced about 1.5 million people, and damaged or destroyed almost 4,000 schools. All those figures add up to one stark reality: beyond the terrible loss of life, this achingly-poor country suddenly had more challenges to face than ever before.

Humanitarian crises also come with a big price tag; they significantly impact, and often derail, a country's path towards development, setting back investments and progress made in areas like health, education and infrastructure. For example, instead of training teachers, building new health clinics or improving the business enabling environment—government resources go to finding the bodies of those killed, housing and feeding displaced people, rebuilding homes, schools, roads and so on. It's pretty daunting to think about how hard it is for a poor country to claw its way back from a humanitarian crisis, just to arrive back at the point where it can once more start improving the fragile lives and livelihoods of its citizens.

Vulnerability in a Time of Crisis...

Women, minority populations and LGBTQ persons are uniquely vulnerable in the aftermath of disasters, humanitarian crises and in complex emergencies. Their vulnerability as socially-excluded groups is heightened and exacerbated by the chaos of humanitarian situations, because their vulnerability makes them easy targets of violence and abuse. This manifests itself in sexual assault, lack of access to resources (food, shelter, medical treatment, etc.) and exclusion from reconstruction efforts.

Practitioners in the field of humanitarian assistance have come to understand the unique vulnerability of marginalized groups during and after humanitarian crises and, as a response, have created the field of 'protection' within humanitarian assistance. These are specific individuals who work on ensuring that marginalized groups are protected after a crisis, which means planning for their needs before a crisis even begins. It's a heart-wrenching and meaningful field to have a career in, and I encourage you to learn more about it if it sounds like something that you have the heart – and guts – to handle.

Every year, humanitarian situations affect roughly 125 million people—about equivalent to the population of Japan. Natural disasters (such as earthquakes, hurricanes, droughts, flooding, pandemics, volcanic eruptions, tsunamis) top the list of causes of humanitarian situations. Annually, about 26 million people are displaced as a result of natural disasters. As a result of climate change, we experience an increasing number of extreme weather events, which quickly turn into natural disasters and create humanitarian situations.

As you might expect, developing countries have less of what's called 'structural resiliency' to cope with natural disasters. This means that there is a higher potential for massive damage from a natural disaster because there are fewer mechanisms in place for preventing disasters and less infrastructure that can mitigate the damage inflicted by a natural disaster.

To take a specific example, often times developing countries have minimal (or non-existent) levels of construction regulations (or those that they do have are not adequately enforced—hello corruption!). When there's no legal requirement for new buildings to be well-constructed, you find that people opt for cheaper (flimsier!) construction methods that won't necessarily withstand an earthquake or a hurricane. Or, buildings and houses might be built in floodplains; so flooding wreaks more havoc than in a country where regulations limit building in floodplains. (Regulations are your friend!) In the US, national law requires you to purchase flood insurance if you build on a floodplain. This means that, if your house gets destroyed, you'll have access to funds to rebuild it, and in theory, it should encourage you to consider ways to reduce the potential impact of a flood through innovative building methods.

Not only do most developing countries not have the capacity and infrastructure to prevent a natural disaster, but they also don't have the internal capability to adequately respond to natural disasters. This is where the international community comes in. Donor countries and international organizations usually provide humanitarian assistance to help these governments respond to disasters.

The US Government is the world's single largest humanitarian assistance donor. We've contributed almost *$26 billion* over the past five years alone to more than 60 new and protracted emergencies worldwide. The majority of US Government assistance is directed toward meeting the needs of the victims of long-running conflicts, but it also helps respond to the humanitarian situations created by new conflicts, natural disasters, health epidemics and refugee crises.

Of course, no country is immune to disasters, and no country ever aces the 'disaster response test'. Hurricane Katrina in New Orleans (in 2005) is the perfect example of flawed disaster prevention and response. An estimated 2,000 people died during, and immediately after, Hurricane Katrina. Even though in theory there was preparation and infrastructure in place to prevent a natural disaster—the levees that were supposed to protect the city from flooding broke. Even proper regulations couldn't protect against shoddy construction, in that case. Then, the government responded slowly in terms of evacuation, and many people trapped by the flooding died. Finally, the government was really slow to get reconstruction underway in the damaged areas of New Orleans. Bad infrastructure, slow emergency response and slow reconstruction: it was a textbook trifecta of ill-preparedness.

That having been said, there's a silver lining to this very dark cloud in US history, namely that we learned that humanitarian assistance is a two-way street. As the disaster unfolded, and it became apparent that our response would be inadequate, the global community rallied around the US, and 90 countries pledged disaster relief.

As we experienced during Hurricane Katrina, and indeed in most humanitarian situations, it can be challenging to access the victims of a disaster. We refer to the victims of natural and man-made disasters who have to leave home as 'refugees' or

CHILD INTERRUPTED...

Half of all refugees worldwide are children, a fact that absolutely claws at my heart. Being a refugee is scary and challenging even for adults, but I can't even imagine how utterly terrible it is for children—the deprivation, uncertainty, the danger.

'internally displaced people' (IDPs), depending on whether they cross international lines. Think of IDPs as 'domestic refugees': they flee their homes, but stay within the country.

It can be challenging to provide humanitarian assistance to refugees and IDPs. The list of reasons why is long: perhaps they're in very remote areas, or there is still fighting, or people are still on the move, or flood waters haven't yet receded, or the government is unwelcoming of refugees, or there just aren't enough resources to go around.

Providing humanitarian assistance is also complex because you need to utilize infrastructure (roads, airports, etc.) to get supplies into the country, but that infrastructure might have been pretty inadequate even before the disaster hit.

Furthermore, the logistical requirements of an emergency response are quite intimidating! You have to procure (a fancy word for 'buy') supplies, ship them to the site of the disaster, find a port or airport in which to unload all of the stuff, get staff on the ground ahead of time to receive the stuff once it arrives (and make sure that it's not diverted by corruption), procure vehicles or some other transport to get your stuff to those that need it, get staff in place at camps for displaced people to work out a system of resource distribution and hand out supplies and ensure that resources are distributed equitably. The situation gets even more complicated when the humanitarian assistance is in response to a conflict because this means there might be 'bad guys' (combatants) in the area that would love to get their hands on your disaster relief supplies as a way of controlling the affected population.

* * * * *

NEARLY 60 MILLION PEOPLE around the world have been forced to flee their homes in the wake of conflict or human rights abuses. But the hardship doesn't always end when they do.

When refugees apply for asylum in a new country they need to prove that their life was in danger, and/or that they were targeted in their countries of origin because of their unique identity (religion, race, political affiliation, sexual orientation, etc.). This is a long and complicated process, and asylum seekers can be kept in detention centers and made to feel like prisoners until a decision is made on their application.

Worse, when an individual chooses to flee their home due to persecution and embark upon a sometimes hazardous journey to a new country, it's quite common for the paper trail on who they are (e.g. identity papers), and what they suffered at home (e.g. police reports), to become lost along the way.

Other times, the sheer scale of a refugee crisis (for example those fleeing to Europe to escape the war in Syria) creates problems for individuals, as waiting times to start the application process increase, and political will to accept a seemingly endless number of refugees decreases.

Finally, refugees can find it hard to adapt to life in a new country, learn a new language and new customs, and integrate themselves into their host society. And this is all assuming they're lucky enough to move out of the detention center or refugee camp that they've initially been assigned to. Of course, the vast majority of war-affected refugees would prefer for the fighting to stop so that they could return to their homes.

* * * * *

COMPLEX EMERGENCIES (which is what we call it when a veritable smorgasbord of bad things happens all at once) also call for humanitarian assistance. A complex emergency can be a combination of a man-made disaster (e.g. conflict) and a natural disaster. Or it could be a man-made disaster coupled with an outbreak of a major infectious disease.

One example of a complex emergency was a cholera epidemic among Rwandan refugees who had settled in the eastern region of the Democratic Republic of the Congo (DRC). The refugees were Hutus who fled Rwanda in 1994 after members of their ethnic group committed genocide against a different ethnic group, the Tutsis (killing up to one million Tutsis during a 100-day period). The Hutu refugees (driven out when a Tutsi-backed government came to power) encountered instability in eastern DRC because of competing rebel groups, on top of which a cholera outbreak began because of the poor sanitary conditions in the refugee camp.

If you'd been there, you would have witnessed more than two million Hutu refugees, ongoing fighting among Congolese rebel groups, and an outbreak of a highly contagious and extremely deadly disease. To make matters worse, members of the *genocidaires* (the Hutus who committed the acts of genocide), had infiltrated the refugee camps to escape prosecution and regroup before launching a counter-offensive.

The only silver lining (if you can even call it that) was that when Mount Nyiragongo (a massive, active volcano in eastern DRC), exploded, the damage was limited. Don't get me wrong: it exploded, but not as badly as it did a few years later in 2002 when it killed almost 150 people and left 250,000 displaced. This next explosion created a whole other disaster situation that needed humanitarian assistance. When I was in eastern DRC in 2009, there was still evidence of the 2002 explosion: walls built out of the lava rocks and a threat level sign indicating the likelihood of another explosion in the near future.

Suffice it to say: humanitarian assistance is a challenging and complex field. If you've got guts and grit, it might be just the career for you. I've only really just scratched the surface of these issues here, but hopefully, I've whetted your appetite to go out and learn more. Many organizations do excellent development and humanitarian assistance work; check out *Annex One* for some suggestions.

REMEMBER!

- Humanitarian assistance is a response to situations caused by natural or man-made disasters
- Humanitarian aid transitions into development when the situation is stable enough
- The protection field within humanitarian assistance addresses the unique vulnerabilities that marginalized groups experience during humanitarian situations
- Victims of disasters who have to leave home are 'refugees' or 'internally displaced people', depending on whether they cross international lines
- A complex emergency is a combination of several disasters and/or threats.

CHAPTER 13
CONFLICT

●┄┄┄┄┄┄┄┄┄┄●━━●━━●┄┄┄┄┄┄┄┄┄┄●

THE NUTSHELL...

Conflict (usually of the violent variety) is a big area of concern within the international community. Not only does it threaten lives and livelihoods, it puts our development efforts at risk. No two conflicts are the same, but they can generally be categorized as being either interstate, intrastate, or extrastate. Just as there is every flavor of conflict, so too do we have a large arsenal of peace-building tools at our disposal (including truth and reconciliation tribunals and the Kimberly Process). At the intersection of conflict and gender: we see rape being used as a weapon of war, but also improving practice around bringing women into the peace-building process.

WHAT KIND OF JOB COULD THIS BE?

Conflict prevention officer for the UN • Mediator for a peace-building NGO • Peacebuilding and conflict transformation expert at a think tank • Crisis and stabilization officer for the US Government • Community development advisor for an NGO

●┄┄┄┄┄┄┄┄┄┄●━━●━━●┄┄┄┄┄┄┄┄┄┄●

THE ISSUE OF CONFLICT GETS A LOT OF ATTENTION in global affairs—we want to know who is experiencing it, who is trying to perpetrate it, and who is trying to resolve it. Conflict can cause widespread disruption to the global economy, global political relationships, the environment and the lives of ordinary people.

While non-violent conflict is technically possible, generally the term 'conflict' is synonymous with 'violence', whether this is in the form of state-sanctioned conflict, terrorists, narco-traffickers or gangs. The pen may be mightier than the sword, but these people are armed with serious weaponry, and they often use it to advance their agendas.

America's role in global conflict is complicated (that's putting it mildly). In the case of the recent conflicts in Iraq and Afghanistan, we have initiated the conflict. Other times the US (because of our geopolitical strength and massive military capability) has been called upon to help resolve conflicts we are not directly involved in. As you might have guessed, when the US plays 'global police officer', reactions around the world vary. Some think that the US is sticking its national nose where it doesn't belong (and sometimes with the unspoken aim of furthering our own national security priorities across the globe).

Others believe that the global community relies too much on the US to sort out their conflicts and that the country should take a more isolationist approach, which would mean we'd only intervene in conflicts that directly affected us.

Still others think that the US is best-placed to resolve a conflict because we are in a good position to promote democracy, the rule of law and human rights. And finally, some people think that we should intervene because it's the price that we pay for being the last hegemon standing—at least for now.

Whatever your stance on the moral/ethical issues, the fact remains: through the commitments outlined in defense pacts that the US has signed, our country is legally obligated to defend over 60 countries on five continents, which equals a quarter of the world's population, and nearly three-quarters of global economic output. Of course, whether this commitment makes the world a safer or a more dangerous place is definitely up for debate.

Most conflicts around the world typically don't get much attention from the US military or media. Our foreign policy determines whether we intervene or not, and when we do: it should be extremely clear how doing so supports our own national security. When the media picks up the story, it's generally only at the peak of the violence (until the next big story comes along).

For example, the conflict in Sudan (ongoing intermittently since independence in the mid-1950s), only really hit our news-papers when the ethnic cleansing in the Darfur region reached near-genocidal proportions. And while US cameras have stopped rolling, the region is still mired in conflict. So too is the south of Sudan—which seceded from the north to form the independent nation of South Sudan.

The same can be said of other Sub-Saharan African countries: the Central African Republic, DRC, Mali, Somalia—and that's only part of the list. Of course, Sub-Saharan Africa isn't the only place that gets ignored by Western media; take for example the row between Armenia and Azerbaijan over the disputed territory of Nagorno-Karabakh, the narco and gang violence plaguing much of Latin America and the Islamic insurgency in the Philippines.

The conflicts that do get airtime in the US are usually those that the US has initiated (such as Iraq and Afghanistan), those that are considered geopolitically significant (such as Syria) or those that affect a US ally (such as the Paris terrorist attacks).

SOURCES OF CONFLICT

VIOLENT CONFLICT IS JUST WHAT YOU'D EXPECT: using violence to get what you want. Conflict is as old as the human race, and humans fight for all sorts of reasons. As a conflict expert, I'm pretty pragmatic about the topic. Conflict is inevitable because disagreements between different people and different nations are inevitable in the grand scheme of things.

However, I also know that not all conflict needs to turn violent. There is a role in this world for non-violent conflict: Gandhi led a peaceful revolution in India; Mandela in South Africa; Martin Luther King Jr. in the US during the civil rights era. Yet sadly, it's the exception rather than the rule. Whether violence is seen as simpler or easier, or whether it's seen as the only option, violent conflict litters the annals of human history.

Understanding the real drivers of conflict is the critical first step in solving it. When I say *drivers*, I'm referring to the people, groups, events and institutions that engage in and perpetuate a conflict. Bear in mind: conflict is complex, and often there is more than one driver.

Armed conflict and endemic violence are caused by a myriad of factors. To name just a few: conflict can be sparked by tensions due to differences in religion, ideology, ethnicity or culture. It can be caused by competition over territory (domestically or across borders), or a fight for political power. It can be a struggle for freedom from oppressive governments, or it can be for access to natural resources. Sometimes it's a global coalition of forces trying to topple the latest designated 'bad guy'. The reasons are endless, yet to my mind never good enough to justify violent conflict. Nobody wins in war. Everybody loses.

In many former colonies, especially in Sub-Saharan Africa, the aftermath of World War II never really ended. Rather, the conflict has been simmering (or worse) since the mid-fifties. Many of these conflicts started because of people fighting to gain power in the political vacuum left after independence. Some of these have endured as a direct result of the ineptitude of post-colonial dictators in improving their countries after they grabbed power. As you might expect, most of these dictators abused their position for their own gain and left people to fend for themselves.

On top of bad governance, these nations were also dealing

with ethnic tensions arising because many of these new countries didn't have state borders that aligned with their national (cultural) identities. Even where different ethnic groups had historically co-existed peacefully, the colonial powers often used a 'divide and conquer' tactic to pit them against each other—creating ethnic tension that would linger for decades. As if that wasn't bad enough—add in the struggle to control lucrative natural resources (e.g. diamonds in Angola, oil in Nigeria, gold in Liberia), and you've got yourself a tinderbox.

* * * * *

'THE RESOURCE CURSE' IS what we call armed conflict and violence aimed at controlling lucrative natural resources. You would think that having a lot of natural resources (timber, coal, gold, oil, etc.) would be a good thing for a poor country, right?

In an ideal world, the state could sell its natural resources to make money to help the country develop. But, when the government is inept or corrupt, none of that actually happens. Instead, sometimes the government (especially a dictator) uses the profits from the sale of the natural resources for their own profit (by embezzling the money from the government). Other times, competing militias want to use the natural resources for their own benefit. We've seen this happen time and again in the form of bloody and protracted conflicts over the control of natural resources in Burma, Angola, Pakistan, Nigeria, Papua New Guinea and others.

The *Kimberly Process* is one way that governments, civil society and the private sector try to work together to reduce the resource curse. Historically, diamonds have been one of the most fought-over resources. Diamonds that came from diamond mines in countries in conflict were called 'conflict diamonds'. These conflict diamonds would bankroll the rebel groups terrorizing the local population (a model sadly replicated in other conflicts, over other resources, still today). At the turn of the 21st century, governments, civil society and the diamond industry agreed upon the Kimberly Process (named after the town where the first meeting occurred), to certify that diamonds are conflict-free.

Unfortunately, it's unclear whether the Kimberly Process has created the dramatic reduction in conflict diamonds that the international community had hoped. Government corruption and smuggling by illicit groups are clearly impeding the Kimberly Process' success, but no one is certain to what extent.

Nonetheless, it's an outstanding example of how what you buy affects lives halfway around the globe, and the good that can happen when ordinary people put pressure on the government, civil society and the private sector to reduce the harmful impact of their products. Vote with your wallet!

So what does the 'resource curse' look like for the ordinary people that live in a country? For the answer to that question, let's consider the Democratic Republic of the Congo (DRC) for a moment. The DRC is one of the poorest countries in the world and has been in a state of conflict for decades, mostly due to competition over its resources. The DRC is a wealthy nation: it has diamonds, gold, cobalt, copper, tin, tantalum and other resources—the total market value of which comes to *trillions of dollars*. However, countless factions are locked into conflict over these resources (militias, rebels and the government), which has made life in eastern DRC a living hell for millions of people.

93   I'm not exaggerating. More than 5 million people have died since 1996 because of the disease and starvation caused by the fighting. At the height of the reporting on the atrocities in 2006, *nearly 50 women were raped every hour* in the DRC.

The heartbreak doesn't end there. Not only are people murdered, raped and enslaved by the different factions who try to gain access to and control natural resources, the country is also locked in desperate poverty when foreign companies won't invest there due to the political instability.

So, even though the people of the DRC are living on top of a gold mine (not even a metaphorical one!), they don't have enough food, electricity, running water, medicine, school materials, or roads that they need to lead healthy, productive and dignified lives.

Meanwhile, those natural resources from the DRC are sold on the international market and can be found in electronics and jewelry stores throughout the world. From smartphones to laptops, gaming systems and gold jewelry—these all have raw materials that could have originated from a mine in the war zone that is eastern DRC.

I even heard a crazy story from a friend who's a conflict specialist. He mentioned that China reportedly wants access to the minerals, but doesn't trust the DRC to be involved. As such, it ships boatloads of raw dirt to be 'mined' and processed in China. This means that China isn't even paying local Congolese to sift through the dirt, or sending their own employees to the DRC to do it. It means they're shipping the dirt to China to use their own systems and employees to mine the dirt for valuable resources. Countries want the natural resources, but don't want to have to invest in the DRC.

CONFLICT PREVENTION

CONFLICT SUCKS. I think we can all agree on that. That's why it's so important to prevent it from happening in the first place. *Conflict prevention* is an effort to keep tensions between two parties from escalating to a point where violence seems to be the only means of resolving the issue. Conflict prevention relies on teaching the parties to resolve disputes peacefully (it's a learnable skill, just like fighting), and working through and talking about the underlying problems that created the disputes.

I chose to pursue a master's degree in International Peace and Conflict Resolution because I think that helping to resolve conflict and create stability is vital to making the world a better place. Some of my wise-cracking friends asked me, at the time, whether I really believed that I would be able to create world peace. For me, the point is to recognize that, while perhaps a world that is completely free of conflict isn't possible—current levels of conflict are too high, much of the violence is unnecessary, and we should be trying to create the conditions that help to prevent conflict in the future. It's worth a try at least, right?

Conflict prevention and conflict resolution are inextricably linked because many conflicts reignite after lying dormant for a stretch of time. Nearly 60 percent of countries that have experienced a civil war are likely to face at least one additional conflict after the initial resolution. This is why efforts towards post-conflict reconstruction are really important for preventing further conflict. And it means that there are efforts that can be made in conflict-prone neighborhoods (such as eastern Africa) that can try to help prevent conflict.

Conflict prevention and development are also tightly linked, for reasons we've already touched upon. A lot of conflict is driven by people not having enough resources to secure themselves a positive future (especially in countries with a youth bulge and high unemployment levels). Where you find a lot of desperate young people without many options, you also find them being lured into activities that can lead to violence and conflict. Fostering well-functioning countries that respond to the needs of their citizens creates the condition where people can live fulfilling, productive lives—without resorting to violence to meet their basic needs.

In the past, I worked at the Department of State as a Conflict Prevention Officer for what's now called the Bureau of Conflict and Stabilization Operations. My portfolio was Sub-Saharan Africa—nearly the whole continent! Obviously, that was a vast portfolio and (spoiler alert) I did not successfully prevent all conflict in Africa. That said, a lot of what we (State and the interagency) focused on is noteworthy because much of it took the form of basic development projects. This included helping to establish radio stations and content to counter extremist narratives, improving access to education for children in at-risk areas, strengthening civil society's advocacy skills, and training community and religious leaders on conflict resolution.

THEY'RE NOT TOY SOLIDIERS...

Let's talk about child soldiers: actual kids with actual guns. Today, child soldiers are fighting in at least a dozen countries, and scores of other countries recruit soldiers below the age of 18. Child soldiers, sometimes as young as eight, are used in Afghanistan, Central African Republic, Colombia, DRC, Iraq, Mali, Myanmar, Nigeria, Philippines, Somalia, Sudan, South Sudan, Syria and Yemen.

Child soldiers are often 'recruited' by kidnapping them from their homes or refugee camps, lured into fighting because they are orphans and can't survive on their own; because they are given away by impoverished parents who can't take care of them (or because they think it's their best chance of survival in a conflict).

Child soldiers are often forced to commit atrocities – rape, murder, mutilation – even upon their own family members. They are frequently forced to take drugs to get them addicted and more dependent on their leaders. And it's not just boys that are used as child soldiers—about 40 percent are girls. In Nigeria, Boko Haram uses young girls as suicide bombers; girls can also be forced to fight and may be compelled into sexual slavery.

94

Types of conflict

Conflicts come in every size and shape that you can imagine. The two primary kinds are *interstate* (between countries) and *intrastate* (within a country)—the latter being the most common type of conflict by far. Civil wars are a type of intrastate conflict where two (or more) competing sides (one of which is the government) fight for control of the country. Sometimes in an internal civil war (for example in Syria), you'll see other countries getting involved (providing funding and support to one side or another).

As you know, the US had its own civil war in the 1860s, in which the north and the south were pitted against one another largely over the issue of slavery. If you think about it: 1860 isn't that long ago—and if things had gone differently, either slavery would have continued, or we'd be two different countries today.

Another type of intrastate conflict is an *insurgency* or *rebellion*, where you find an armed group fighting to overthrow the entire government, or just establish control over a smaller portion of a country's territory. Technically, the US was founded by an insurgency: the colonists fighting for independence from England! Insurgencies are similar to civil wars but are usually more asymmetrical. That means that the rebel group is much less powerful than the government forces.

Insurgents often try to establish control over a portion of territory, either to hunker down, run up their flag and have free reign over their own chunk of land; or to establish a power base from which they can fight their way to the capital city and overthrow the central government. Overthrowing a head of state (i.e. the president or prime minister) through conflict is called a coup (rhymes with 'who'). Coups are a non-democratic (usually violent) way of creating political change. And more often than not, violence begets violence—as they often result in dictatorships that use force to stay in power.

Interstate conflict occurs between two countries, typically when one invades the other. This doesn't happen too often these days, but one example is when Russia invaded Ukraine in 2014 to reclaim its historic control over Ukraine's region of Crimea.

The wars in Iraq and Afghanistan were also technically 'interstate', but in a slightly different way: the US did not invade these countries unilaterally. Rather, we went through the United Nations Security Council. (The UN Security Council is like the referee in a global soccer match: it arbitrates peace agreements, coordinates joint security actions, and takes countries to task when they invade each other without exhausting peaceful options first.) The Security Council authorized the invasion of Iraq and Afghanistan, and formed a coalition of countries to support these attacks, which is why we consider them as 'global responses', rather than as one country attacking another. In terms of geopolitics, the distinction is important—but at the end of the day, it's still an invasion of a sovereign nation and so considered interstate.

The terms 'interstate' or 'intrastate' don't actually work when we talk about terrorism. Terrorism can be intrastate when a terrorist group conducts attacks in their country of origin, such as Boko Haram's activities in Nigeria. Or, terrorism can be extrastate—individuals or groups of terrorists carrying out attacks in other countries, such as in the case of Daesh (the Islamic State of Iraq and Syria) bombing the Brussels Airport.

Whatever you call them: extrastate attacks are on the rise. Between 2013–2014, there was a 35 percent increase in terrorist attacks, and an 81 percent increase in fatalities as a result of terrorist attacks. The power of these non-state actors has grown due to the use of terrorism. Because terrorists use non-traditional tactics, it can be a challenge for the US and other superpowers to respond, given that our experience and instruments of war (planes, tanks, etc.) relate to mostly traditional warfare.

Another example of extrastate conflict is the activities of gangs and narco-traffickers. These entities regularly perpetrate organized crime across national borders. Narco-trafficking organizations often use gangs to sell drugs or to physically intimidate or harm people that endanger their business interests. The way narco-trafficking organizations and gangs work together has created an enduring conflict in many countries around the world with a high concentration in Latin America. And now, experts suspect growing linkages between Latin American narco-traffickers and militant Islamic groups, wherein the militant groups can raise money from the drug trade.

VIOLENCE IS THE NEW WAR

TRADITIONAL CONFLICT IS BECOMING less frequent, yet violence still plagues the world. For example, traditional wars (including civil wars) were common in Latin American during the sixties, seventies and eighties. Since the nineties, the use of traditional warfare has fallen, but violence committed by non-state actors (gangs and narco-traffickers) is on the rise. It's tempting to dismiss a drug war as 'not being a real war', but it's violence all the same—violence to secure or maintain dominance over resources or territory. This bloody trend is only encouraged by poorly-functioning governments that fail to deliver economic growth and a robust judicial system.

I lived in Guatemala from 2010–2012, during my first tour as a USAID Foreign Service Officer. In many ways, it felt like life in a war zone. I once saw a dead body on the street outside of my apartment; the road was nicknamed 'Murder Avenue', despite being in a more upscale part of town. Like I've mentioned, Guatemala has one of the highest murder rates in the world, and its neighbors (El Salvador and Honduras) have even higher murder rates. With so many people dying every day, it really did feel like one long, slow war. And worse, it felt like a war that everyone just accepted as 'business as usual'.

A culture of violence perpetuates the high murder rate of many countries around the world. Violence becomes commonplace, even acceptable, when children are raised in an environment where they are constantly exposed to violence everywhere, every day, and often at home.

They may have fathers who abuse their mothers, and possibly the kids too. The statistics on domestic violence alone make you wonder what example we're setting for our children. Nearly one third of women around the world have experienced violence from their partner, and 38 percent of female murders are perpetrated by intimate partners. It's estimated that every year, 40 million children are abused around the world. The real numbers are likely much higher, but not everyone reports it because abuse is considered a private matter, or people are ashamed, or are discouraged from reporting it by others.

When you're raised experiencing violence on an almost daily basis, it becomes routine. Normal to witness; normal to perpetuate; normal to receive. Violence is a learned behavior, so if you're constantly exposed to it, you are more likely to abuse your partner and children, and you are more likely to use violence to resolve disagreements. It is also normalized for the one who is the victim of violence. If a woman grows up seeing her mother beaten by her father, this can be seen as normal couple behavior. Violence begets violence.

The gang culture incorporates this culture of violence and perpetuates it because violence is the main tool used to maintain a gang's power and prestige. In many parts of Latin America, gangs, working alongside narco-trafficking organizations, are often more powerful than the national government.

Latin America's gang problem is more or less a consequence of gang culture in Los Angeles. It started after the LA riots in 1992 when California enacted new, stricter anti-gang laws, which sent an increased amount of young criminals to jail. By 1994, California had passed legislation that dramatically increased jail time for third-time offenders of felonies, which sent even more young criminals to prison. Two years later, the US Congress passed a stricter immigration law which stated that if sentenced to a year or more in prison, non-citizens would be repatriated to their home countries. With this new law, foreign-born US citizens could have their citizenship taken away and be sent back home. The crimes that were considered 'worthy of deportation' were also expanded to include minor offenses, such as petty theft and drunk driving.

Because of these new laws, from 2000–2004 we sent 20,000 young Central American criminals packing. It's a good example of the 'law of unintended consequences'. When US jails started exporting young offenders, many of whom were already caught up in the US gang culture, they didn't think through what would happen to the men once they returned home. Although it really wasn't 'home', because many of these men had been in the US since a young age—which meant that many of them didn't speak Spanish, didn't understand the culture, and didn't have family support networks awaiting their arrival.

In that context, survival often meant going back to the one thing they were good at: being a part of a gang. As you'd imagine, this has had devastating effects. Latin America has the highest rate of criminal violence in the world. In fact, in 2013 Latin America accounted for almost one third of murders in the world, even though only eight percent of the world's population lives there.

RAPE IN WAR

RAPE IN WAR IS AS OLD AS WAR ITSELF. Rape is used as a systematized approach to inflicting suffering on non-combatant civilian populations during conflict. The logic is this: attacking a woman's perceived purity is an effective means of defiling a group's identity. Women and girls are often targeted for violence based on their group identities, whether it is ethnicity, religion, culture or nationality. Women are seen as the emblem of cultural heritage, which means that their safety, purity and identity are an especially attractive target for enemy groups.

In Yugoslavia, Serbian men raped Bosnian Muslim women; in Somalia, women from rival clans are targeted; in Sudan, Arab soldiers have used rape to terrorize the black Africans in the region of Darfur; in Iraq, Daesh enslaved Yazidi women to eradicate the ethnic group. The rape of enemy women can be used as a weapon of ethnic cleansing and the public raping of women by invading forces has been used to systematically force families to flee their villages.

The consequences endured by the victims of rape are immense. When the victim is lucky enough to survive the attack, she might still suffer for the rest of her life from serious physical and psychological problems, including post-traumatic stress. These crippling impacts can prevent her from leading a normal life once the conflict has ended. Women who are raped can also be infected with any number of sexually-transmitted diseases (including HIV), and suffer from forced pregnancy or infertility as a result of rape. Impregnating women is part of the motivation behind rape as a weapon of war, especially when it's used to attack a group's identity. Raped women face the likelihood of being stigmatized or rejected by their families, communities and husbands—or not being able to get married in the future.

Although the use of rape in war has been widespread throughout history, it has (until very recently) been an underreported aspect of armed conflict. Still today, though it's technically a 'war crime', it's often considered more as 'collateral damage'.

The conflicts in the former Yugoslavia and Rwanda during the 1990s brought international attention to the use of rape as a weapon during war. The United Nations estimates that up to 250,000 women and girls were raped during the three-month period of genocide in Rwanda. In eastern DRC (the so-called 'rape capital' of the world), rape has been used by rebel militias to systematically terrorize communities. There was a peak of rape

95

96 cases in eastern DRC around 2006 when it was estimated almost 50 women were raped every hour. Reducing conflict is one way to reduce the number of women and girls being raped during conflict. So too is changing the way that women are viewed by, and valued within, society.

PEACE PROCESSES

NO DISCUSSION ABOUT CONFLICT IS COMPLETE without a discussion about peace. A peace process is where we all agree to stop shooting at each other for long enough to sit down and negotiate a resolution. Sometimes the peace process can even be decades long, as in the case of the Israel/Palestine conflict. But just because it's long doesn't mean it's not worth doing— because you never know what might actually work, and when.

Just consider the conflict in Northern Ireland between Catholic separatists (who wanted Northern Ireland to join the Republic of Ireland) and the Protestant nationalists (who wanted to remain a part of the United Kingdom). After 30 years and thousands of deaths, the two sides finally agreed upon conditions by which they were willing to stop fighting and work on their differences through political, not violent means.

A peace process involves negotiations and relationship building and can take many different forms, using many different tools. There's the official governmental form called 'Track I' and there's also a form that can be undertaken by people outside of, but with close ties to, the government. And the peace process can even be undertaken by civil society representatives that build linkages between the warring parties to resolve conflict. And, sometimes, a combination of all different forms is utilized.

Once an agreement on peace conditions has been established, a peace treaty is created to record these conditions and create a roadmap for building peace. Peace treaties succeed to varying degrees. In 1995, a peace treaty called the Dayton Accords successfully ended the Bosnian war, which occurred

PEACEFUL WOMEN...

Women are vital to creating lasting peace. This isn't just wishful thinking; it's true. When women are a part of the peace process, it's estimated that there is a 20 percent increase in a peace agreement lasting two years and a 35 percent increase in the probability of it lasting 15 years.

97

The UN states (in Resolution 1325) that women's participation in the peace process is essential for international peace and security. Women have a different experience during conflict (and peace time) than men—and they represent half of any population. Yet still, women are often not involved in formal peace processes. In those peace processes occurring from 1992–2011, women were only two percent of chief mediators, four percent of witnesses and signatories and nine percent of negotiators.

As a result, women's specific needs and concerns are excluded from the priorities of the post-conflict reconstruction and, inevitably, from the future of the (hopefully!) peaceful society.

Part of women's needs and concerns are related to gender-based violence, or other forms of violence perpetrated against them or their families. Often restitution for what they suffered during a conflict is just an afterthought, something to deal with after the 'real peace' has been restored.

Ensuring women are an equal part of peace processes means that their issues are addressed up front. To have their voices heard in the process, women need to sit at the table (literally and figuratively) so that their experiences, needs and ideas shape the peace process.

The omission of women from the peace process, and gender inequality in general, is a form of structural violence. A society with lots of structural violence will beget other,

98

and continuing, violence—ultimately undermining the success of the peace process. For more on how gender inequality furthers global instability, read a great book called *Sex and World Peace*. I'd also encourage you to watch Zainab's Salbi's 2010 TEDGlobal Talk entitled *Women, Wartime and the Dream of Peace*.

When I worked at the State Department, I had the honor of hosting Nobel Peace Laureate, Leymah Gbowee, and showing the documentary film about her and the Liberian women's peace movement, *Pray the Devil Back to Hell*. It told the story of how, in 2003, this non-violent movement helped end the country's 14-year civil war and bring Ellen Johnson Sirleaf to leadership as Africa's first female head of state. The clear message of the film is: if you're not invited to the table, sometimes you have to make your own seat.

If the negotiations behind the 2016 peace deal between the Colombian Government and the country's largest rebel group, the Revolutionary Armed Forces of Colombia (called the FARC), are any indication, then I have hope that gender integration in the peace process is improving. During the negotiations, women made up one-third of the participants at the peace table. Women were 60 percent of the victims and experts present, and the process had a gender subcommittee, which was the first of its kind. Also a first: the final peace agreement has an entire chapter on gender, and gender is mainstreamed across all areas of the agreement. Maybe we are actually learning from past mistakes?

after the dissolution of Yugoslavia. In contrast, the Khasav-Yurt Accord signed in 1996 between Russia and the separatist region of Chechnya did not successfully prevent a resumption of fighting and another war. Even without knowing whether it will succeed, a peace treaty makes good practical sense because having a 'contract of peace' between the warring sides makes it easier for the rest of the world to hold them accountable to the promises they each made.

To establish a truce or a cessation of conflict, sometimes the United Nations provides peacekeepers. UN Peacekeepers come to the warring country to help it maintain its peace. UN Peacekeepers come from 128 member countries that volunteer over 120,000 of their own military, police and civilian personnel to don the famous blue helmets.

UN Peacekeepers help to maintain peace and security in countries all around the world, primarily in Sub-Saharan Africa. They also help to maintain peace and foster stability through training the police, helping displaced people return to their homes and reforming the judicial system. They also sometimes help to disarm former combatants and reintegrate them into society.

Helping former combatants become civilians again is an important part of the peace process, and is called *disarmament, demobilization and reintegration (DDR)*.

Disarmament is the first step because to participate in demobilization and reintegration, the rebel fighters need to first relinquish their weapons so that they can't keep using them. This isn't as easy as it sounds because of course any one individual could have multiple weapons, and choose to relinquish only some of them. Or, an individual could have been involved in the rebel group in another way (e.g. as a slave used for sex or cooking), and they wouldn't have a gun, so they wouldn't necessarily have access to the resources available through the DDR process. Luckily, these days, people understand that not only adult males with guns need to be part of the DDR process and have created more sophisticated criteria for getting the people who need it into the DDR process.

After combatants are disarmed, they are formally discharged from the armed groups that they had belonged to. This process, called 'demobilization', includes providing ex-combatants with short-term assistance (transitional safety allowances, food, clothes, shelter, medical services, short-term education, training and tools) to help them return to civilian life.

Reintegration is the final stage of this process because it's when ex-combatants return to normal life by reclaiming their civilian status and getting jobs. Part of this stage can also be the rehabilitation of individuals affected by the conflict and even the reconstruction of damaged infrastructure.

Beyond a shadow of a doubt, DDR is a complicated and long process. It can take many years and is difficult for everyone involved. It's difficult for the ex-combatants, who often grapple with the trauma of being involved in the conflict; and it's difficult for communities, who were often on the receiving end of that conflict. Reintegration is a long-term process of healing, building trust and forgiving.

Another tool used during a peace process is what's called a *truth and reconciliation tribunal*. This is an opportunity for opposing sides that had been wronged by one another to come together and forgive each other. It's a frank and open discussion of what happened, where people can take responsibility for the terrible things that they did during the conflict.

In some ways, it's like couples therapy: an effort to process the causes and results of the conflict, and to try to bring communities into a relationship again. More than that, it's a useful way of holding people accountable for their crimes without resorting to court proceedings (especially in those circumstances where arresting absolutely everyone involved in a conflict would be impractical).

Like all of the tools in the peace process, tribunals are implemented in differing ways, and with varying degrees of success. In Rwanda, the National Unity and Reconciliation Commission, and the Gacaca process (based on traditional Rwandan practice) were part of a reasonably successful effort to create justice and reconciliation after the genocide. The Guatemala Truth Commission, on the other hand, after the 30-year long civil war, was seen as a just a band-aid that didn't do much to help bring the government and the indigenous community together. That having been said, even though no one can guarantee the success of a tribunal, it can be an important milestone in the collective healing process for a country or community that has been divided by conflict.

REMEMBER!

- Conflict drivers are the people, groups, events and institutions that engage in and perpetuate a conflict
- Causes of conflict are diverse, including religion, ideology, ethnicity, culture and/or resources
- Conflict prevention tries to keep tensions between two parties from escalating to the point where violence is used to resolve it
- Categories of conflict are interstate, intrastate and extrastate
- Rape in war is used as a systematized approach to inflict suffering on non-combatant civilian populations
- A peace process is a way to resolve conflict peacefully.

CHAPTER 14
GENDER EQUALITY

THE NUTSHELL...

Gender and sex are related, but different concepts. Gender is a cultural construct, while sex is a biological designation. Feminism is the radical idea that women and men are equally-valuable within society, and we need more feminist men in this world so that we can put gender injustice in a museum. Until then, we're left grappling with the many pernicious faces of gender inequality, including gender-based violence, intimate partner violence, child brides, missing women and female genital mutilation. Tackling these problems head-on isn't just a moral and ethical question: gender equality could actually add *trillions* to the global GDP.

WHAT KIND OF JOB COULD THIS BE?

Gender integration and training assistant at a charity • Advocacy officer for a women's rights NGO • Gender-based violence researcher in a think tank • Gender and diversity coordinator at an NGO • Anti-trafficking officer at a multilateral organization

GENDER HAS COME UP A LOT IN THIS BOOK, in relation to issues such as education, health, political voice, conflict, etc. This chapter is our chance to get some clarity on this whole 'gender' thing. And you might (or might not) be surprised to learn that 'gender' is not just about women!

All too often, people use the words 'gender' and 'sex' like they mean the same thing. However, sex refers to the biological characteristics that define humans as female or male (think body parts).

Gender refers to "the economic, political, and cultural attributes and opportunities associated with being male or female. Social definitions of what it means to be male or female vary between cultures and change over time. Gender refers to the array of socially-constructed roles and relationships, personality traits, attitudes, behaviors, values, and the relative power and influence that society ascribes to the two sexes on a differential basis. Gender is an acquired identity that is learned, changes over time and varies widely within and across cultures. Gender is relational and refers not simply to women or men but to the relationship between them." 99

Wondering what *gender equality* is? Well, lucky for you, I've got the answer right here: gender equality "refers to the absence of discrimination, on the basis of a person's sex, in the allocation of resources or benefits or in the access to services. Gender equality entails the concept that all human beings, both men and women, are free to develop their personal abilities and make choices without the limitations set by stereotypes, rigid gender roles, or prejudices. Gender equality means that the different behaviors, aspirations and needs of women and men are considered, valued, and favored equally. It does not mean that women and men have to become the same, but that their rights, responsibilities and opportunities will not depend on whether they are born male or female. Inequality, discrimination and differential treatment on the basis of sex can be structural (i.e. it is practiced by public or social institutions and maintained by administrative rules and laws

100 and involves the distribution of income, access to resources and participation in decision-making)."

People also talk about *gender equity*, which "means fairness of treatment for women and men, according to their respective needs. This may include equal treatment, or treatment that is different but considered equivalent, in terms of rights, benefits, obligations and opportunities (e.g. equal treatment before the law, equal access to social provisions; education; equal pay for
101 work of the same value)." Women and men have different experiences in most areas of life—access to health, access to justice, voting, education, how they experience poverty, their ability to get formal jobs, vulnerability in humanitarian situations, climate change, etc. Because women experience the impacts of these things differently, sometimes they need *a bit more help* than men to cope with them. That's how equity and equality differ.

So why are women so often the focus of the gender equality debate? It's because currently, in most of the world, they are not seen as being equal to men. This doesn't mean that men don't have a significant role to play in the fight for gender justice. On the contrary: we'll never reach gender equality if men aren't aware of the issues and advocating for it. This is particularly true when it comes to busting the myth that gender equality is a zero-sum-game. Giving women more equality doesn't mean that men need to lose out. In fact, men benefit from gender equality. It allows them to shed outdated approaches to masculinity and it helps them live in a healthier and more prosperous world where the women in their lives have opportunity and agency—and can live free from violence.

SO HOW ABOUT THE WOMEN?

WOMEN ARE HALF OF THE WORLD'S POPULATION. And in most countries in the world, being a woman has distinct challenges (to put it lightly). In some of the developing countries I've visited, women's social status ranks somewhere between 'dog' and 'slave'. Globally, women enjoy second-class citizenship. Russia recently decriminalized domestic abuse. Saudi Arabian women aren't allowed to drive. Even in the US (where women have more rights than in a lot of countries) women still live in fear for their safety, there has never been a female president, and women are underrepresented in government

SAY THE 'F' WORD...

Let's clear up an unhelpful misunderstanding. Feminism isn't about valuing women more than men. Feminism is about creating equality for all populations regardless of sex, sexual orientation, gender identity, socioeconomic status, ethnicity, religion, disability status, etc. It's about a world where everyone can receive equal access to economic opportunities, political participation and representation and social services, such as healthcare and education. Feminism is about women enjoying the same physical safety as men; valuing women's unique contribution; respecting our differences.

Yet for the feminist agenda to take hold, we need to educate everyone, particularly men. Men and boys need to understand that feminism is about equality, and that equality benefits everyone. We especially need to tell the men that if they can't see the inequality inherent in society—that's a signal that something is seriously wrong, and that gender inequality is a cultural norm rather than an exception. After all, those with privilege rarely spend any time thinking about that privilege, because it's invisible to them.

It's high time that we start, and continue, that very important conversation, because I believe that if men knew the disadvantages and risks facing women today, then they would be scrambling to find a solution—out of respect for their mothers, daughters, wives and friends. Only by working together can we create an equitable world.

and in the boardroom. Only five percent of Fortune 500 companies have a female CEO. And at every level, women still make less money than men—especially African-American and Latina women.

Simply put: global peace and prosperity are not possible when half of the world's population are not given the same agency and respect enjoyed by the other half. Equality is important because the way a country treats its citizens – *all* of its citizens – translates into its ability to be a well-functioning state. Well-functioning states provide for their citizens and don't depend on aid from other countries. Well-functioning states have citizens who are less likely to engage in conflict because they have fair and reliable mechanisms for resolving their disputes and grievances. A country that only gives voice, opportunity and respect to the male citizens is not a country that is being responsive to the needs of its citizens. Half the population is missing out. The authors of *Sex and World Peace* point out that "the best predictor of a state's peacefulness is not its level of democracy, wealth or ethnoreligious identity; it's how well women are treated." They're right on the money.

Prosperity is strengthened when women have opportunity, agency, and lives free from violence—this is the holy trinity of gender equality. When women can go to school, get jobs and be active in the public sphere; they can contribute economically, intellectually and politically to making society a better place. Women have so much to contribute to society, and frankly, a country that isn't using half of its human resources is losing out. Who knows what might've happened if we'd tapped into the potential of women sooner: we might've found a cure for cancer, be living on other planets, or have eliminated hunger by now.

Sexual assault, discrimination, abuse, neglect and the other ugly faces of gender inequality often cause women and girls to turn to suicide as a means of escape. In fact, suicide is one of the leading causes of death worldwide for girls 15–19. When I lived in Tajikistan, it was all too common to hear about

102

female suicides in the news. More disturbingly, women would use self-immolation (setting themselves on fire). If a woman is willing to put herself through that, her life must be unimaginably difficult.

Gender inequality perpetuates in a world where women are not valued and are not safe. Lots of people and lots of organizations are working on these issues, but if you feel that change just isn't happening fast enough, I sympathize. From 2006–2016, the global gender gap (a measure of gender inequality) closed by only four percent across health, education, economic opportunity and politics—which means that at the rate we're going, it will take an additional 170 years for it to close completely. **103**

GENDER-BASED VIOLENCE

LIVING FREE FROM VIOLENCE is the third and final part of the 'gender equality equation' (I talked about the first two parts, women's access to opportunity and agency, in other chapters). What is this violence we're talking about? It's what we call gender-based violence (GBV).

Here is a helpful definition from the US Strategy to Prevent and Respond to Gender-Based Violence: "GBV is an umbrella term for any harmful threat or act directed at an individual or group based on actual or perceived biological sex, gender identity and/or expression, sexual orientation and/or lack of adherence to varying socially constructed norms around masculinity and femininity. It is rooted in structural gender inequalities, patriarchy and power imbalances. GBV is typically characterized by the use or threat of physical, psychological, sexual, economic, legal, political, social and other forms of control and/or abuse. GBV impacts individuals across the life course and has direct and indirect costs to families, communities, economies, global public health and development." **104**

There's a lot to unpack there. First, women are most frequently the victims of gender-based violence (rather than men). For that reason, many people use the terms 'gender-based violence' and 'violence against women' interchangeably. However, GBV has a further subtlety in that it is related to people's adherence (or not) to perceived gender norms: so both men and women can be victims of GBV. That's why violence against the LGBTQ community is considered GBV. Here, I use the more general term of GBV even though I'll primarily talk about its impact on women.

105 GBV is a clear reflection of gender inequality and women's lack of physical safety. Globally, one in three women has experienced physical or sexual violence, usually at the hands of men. If you had to guess, you might imagine that car accidents, malaria, cancer and war account for the most deaths in the world. Shark attacks are definitely low on the list. But would you believe that more women (aged 15–44) die as a result of male violence than any other cause? Why do they die? For the crime of being a 106 woman.

I'm not trying to downplay the issue of men dying—it's just that violence against men is rarely gender-based; rather, men are typically killed as a result of armed conflict (i.e. war) or a gang conflict or an armed robbery or similar such activities. In Guatemala (with its sky-high murder rate), there's even a separate court for *femicide*. Femicide is a term for the sex-based hate crime of killing a woman just for being a woman.

GBV has many different manifestations—including intimate partner violence (IPV). IPV was traditionally called 'domestic violence', but these days 'domestic violence' more often refers to any violence that can take place in a home (child abuse, elder abuse, etc.), so to specify the type of domestic violence, we talk about 'intimate partner violence'. GBV also includes female genital mutilation, child marriage, honor killings, femicide, acid burnings, trafficking in persons, widow burning, bride kidnappings, and violence against the LGBTQ community. I don't have room to do justice to each of these topics within the pages of this book, but where you are inspired to learn more, I'd encourage you to do so.

⫸ ➔ Missing women

Poor access to health. Poor access to education. Poor access to income-generating opportunities. Poor representation within the political process. These are but a few of the serious issues plaguing women living in the world today as a result of being perceived as second-class citizens.

Now let's talk about the women who aren't alive today, but frankly should be. More women have died *for being a woman* than all of the people who died during all of the conflicts of the 20th century, including (but in no way limited to) World Wars I and II, the Korean and Vietnam wars and the Rwandan genocide. **107** These girls and women are missing from the world because of sex-selective abortion (i.e. aborting babies when the ultrasound reveals the sex is female), female infanticide (killing newborns who turn out not to be a boy), maternal mortality, insufficient food, inadequate healthcare (compared to boy children), femicide, honor killings, IPV and sexual violence.

No one can pin down the exact number of missing women, but experts estimate that there are over *126 million missing women* in the world, half of those dating from the past 40 years alone. Take a moment to let it sink in. That's the same as the pop- **108** ulation of Japan. That's what happens when society places a higher value on a man's life than a woman's.

Quick side note—these lethal discriminatory practices rear their head all over the world, but some countries are bigger culprits than others (like China, South Korea and India). For example, in South Asia in 2012, almost 30,000 girls died as a result of violence, which is a death rate twice the global average for adolescent girls. (I'd also like to acknowledge that **109** talking about 'missing women' does negate the importance of 'missing men' who are at risk because of certain types of jobs, their involvement in gangs or other structural discrimination and violence that uniquely affects them.)

You might be thinking: *So what?* The whole missing women thing is unspeakably awful, but what can we actually do about it now that it's happened? And why should we even get involved in cultural issues such as sex and gender discrimination? Anyway, isn't imposing our 'gender equality' agenda just another form of cultural imperialism?

Good questions. Here's my take on things: first of all, cultures change. That's what they do. In fact, cultures are changing more rapidly today than ever before, thanks to globalization. Increased travel and improved technology mean that cultural norms are shifting through exposure to other cultures. Second, the claim that female empowerment is the imposition of Western values on other cultures ignores the reality that universal human rights must be applied to all people, not just the half of the world's population that happens to have been born male.

South Korea provides an excellent example of how cultures can change—in that case over just one generation. In 1990, the South Korean population had the world's widest gender gap: 116.5 males for every 100 females. There were fewer women because of sex-selective abortion, female infanticide and other factors favoring boy children over girl children. Now, just a quarter century later, they value girl babies just as much as boy babies, and this distortion is no longer evident in their population. Now there are as many women as men in the country.

Don't get me wrong, there is still rampant gender inequality in South Korea, but the fact that girls are being allowed to live reflects the cultural progress that has been achieved. That progress is, in large part, thanks to the Korean Government realizing that there was a problem and then doing something about it. In the past 30 years, the government passed several laws to reduce gender inequality in employment, and also revised the law that now grants women equal rights to custody of children and material property in case of divorce. In 2001, the Korean Government even created a Ministry of Gender Equality and Family and, in 2005, abolished the law that made men the legal head of the household.

110

These legal efforts to improve women's status have translated into an evolution in cultural practices. Historically, sons were the only ones who could care for elderly parents, inherit property and worship ancestors. This meant that girls did not get to play this important cultural role, which meant they weren't valued as much as boys. When girls started to be appreciated more, the culture adjusted so that they could play similar cultural roles to boys.

Of course, this gets us back to the question of the chicken and the egg. Were girls allowed to play these important cultural roles because they were valued more, or were they valued more because they were able to play these important cultural roles? Economics and legal protection play such an important part in changing the perceived value of women—there is a strong correlation between the Korean Government's attempt to legally protect women's economic rights with an increased cultural value placed on girls and a decreased gender population gap. Cultures change, and we help nudge them gently in that direction.

I'm not saying that all cultures change at the same rate—because they don't. But in those places where change isn't happening fast enough, millions of women are dying in the meantime. In fact, technology is even compounding the problem. Take for example ultrasound technology, without which sex-selective abortion wouldn't occur at all. Ultrasounds increase the risk of girl fetuses being killed where female infanticide was a practice historically used, or still used today in countries without ultrasound technology.

China's infamous 'one child policy' (which ended in 2016, after nearly 40 years) resulted in very high rates of female sex-selective abortion and infanticide because boys are more valued within the culture. Also, part of the logic was that if parents were only allowed have one child, it made more economic sense to have a boy because he could earn more money—which he'd use (among other things) to care for parents in their retirement. Boys were insurance against old age, whereas girls were considered a liability. One reason why China finally put an end to this policy is that it had a huge negative demographic impact. With too few girls being born, there were too few women for men to marry, and mothers to give birth to the workforce of tomorrow (whose taxes would cover the enormous cost of social welfare for older generations). The Chinese Government has even tried to incentivize parents to not abort their girl babies by developing a nationwide program called the 'Care for Girls Campaign'. The campaign sought to decrease sex-selective abortions by awarding money to parents with daughters and reducing the use of ultra-sounds to detect the sex of the fetus.

As promising as the campaign sounds, it will take decades for the payoffs to appear. In the short term, the gender gap problem persists, and China is seeing an increase in rape and trafficking in persons, because there are not enough women to go around.

⇒ Sexual violence

Sexual violence is a sexual act committed against a person without their consent. Rape (forced penetration) is one of the most common acts of sexual violence. In the US, a woman is raped every two minutes; 1 out of every 6 US women (and
111   1 out of 33 US men) is a victim of rape. Women in the US between the ages of 18–24 are at an even higher risk of sexual violence: three times higher if they're in college, and four times
112   higher if they're not. Around the world, every year, 150 million women and girls are the victims of sexual violence. Half of all
113   sexual assaults are committed against girls under 15.

So just what are we doing about this problem? Good question. In 2013, the United Nations undertook a study of 10,000 men in Asia and the Pacific, to better understand and address the issue of sexual assault. The study found that depending on the country, between 26–80 percent (on average half) of the men interviewed reported using physical and/or sexual violence against a female partner, and almost a quarter reported raping a
114   woman or girl. It found that rape was particularly common within

relationships, but that one in ten men admitted to raping a woman who was not their partner. 115

The study showed that to prevent rape, it's important to work with men when they're young; more than 50 percent of the non-partner rape perpetrators first did so as teenagers, some were 14 years or younger when they committed their first rape. 116 The study also found that the most common reason (75 percent) why a man rapes a woman is on the grounds of 'sexual entitlement': they felt like it was their right to have sex with a woman, even if she didn't consent. This means sexual violence is far from inevitable. If women's value increases within society, and if men learned that it wasn't their right to sexually assault women, then assault rates would decrease. If women were not considered lesser than men, both at home and in society, they would enjoy more physical safety. Perhaps the most worrying finding, however, was that most rapists (between 72–97 percent) didn't face any legal repercussions for their crimes. Creating (and enforcing) legal consequences for rape and other sexual assault is the key to retiring the practice for good. 117

Intimate partner violence

Intimate partner violence (IPV) is violent or aggressive behavior within a relationship, usually involving abuse (physical, sexual, psychological, economic or emotional) by a spouse or partner. This type of violence can occur among both heterosexual and same-sex couples, and isn't based on sexual intimacy. While women are the majority of the victims and survivors, it can also happen to men—an estimated ten percent of men in the US experience violence from an intimate partner. 118

IPV is a vicious cycle because if boys see their fathers hurting their mothers, or if they are beaten themselves, those boys are more likely to grow up and be violent towards their own families. Girls who grow up seeing their mothers abused by their fathers assume that it's 'normal relationship behavior'. This perhaps explains the fact that IPV can start at a young age. In the US,

119 almost a quarter (23 percent) of females and 14 percent of males who have ever experienced rape, physical violence or stalking by an intimate partner first experience some form of IPV between the age of 11 and 17.

Beyond the moral arguments against IPV, there's the practical impact. Between the medical and legal costs, and lost productivity—IPV costs the US economy more than *$8.3 billion every year*. You could buy a lot for $8 billion. In fact, you could buy the Chicago Cubs and still have $7 billion left in your pocket.

But let's not make light of this: living with IPV is not only terrible, it's dangerous. In the US alone, the number of women murdered as a result of IPV in the four years following 9/11 exceeded the number of victims on 9/11 itself and all of the US soldiers subsequently killed in the wars in Iraq and Afghanistan
120 *combined*. It makes you wonder why the media pays so much attention to terrorists and crazy lone-wolf shooters, but ignores the many thousands of women killed by their partners.

⫸➔ *Child marriage*
A grave risk facing girls in developing countries (in an already-long litany of horrors) is the danger of being a child bride. It's far from a fantasy wedding: a third of all girls in developing countries are married before they reach the age of 18—and that's just the *global average* (you know what I think about global averages). South Asia has the highest number of
121 child brides in the world; there, almost all girls are married off before they turn 18. In Niger, three out of every four girls are
122 married before the age of 18.

Elsewhere (like Yemen), girls as young as 8 years old are married off—and because 'sexual consent' is a virtual impossibility at that age, they're left vulnerable to marital rape. Across the world, girls die as a result of internal damage caused by their husbands raping them. Child brides' lives are also at risk during childbirth, because their bodies are not fully developed to deliver babies; and they live in countries where caesarean sections are rare. I've said it before, and it's worth repeating here: globally, for girls aged 15–19, pregnancy is one of the leading causes of death. **123**

The terror of being a child bride doesn't even end there. In Sub-Saharan Africa, girls (aged 15–19) are 2–6 times more likely to contract HIV than boys of the same age. A big part of **124** this is because they are married off to older men who have had many sexual partners during their lives. They may also be their husband's second or third wife, in the case of cultures where polygamy is still practiced. Child brides are also at a higher risk of IPV.

Every year, at least 14 million girls are married before their 18th birthday. That's more girls than all of the people that live in **125** New York City and Los Angeles *combined.* That's 14 million too many girls who should be enjoying their childhoods, rather than being forced to marry men (sometimes as old as their grandfathers) who don't think twice about raping them—because in the confines of the relationship, sexual relations are expected and, in some countries, marital rape is not a crime. That's 14 million too many girls who will never finish school or fulfill their dreams or aspirations. Is that the life you'd want for your own daughter or sister?

Poverty, coupled with cultural norms around gender inequality, is the leading cause of child marriage. Girls are married young because their families are poor; marrying off girl children means having one fewer mouth to feed.

Child marriage may increase during natural disasters or conflicts because families need additional resources, one less mouth to feed, and/or think they're protecting the girl fearing she may be raped, making her unmarriageable.

Girls are married off young in those cultures that place an extremely high value on a girl's purity. It is thought that, if she is allowed to go through puberty or become an adult, it is more likely that she will dishonor the family by engaging in pre-marital sexual relations or, more likely, that she will be sexually assaulted before being married, which would still be considered a dishonor to her family. In many countries around the world, including Malaysia and

Afghanistan, would-be suitors rape the woman they want to marry, because it is culturally acceptable to force a woman to marry her rapist (because no one else would want to marry her after she'd been raped). Some women in other places fare better. For example, in places like Kyrgyzstan, men don't use rape to claim a bride—they just use kidnapping.

Educating girls is one of the best weapons against child marriage. Girls with eight years of education are four times less likely
126 to be married as children. Roughly 60 percent of girls with no education are married by the age of 18 in Mozambique, whereas only 10 percent of girls with secondary education are married young, and less than one percent of girls with higher education are married young. In countries in Asia, like Indonesia, Sri Lanka and Thailand, educating girls has been a key factor in increasing
127 the age of marriage. Education not only delays marriage, but it also increases a girls' value within society, which is essential for changing the awful way that much of the world treats girls.

⫸➔ *Female genital mutilation*

Female genital mutilation (FGM), or female genital cutting, is another example of violence inflicted upon girls. Campaigns against female genital mutilation have helped to decrease the practice, but millions of girls around the world still fall victim
128 to it. More than *130 million girls* and women alive today have been cut, and those are just the ones we know about. For reasons you can probably guess, it's impossible to get precise statistics on FGM.

In case you're wondering, FGM is a spectrum of genital cutting, and none of it is ok. The first type of FGM is the partial or total removal of the clitoris and/or the skin around the clitoris. The second is the partial or total removal of the clitoris and the labia minora; the third is the narrowing of the vaginal orifice with a covering seal (and could also include cutting out the clitoris).

It's often done before the age of puberty, with the understanding that it will help women be 'pure' by not craving sex. It's a custom done in societies throughout Africa, Asia and the Middle East. Often it's a woman who carries out the cutting ceremony, and it's often women who perpetuate the custom because they think that their daughters won't be able to get married without having it done. The ceremonial cutting is often undertaken using unclean instruments, which leaves the girl susceptible to a huge range of infections and other complications. (Don't picture a clean hospital room. Picture a girl lying on the ground being cut with a sharp rock or knife, and without any anesthetic.)

In the immediate term, FGM can cause hemorrhaging and infections—both of which could lead to tetanus, blood poisoning, or death. Potential long-term effects include complications during childbirth, anemia, the formation of cysts and abscesses, keloid scar formation, damage to the urethra resulting in urinary incontinence, vaginal obstruction leading to the accumulation of menstrual flow in the vagina and uterus, painful sexual intercourse, maternal mortality, sexual dysfunction and increased risk of contracting HIV. A woman's vagina might also have to be 'cut open' to have intercourse or for childbirth. In addition to these physical impacts, there can also be psychological damage, including the girl's loss of trust in her caregivers and long-term feelings of anxiety and depression.

129

PAYOFF FOR INVESTING IN WOMEN

GENDER INEQUALITY HURTS EVERYONE, not just women. Women are half of the world's population. Of the list of current pressing human rights issues, gender is definitely the one with the largest constituency. But beyond the moral and pragmatic arguments for a gender-equal world—it's important to realize that gender equality is good business. As it so happens, investing in girls and women seriously pays off—for her, her family, her community and her country.

If families start seeing a payoff from investing in their girl children, the potential cultural impacts are also huge. Girls will earn more as adults, and when they do they'll be more valued in the family (as income-earners) and be more valued within society as a result.

Moreover, their children will grow up with a different type of female role model: one who is empowered to earn money, make decisions about her own body, and who can't be threatened into submission. And remember all of the benefits of girls' education: higher earnings, higher national GDP, healthier children, fewer child marriages, etc.

Here's another example of a big potential payoff for a relatively small investment in women: agriculture. Farming women do more unpaid labor, have fewer (and poorer quality) inputs (like seeds and fertilizers), smaller pieces of land, smaller and weaker animals, less education to read instructions, less power to negotiate, less access to credit and other financial services, etc. Yet if women farmers had similar access to the sorts of resources that male farmers have, their crop yields would increase (by up to 30 percent), which would help slash the number of undernourished people in the world (by up to 150 million!). With so many people going hungry, it's crazy not to grab every chance we can to grow more food!

Another argument for investing in women is that, often, when a woman begins to have an income or increases her income, she spends that money on her family's well-being (in the form of food, education and healthcare). Whereas when men have an increased income, they typically increase their expenditure on alcohol and cigarettes. This isn't just a harsh stereotype: a recent study found that a $10 increase to a woman's income had the same health and nutritional benefit to children as a $110 increase to a man's income.

Investing in women is good for women, good for their families and good for the global economy. Think about all of the potential innovation that we have missed out on not investing in women. If men have been able to come up with such cool things (like the internet or planes or penicillin), just think of what else could have been created, if we'd had twice the brainpower trained on the challenges of the world.

As I mentioned, the World Bank recently determined that improving employment and entrepreneurial opportunities for women could increase the potential GDP of Armenia (where I'm currently living) by 14 percent. A recent United Nations study highlighted how Sub-Saharan Africa loses $95 billion every year **133** because of gender inequality.

The shocking statistics around the economic impact of gender inequality don't even end there. Get this: gender equality can add *$12–28 trillion* to the global GDP by 2025. I work with **134** numbers all the time in my job, but this one just boggles my mind. Forget what I said about there not being a silver bullet for the problem of global poverty and suffering. If we can move the needle on just this *one issue*, we stand to make enormous gains in stability, peace and prosperity.

Because of this, whether you focus your career on gender equality or not, I encourage you to integrate a gender lens into whatever you do end up doing. If you're designing an agricultural extension project, ask yourself whether both women and men **132** will benefit (and if not, then revamp your design). If you're training journalists, do a headcount to find out how many women are in the room (and if they're not, work harder to get them there in future). If you're helping to negotiate a peace settlement after a conflict, make sure that women's voices are present in the debate. If you're mining data on financial inclusion in a country, ask yourself whether women are less financially-included than men. If you start asking those questions in your daily work, and if we all ask those questions in our daily work, and we do something positive as a result—then we're one step closer to gender justice. Think about it, then act on it.

REMEMBER!

- 'Gender' is cultural and 'sex' is biological
- Gender equality is the absence of discrimination, on the basis of a person's sex
- Gender-based violence (GBV) is a harmful threat or act directed at an individual or group based on sex, gender identity and/or sexual orientation
- Types of GBV include female infanticide, femicide, intimate partner violence, sexual violence, female genital mutilation, child marriage, honor killings, acid burnings, trafficking in persons, widow burning, bride kidnappings and violence against LGBTQ persons
- Gender justice isn't just an ethical issue: it is essential for global peace and prosperity, and could add trillions to the global GDP.

Chapter 15
Environment

———————————•···········•——•——•············•———

The nutshell...
Our climate is becoming more severe and erratic, and the effects of climate change refuse to respect national borders. Climate change most heavily impacts poor countries because they have weaker coping mechanisms. Environmental degradation creates conflict over diminishing resources and forces the displacement of millions of people every year due to climate-related disasters. Governments are coordinating their efforts to respond to this threat—but don't forget your role as an ordinary hero in the fight for global economic justice. Small changes really do add up!

What kind of job could this be?
Environmental officer with the US Government • Climate change analyst at an environmental watchdog organization • Natural resources project assistant with a multilateral organization • Energy and climate change consultant • Climate resilience officer at an international organization

———————•············•——•——•············•———

LET'S NOT BEAT AROUND THE BUSH. There's no point in making life better for humans if we're destroying the planet that those humans live on, or if the impacts of environmental degradation undermine all our efforts to raise living standards around the world.

Climate change isn't just a problem for people living in the global south. It's everyone's problem. The impacts of natural disasters (many of which are linked to climate change) simply don't respect national borders. Climate change causes all sorts of crazy weather events (floods, storms, torrential rains, typhoons, etc.). When it does, poor people often pay a higher price because their infrastructure is typically poor-quality, and therefore less re-silient to extreme weather, and because many are farmers at the mercy of the weather and Mother Nature.

135   In 2013, *21 million people* were displaced because of climate-related disasters. If you were to do a headcount, you'd find that's *nearly three times the total population* of New York City! Worse, most of that displacement happened in countries with weak, or non-existent, coping mechanisms. With more and more of the world's land becoming uninhabitable (due to desert-ification or flooding) and governments unable to respond, global migration is increasing.

Environmental disasters can also compound the effects of man-made disasters, creating complex emergencies that lead to increased global instability. For example, a climate change-

WE'RE ALL IN THIS TOGETHER

As I'm sure you've guessed (after reading the previous chapter) women and men interact with the environment differently, use natural resources differently, are affected by climate change differently, and are equally vital to creating solutions to reduce environmental degradation. Keep this in mind as you read on!

induced drought in Syria magnified the impacts of the civil war and could have contributed to the rise in power of the Islamic fundamentalist terrorist group, Daesh.

POLITICS AND THE ENVIRONMENT

WHERE THE ENVIRONMENT AND GLOBAL AFFAIRS INTERSECT, countries need to work together to slow environmental destruction, especially climate change. The Paris Climate Conference held at the end of 2015 is the latest round of talks between countries to reduce carbon emissions. Through the United Nations, countries are making commitments to reduce their carbon emissions and strengthen climate resilience, in the hope of slowing climate change.

While climate change affects everyone, it doesn't affect everyone equally. Developing countries tend to produce less carbon than their developed counterparts, yet are more affected by environmental shifts caused by climate change. Also, most developed countries started emitting more carbon dioxide when they began to industrialize their economies (following the example of now-developed nations, like the US and the UK). Today, however, rich countries are asking poor countries to develop their economies *without* damaging the environment. Fortunately, rich countries have committed (through the UN) to give poor countries $100 billion every year to help them reduce their carbon emissions and to help them mitigate the effects of climate change.

Politics and the environment also get tangled up when it comes to the question of oil. To put it bluntly: Americans are addicted to oil. Oil gets turned into gas for our cars and is also used in manufacturing (to produce all that plastic you see everywhere, to give you one example). The US is currently one of the largest global suppliers of oil, but we need more than we produce, so we rely on Canada, Mexico, Saudi Arabia, Venezuela and Nigeria to make up for the 50 percent shortfall in domestic production.

Our reliance on imported oil means that we are beholden (economically and politically) to oil-producing countries whose values or political goals we don't necessarily share. Worse, changes in the price of oil tend to hit our economy, when it goes in the wrong direction. Not to mention that oil is running out. Some **136** estimate that we've only got 47 years left before supplies dry up.

As a short-term (some say short-sighted) solution to reducing our dependence on foreign oil, US companies are increasingly using environmentally-destructive methods of sourcing natural gas, such as fracking. Fracking means drilling into the earth and pummeling underground rocks with a high-pressure water mixture to release the gas inside. Environmental concerns around this practice are high—especially on the question of whether it causes earthquake tremors.

Adding insult to injury, our reliance on wood for construction and consumer goods means that every year, around the world, we cut down roughly the size of Panama in forest **137** (an estimated 18 million acres). And our dependency on coal creates air and water pollution that crosses state and international boundaries.

Here's the bottom line: when it comes to the environment, the choices we make today affect the future of our planet, and our endless appetite for cheap fuel, cheap food and cheap consumer goods is ravaging the ecosystem. (Remember that next time you drive to the mall to buy that cool new t-shirt that you want.)

The good news is: renewable energy sources offer a clean alternative to energy production. And, when it comes to developing renewable energy sources, the government can and should have a significant role to play in encouraging business innovation and encouraging individuals to adopt new technologies (such as providing tax breaks for installing solar panels). These alternative energy sources (including solar, wind and hydroelectric power) are gaining in popularity, and are a great way of cutting carbon emissions—especially in developing countries.

DEFORESTATION

LEARNING ABOUT THE DESTRUCTION of the Amazon Rainforest when I was in the sixth grade sparked my life-long interest in the environment and global issues. Here's what I learned: the Amazon River Basin is the world's largest rainforest. It stretches across eight countries (Brazil, Bolivia, Peru, Ecuador, Colombia, Venezuela, Guyana and Suriname) and covers about 40 percent of South America (about the same size as the mainland US). The Amazon is home to thousands of plants and animals and (of course) trees.

The trees aren't just valuable because they're homes for the animals: they're vital to our planet's health because they help process carbon dioxide. You know: the very same carbon dioxide that happens to be fueling all that climate change? Yep. When it comes to carbon dioxide, trees are our best friends. And we're doing all we can to kill them off. That means fewer trees to absorb carbon, and also more carbon released; when the soil is disturbed, all the carbon that has been captured in the subsoil (over a process of centuries) is suddenly released into the atmosphere. Frankly, deforestation is a climate change 'lose-lose' scenario.

Because the Amazon is so large and sits across international boundaries, it's incredibly challenging to create and implement the laws to protect it. Yet protection is just what the Amazon needs. Humans are putting unsustainable pressure on the Amazon's ecosystem through logging, mining, oil and gas drilling, cattle ranching, agriculture and fires. In the last four decades, an estimated 20 percent of the Amazon has been deforested. **138** Scientists estimate that an additional 20 percent will be lost over the next 20 years, causing irreversible environmental damage. **139**

The Amazon isn't the only forest that needs our help. From Indonesia to Haiti to the DRC—deforestation is causing serious threats to the environment and the citizens of these countries. Worse, because developing countries have fewer environmental regulations, deforestation in those places often goes unchecked. Maybe if trees didn't take so long to grow, this wouldn't be as big of a problem. As it is, even if you replant trees (which typically doesn't happen in developing countries), young trees just aren't as helpful for reducing carbon as the ones that were chopped down.

Deforestation is also a problem in developing countries because many people throughout the world still use traditional firewood stoves for cooking. This means that women (it's mostly girls and women) have to spend a lot of their time finding firewood (rather than, for example, going to school or running a business). Wood collection is risky business: not only is it hard physical labor, but women traveling far from home are vulnerable to being attacked. Once the women return home, however, the risks don't stop. If a home is inadequately ventilated, children can develop respiratory diseases from inhaling too much smoke. Yet despite all the hardship that traditional cooking methods cause, poor families often don't have any other option.

Soil erosion is also caused by deforestation. Without the trees' roots to stabilize the soil, it can blow or wash away. This can lead to the soil getting into water streams and polluting or creating too much silt in rivers. It can also lead to more landslides because if you don't have the trees to suck up the moisture and hold back the soil, the land gets destabilized and is more likely to be displaced by rains and floods. Landslides can cause a lot of destruction and fatalities in developing countries because they don't have rigorous housing or zoning regulations and neighborhoods made out of flimsy materials can be precariously perched on the side of hills.

You'd think that knowing all the risks of deforestation, we'd be doing more about it. Yet economic factors often take precedence: for example, the world's thirst for rubber. We need rubber for most industrial machinery, not to mention all of our car tires, pencil erasers, soles of our shoes and much more. Over 40 percent of all rubber comes from trees, and 92 percent of those rubber trees are in Southeast Asia. It takes about a month of sapping four trees to collect enough rubber to produce just one car tire. Now imagine how many rubber trees you'd need to meet the total global demand for rubber (including the one billion tires produced every year).

Because manufacturing depends on rubber, there are clear economic benefits to increased rubber production. We shouldn't overlook, however, the massive ecological ramifications from the amount of deforestation that is accompanying the rubber boom. In 1983, global annual rubber production came to about 4.5 million tons; today it's triple that. To meet this increased demand, farmers in Southeast Asia have cleared about 18,000 square miles of forest to plant rubber trees—about the size of Massachusetts **140** and Vermont combined.

CLIMATE CHANGE

GLOBAL TEMPERATURES ARE BECOMING more erratic and menacing, which has been proven to be linked to climate change. Hot places are becoming hotter, and cold places are becoming colder. Climates everywhere are becoming more unpredictable. We're seeing more floods and rising water lines. If these trends continue, much of the land that's currently inhabited by humans will soon be underwater.

Climate change is primarily caused by having too much carbon dioxide in the atmosphere. Increased carbon dioxide creates the 'greenhouse effect'. Greenhouse gases love to linger in the atmosphere, forming a 'blanket' that covers the earth. So: when heat from the sun hits the earth, it should (under normal circumstances) be reflected back through the atmosphere; however the blanket of greenhouse gases traps the heat, raising the earth's temperature. Most scientists point toward human activity as the primary cause of the recent climate change, because deforestation and burning fossil fuels significantly increase carbon dioxide emissions, which then worsens the greenhouse effect.

The Paris Climate Conference is the latest attempt for countries to agree to reduce their carbon emissions—but it's easier to agree to something in theory than to do it in practice. Cleaning up industries costs money (and polluting the environment is cheaper than being green). The question then becomes: *Who pays to clean up the environment? Governments or companies?* Between these two, if you're the one meant to be picking up the huge bill at the end of the industrial meal—it's unlikely you're going to lobby hard for strong action on climate change in the first place. Of course, not cleaning up industries also costs money, it's just that the bill for doing nothing tends to arrive late. Getting the balance between theory and practice right can be tricky business.

The Kyoto Protocol is a United Nations treaty committing member states to reduce their greenhouse gas emissions. It acknowledges that the main responsibility (ethical and financial) for climate change falls on *developed countries* since it's their industries pumping most of the greenhouse gases into the atmosphere. Alas, the Kyoto Protocol hasn't been very successful in getting countries to reduce their carbon footprint—in large part because the US Congress refused to ratify it. The US is the second largest polluter in the world (behind China), which is why any meaningful action on climate *must* have US support if it is to succeed.

Kyoto might have failed in part because the UN set the carbon emissions targets for the signatories. In the Paris round, the United Nations is taking a different tack: allowing countries to set their own goals. During the Paris talks, the US had set a goal to cut carbon emissions by 27 percent below 2005 levels by 2025. However, just before this book went to press, the US announced that it will pull out of the Paris Agreement. This will have huge implications on the potential success of the agreement, but it is too soon to know the full impact of this news. The European Union has agreed to cut emissions by 40 percent from 1990 levels by 2030; whereas China, the world's largest carbon emitter, is projecting that its emissions will peak in 2030 and that,

NOT THE KITCHEN SINK

We talk about two types of climate change coping strategies: *mitigation* and *adaptation*. Mitigation is an attempt to reduce climate change by either reducing the sources of heat-trapping greenhouse gases or enhancing the carbon 'sinks' that can store these gases (like oceans, forests and soil). Adaptation is dealing with how we're going to live with the effects of climate change by reducing humans' vulnerability to the harmful effects of it (like rising sea levels, extreme weather and food insecurity).

in the same year, they will increase their share of non-fossil fuels in primary energy consumption to roughly 20 percent.

Promising as those targets may sound, they're meager when compared to the dire warnings around the impacts of global climate change. The Paris Agreement was the first time that governments agreed to legally-binding limits to global temperature rises, though in reality, the limits could be hard to enforce given the nature of global politics.

NOT A DROP TO DRINK

WATER IS ANOTHER VITAL NATURAL RESOURCE that is being affected by climate change. Water (clean water, I should say) is vital to human survival, and it's another thing that doesn't respect national borders. We use water to drink, to grow our crops, to raise our livestock, to cool our nuclear reactors, cook food and much, much more.

Most economies (make that *all* economies) depend on access to water. You might have heard the statistic that up to 60 percent of the human body is made up of water? Well, get this. Nearly 80 percent of all jobs on the planet depend on having access to an adequate supply of water and water-related services, including sanitation. Water is vital, yet access to water is diminishing throughout the world.

141

Climate change, pollution and water overuse are driving desertification (drying up rivers, lakes and inland seas) and destroying ecosystems. Forty-four percent of rivers in the US are too polluted for swimming, fishing and drinking, despite the fact that our environmental regulations and rule of law are pretty decent. Given that, how much do you want to swim in a river in a developing country, let alone drink its tap water?

142

Some people speculate that we will fight the wars of the future over water. Even now, water issues are creating geopolitical tensions. For example, the Amu Darya River flows from Tajikistan to Uzbekistan. Uzbekistan is dependent on this water, but Tajik farmers divert much of it for their own use. You'll also find water at the heart of inter-clan tension in Somalia, the conflict between Afghanistan and Iran over the Hari Rud River, rural conflict in Yemen over scarce water sources, disputes over the Nile River between Egypt, Sudan and Ethiopia and tension between the Mexican police and community protestors. The list goes on and on.

Climate change also affects our oceans. As atmospheric carbon increases, so does the temperature of our oceans, melting the Arctic ice caps. Sea levels are on the rise; it's called the *thermal expansion phenomena*. What happens as water warms up? It expands! Specifically, ocean and seawater expand and creep into low-lying coastal areas, causing inundation. During the entire 20th century, the sea level rose by between 4–8 inches, whereas since the turn of the century the *annual* rate of rise has been 0.13 inches, which is about twice the average speed of the preceding 80 years. Seas are rising, land is disappearing. Why is this a problem? Think of all the people that live in cities on the water. Think of Manhattan!

143

The flood damage in cities near coastlines could cost nearly *one trillion dollars every year* if sea levels rise a mere 16 inches

by 2050. Think of all the things we could spend that money on **144**
instead. We could buy over a *billion* new iPhones and hand them
out to poor people in developing countries. Imagine the potential
benefits, especially for women and girls, of creating free universal
access to communication and information! At home, if we had a
trillion dollars, we could give over 8 million people a free 4-year
education at a top US university. Or, for Christmas, you could
buy every single team in the National Football League and have
enough left over to give a million bucks each to 45,000 of your
closest friends. Are you starting to get the picture?

There are currently 136 large coastal cities at risk from rising
sea levels, and about 40 million people are at risk in those cities. **145**
Experts disagree on how quickly sea levels will rise because no
one knows how high global temperatures will rise, or how quickly
the polar ice sheets will melt. Some estimate that the sea level
will rise by at least 36 inches by 2100, which might be in your
lifetime. Other scientists predict more (up to six feet!) and others
predict less. If even 16 inches could cause mass chaos in coastal
cities (Miami, New York, Amsterdam, Hong Kong, Shanghai and
Mumbai to name a few), another 36 inches of sea level rise could
be catastrophic.

SMALL CHANGES

REDUCING GLOBAL CARBON EMISSIONS might seem like
a really big effort. And I bet you think that there's very little
that you can do to help. Not so, my friend. Don't discount small
differences: they really do add up.

When I was living in Washington, DC, I signed up for the
more expensive, environmentally-friendly electricity source for
my house. While I know that just one home using green energy
isn't going to save the world, without market demand for alternative energies, market supply will dry up (aren't you glad we
learned about supply and demand?). And the more of us that get
on board, the bigger difference we can make.

It's the same with turning out the lights when you leave a room. One light won't make a difference, but lots and lots of 'one lights' will. Same too with getting out of your car and opting for walking or mass transit, using canvas bags for your grocery shopping, and recycling like it's going out of style.

Another way you can help to reduce carbon emissions is by eating just a little less meat. Raising cattle (and other livestock) takes a toll on the environment in several ways. I say 'other livestock', but cattle are the biggest culprit because they need the most water, food and land for grazing. If you ate just two fewer hamburgers every month, then it would reduce carbon emissions and free up farmland to grow more sustainable crops. You would have an even bigger impact on reducing climate change if you stopped eating red meat than you would if you stopped driving your car. Chew on that!

Doubtless, you know the slogan 'reduce, reuse, recycle', which dates back to an effort in the 1970s to help tackle the problem of waste (including food packaging). Sadly, most people only heard the 'recycle' part; and even though recycling is better than *not recycling*, the very act of recycling our waste uses up precious natural resources.

If we did more reducing and reusing, we could have a more positive impact on the environment. 'Reducing' means looking for products that have less packaging, or buying products from the bulk section of your grocery store. You can reduce the number of disposable water bottles you use by investing in one reusable water bottle, and take your coffee with you in a travel mug rather than grabbing coffee in a disposable cup.

'Reusing' means washing out your sandwich baggies after you use them rather than chucking them in the garbage can. These are simple, easy things that you can do that, when they're all added up, really do make an impact. Even something as little as turning off the faucet when you're brushing your teeth makes a difference!

Better still, reducing and reusing saves you money in the long run—so it's a win-win situation for both people and planet. And once we get our renewable energy infrastructure in place, the fuel for this infrastructure (sunshine, wind and running water) will be a free gift from nature!

As a citizen, small changes are an important part of your contribution to the world. As an ordinary hero, a career in environmental justice will prove to be rewarding, challenging and meaningful. I encourage you to consider adding it to your list of potential future careers.

REMEMBER!

- The impact of environmental degradation plays an increasingly significant role in global affairs and can lead to global instability
- Climate-related disasters displace millions of people annually
- Countries have mechanisms, like the UN Paris Climate Conference, to try to coordinate on climate change
- Deforestation poses a grave threat to the environment
- Climate change is primarily caused by having too much carbon dioxide in the atmosphere
- Rising sea levels could create devastation in coastal cities
- Make little changes in your life to reduce your carbon footprint—it's easier than you think!

PART THREE

YOUR GLOBAL CAREER

CHAPTER 16
THE JOURNEY

THERE ARE NO ARMCHAIR GLOBAL HEROES. One day, perhaps very soon, you're going to find yourself on the front-lines of the fight against social injustice. Your career in global affairs can lead to jobs where you get to help people, travel around the world, make important decisions, manage budgets of millions of dollars and meet fascinating people all over the world.

What I don't know, what I can't tell you, is precisely which path your journey will take. From poverty, to health, education, human rights and the environment—the list of social injustices is bigger than any one person can take on. That's why we need lots of people to show up. What's more, you can show up in whatever way matches your passions and your skills.

You could be a diplomat working for the US Government. You could be a human rights lawyer; you could become a doctor and train doctors and do surgery in poor countries. You could be a civil engineer and work on water issues. You could study ecology and help developing nations protect their wildlife. You could be a journalist and train indigenous populations to report on the issues that affect them but that aren't being reported in the media. You could be a humanitarian photographer, documenting the trials and triumphs of populations suffering from conflict. Or, you could put your ninja spreadsheet skills to use managing overseas projects from a desk in Washington.

The list of potential career paths is endless, and there's no shortage of surprises along the way. A friend of mine, Brian King, is now in charge (we call this being the 'Chief of Party') of a big USAID project in Georgia. He reflects: "I never expected that I'd end up working in international development. After graduating from the University of Virginia with a degree in economics, I got my first job with Solomon Smith Barney in securities sales, and then spent five years as a financial analyst at Worldcom. I initially enjoyed the work, but working at a company that would file the largest bankruptcy in history amidst a massive accounting scandal made me realize that I wanted a more fulfilling, more personally rewarding career. Trouble is: I had no idea what that would be. I thought about graduate school, but didn't know what to study and whether it was a good idea to rack up student debt if I didn't really have a grand plan.

"That's when chance stepped in. My roommate picked up a Peace Corps brochure at a job fair. I'd never really considered the Peace Corps, but it sounded like a great opportunity to take a break and try to better understand myself and my career prospects, all the while doing something useful in the world. One year later, I was on a plane headed for Romania.

"Once there, I worked on a large USAID project on rural tourism and information technology. The work was eye-opening, meaningful, challenging; it drew on the entire range of my knowledge and experience. When my time at Peace Corps was up, the NGO running the project hired me as the deputy project director to finish out the final 18 months of the project. Since then, I've never looked back!"

My friend, David Rubino, trained to be a lawyer because he wanted to help people, and because he's great at talking to people, distilling complex issues into easily-understood narratives, and a very persuasive writer. As he says: "It seemed to me that if I channeled all of this into a legal career, I could do the most good. Of course, what I hadn't quite figured out was what 'good' really meant. At first, I thought I would become a prosecutor—putting away murderers and rapists and thieves. But as time went on, it became harder to tell who the 'bad guys' really were. Some innocent people served jail time for heinous crimes, and some good people made unbelievably bad choices. Some people lacked the education and guidance they needed to make good choices in life.

"Ultimately, with a mountain of law school debt and no clear path to follow, I began working for large New York City law firms as a litigator. Yup, I was that guy in the suit, like the ones you see on TV, zealously arguing his cases in court. But it was an empty suit; I was defending large corporate clients and never really feeling like I was adding to the greater good. When my name came up in the same sentence as 'partner', I knew I couldn't continue sleepwalking.

"I found the American Bar Association Rule of Law Initiative (ABA ROLI) by chance. Before that, I had no idea that the largest legal membership organization in the world had an international development arm. They were looking for experienced litigators to work in developing countries to train local lawyers in litigation skills, help shape legislation, and work with judges to ensure that these nascent judicial systems were designed to ensure justice. ABA ROLI was concerned with issues like human rights, gender equality, access to justice and anti-corruption—all issues that struck a chord with me.

"Not long after my interview, I was offered a position in Azerbaijan—a place I was certain I couldn't find on a map. The job included directing a Human Rights Legal Aid Center, coordinating a 'Traveling Lawyers' program bringing legal services to remote villages and helping launch the country's first Women's Bar Association. It sounded like a great adventure, and the perfect way to finally put my law degree to the use I had originally intended.

"There was, however, one big catch. The position was only for one year, and only paid a small stipend for living expenses. It was a difficult decision. Financial stability versus work that matched my values. Leaving my family and friends versus going on the adventure of a lifetime. In fact, I'd never been more certain about anything in my life. I accepted the job, and (to quote Robert Frost), taking the road less traveled really did make all the difference."

MY JOURNEY

MY OWN STORY BEGAN in sixth grade, as you know. But, of course, that beginning didn't progress into a career for another 8 years, when I got my first internship the summer after my sophomore year in college. I was studying International Affairs at Lewis and Clark College in Portland, Oregon. My internship was with an international humanitarian NGO called Mercy Corps (also located in Portland).

It was there that I began to understand that development and conflict resolution go hand-in-hand; people will take desperate measures when they can't provide for themselves or their families. Providing food, shelter and, hopefully, a better quality of life are important for helping make the world a more stable, peaceful place. I didn't know it at the time, but that single idea would shape the rest of my career.

I interned with Mercy Corps again during my senior year, and even got class credit for it. After graduation, Mercy Corps gave me a job. It was a great foot in the door.

After a year with Mercy Corps, I moved to Washington, DC to start a Master's Degree in International Peace and Conflict Resolution (with a focus in International Development) at the School of International Service at American University. The general foundation in international affairs that I'd gained in college helped me to specialize once I got to grad school. Of course, there's nothing wrong with specializing in college, if you find a school that is the right fit for your interests.

I chose to do my grad work in DC because so many international affairs agencies, organizations and other entities are headquartered there. New York has its fair share, but no city in the US has the concentration that DC does. That meant that I could pursue more internships during grad school. The first one I had was with InterAction, which is a coalition of US-based international NGOs.

During the summer before my second year of grad school, I interned for Mercy Corps again—this time in Indonesia. It might seem counterintuitive to intern for Mercy Corps after having been on their payroll, but the position offered an opportunity to get hands-on overseas experience. I lived off of my loans in grad school, which meant I could focus on internships that would bolster my résumé, rather than having to get a job, or scrambling for a rare and highly-coveted paid internship.

At the start of my second year of grad school, I interned with Women for Women International, a great organization that focuses on social and economic empowerment for marginalized women living in conflict zones. Near the beginning of my last semester in grad school (when I was finishing my classes and writing my thesis), I got a job as a Gender and Diversity Program Associate at InterAction.

While I was still in grad school, I also applied for the Presidential Management Fellowship (PMF) and got it! I stayed with InterAction for one year before finally landing a job through the PMF—at the State Department in the Office of the Director of United States Foreign Assistance in Washington, DC. It was a brand-new office, and our job was to undertake the largest restructuring of US foreign assistance since the Marshall Plan. No sweat, right?

Once there, I became a Country Coordinator for 11 countries in West Africa, and managed the annual process of formulating their foreign assistance budgets. It was quite a steep learning curve for me to be working in the government when I was only fresh out of grad school, but it was totally worth it for the exposure and experience. I'm grateful that the woman who hired me took a chance on me, and gave me that amazing opportunity.

After the Office of the Director of US Foreign Assistance, I became a Conflict Prevention Officer for Africa at the Office of the Coordinator for Reconstruction and Stabilization, which was under the Secretary's Office. It's now a bureau (which is bigger than an office) called the Bureau of Conflict and Stabilization Operations. Its mandate is to help the US Government prevent and stabilize conflicts globally. It was a really interesting job, because all day I would think about, write about and talk about conflict issues. These issues were as diverse as using community resilience to reduce instability in Mali, undertaking an interagency conflict assessment for the DRC, and reducing conflict in Liberia by improving state services. Both of my positions at the State Department gave me the opportunity to travel and work throughout Sub-Saharan Africa.

After three years, I decided I wanted more hands-on work in development abroad, so I applied to the USAID Foreign Service and left the State Department. My first tour was in Guatemala, where I worked in USAID's Democracy and Governance Office. One of the many cool things about the Foreign Service is that if you go to a language-designated post (i.e. country), then you get to learn the language!

After Guatemala, I served as the Team Leader for Health, Education and Democracy and Governance in Tajikistan, in Central Asia. Tajikistan is part of the former Soviet Union, and is bordered by Afghanistan, Uzbekistan, Kyrgyzstan and China. It's a fascinating, beautiful country and has to be one of the most remote places in the world! For years, Tajikistan's biggest claim to fame was that it had the world's tallest freestanding flagpole. (Alas, Saudi Arabia built a taller one in 2014.)

From there, I went back to Washington to work at the USAID headquarters on gender integration in the Office of Gender Equality and Women's Empowerment. After reading *Part Two*, I'm sure you've guessed that gender equality is a hugely important topic! After that, I took a year off to stay home with my second child and write this book (I'm the ultimate multitasker!).

That brings us to today. As I write, I'm serving a four-year tour as the Director of the Sustainable Development Office in Armenia. My office covers all of USAID's activities there, including projects for economic growth, democracy, health and social reform. The budget is pretty small now—about $14 million a year. But just a decade ago, Armenia had the second-largest per capita US foreign assistance budget, after Israel. It's cool to be in a country where you can see the direct and meaningful impact that USAID activities have had.

Your own career path will be as unique to you as your fingerprint. It can be meandering or direct; it can all be focused in one direction, or it can have many forks, dips, shortcuts or detours. Let's look at some of the typical milestones along that journey.

COLLEGE

COLLEGE IS A GREAT TIME TO LAY A SOLID FOUNDATION for your future career, and you've got plenty of options in terms of where to go and what to study. You might opt for a general foundation, such as international affairs or political science, and then pursue a graduate degree in a more specialized technical subject.

On the other hand, if you want to specialize early, there's nothing stopping you. Somewhere, there's a program that fits your passions—whether this is in public health, education, gender studies or engineering. Or, you might choose a degree program that will equip you with the practical skills you'll need to work abroad and manage complex programs—here I'm talking about language and business or management studies. One of my grad school friends even majored in religion, which just goes to show that all skills sets are welcome in the fight for global social justice.

College will also serve up plenty of invaluable opportunities outside of the classroom. For example, you could volunteer as a research assistant for one of your professors, which will both expose you to new ideas and hone your research and writing skills. You might even get named as a co-author on a publication! Also make sure to sign up for your college study-abroad program. My study-abroad program in Japan was the first time I'd lived overseas, and the experience taught me a lot about myself and about how to navigate a foreign culture. Cultural sensitivity is a crucial skill to develop, and it's not one you can learn from a book (even a book as patently awesome as this one).

The State Department's US Study Abroad Office (study-abroad.state.gov) offers resources to help you find the right exchange program—which is especially important if your college doesn't offer one. The office has information about international exchanges, including ones that are funded by the State Department—such as the Fulbright Program, the Benjamin A. Gilman International Scholarship Program and the Critical Language Scholarship Program. The office also has information on exchanges, scholarships, internships, teaching and research opportunities for high school students, undergraduate and graduate students, scholars, teachers and institutions. Check it out!

In addition, many colleges and universities have international program offices (separate from study abroad). Universities have a lot of technical expertise in the form of professors and researchers, and a lot of free labor in the form of students. With these resources, schools often compete for government-funded international development programs. This isn't so much 'study abroad'—think of it more as 'work abroad'.

These opportunities are more uncommon compared to studying abroad, but if you can nab one, the experience will definitely make your résumé stand out from the crowd. What's more, a lot of times it doesn't cost you a thing to go (or you might actually get *paid* to go). How do you land one of these internships? First try asking the study abroad office. They may handle both study and work abroad. Or at least they may know who does. Try a school directory search for 'international programs' or variations on that theme. Or try googling 'international' and the name of your school along with USAID, USDA, DOD, etc.

If you are in a seemingly non-international field (let's say biology), go to the department chair's office and ask if there are any international projects that professors may be working on in the biology department. Often the competitiveness of a school for federal grant money isn't in the shiny international affairs department, but rather it's back in the dusty halls of some obscure building.

My friend, Mark Kelly, a USAID Foreign Service Officer currently in USAID's Office of Civilian-Military Cooperation, had just this type of experience. "While finishing my Masters in Wildlife and Fisheries, I was trudging through campus one day looking for the grad school insurance office. By sheer chance, I stumbled upon the then-called Office of International Agriculture. I'd always loved travel and didn't think I'd be staying in the exciting field of sulfur amino acids forever. So I went in and asked what exactly the office did. The nice administrative assistant explained and asked me for a résumé (always have some with you). Two weeks later I got a call about spending a summer in Bali working with Indonesian fishermen."

I'm never going to tell you that you need to go to the most prestigious, most expensive and most far-flung college in order to guarantee yourself a good career. Decent grades and internships count for a lot, as does keeping your eye on your next step. Whether you choose to go straight to graduate school, do Peace Corps or get a job, one way or another you should start preparing while still in college (especially by doing internships). Fellowships are also a good option. Organizations provide fellowships as a way of investing in potential talent. They provide an array of opportunities for you to get hands-on experience, funding for research and even possibly a job. I've listed some that might be of interest to you in *Annex One*—check them out!

PEACE CORPS

PEACE CORPS IS A US GOVERNMENT AGENCY that provides service opportunities "for motivated changemakers to immerse themselves in a community abroad, working side by side with local leaders to tackle the most pressing challenges of our generation." For many people with careers in global affairs, doing Peace Corps is the first time they gain fieldwork experience, and it is the stepping-stone for many people into international development.

During its pre-service training, Peace Corps provides language, cross-cultural and technical training—and introduces development theories and concepts. I would suggest doing Peace Corps between college and graduate school (as most do), because having a bit of real-world exposure will help you decide which technical area you might want to specialize in. Of course, you can do Peace Corps at any point, but by the time you're done with grad school, you might not be satisfied with the Peace Corps stipend compared to a paying job.

That said, unlike most 'job' jobs in international affairs, the Peace Corps gives you the opportunity to live in remote rural areas, and often with a family. USAID, State, the UN and most international NGOs have their offices in the capital city of a foreign country—or at least in a major city. Peace Corps, on the other hand, gives you the chance to integrate into a community, and get out of the capital city (although some volunteers get placed in the capital or bigger cities). It's also a good opportunity to get experience managing projects, hone your language skills and develop your cultural sensitivity.

Having international experience is also a bonus for grad school and job applications, because as you're soon going to find out: getting a job in international affairs is one big Catch-22. Most jobs require experience working abroad, but it's hard to gain that experience until you have a job. Peace Corps is a great way in—and you could end up working for the US Government afterwards. Upon completion of service, you get 'Non-Competitive Eligibility' status for 12 months, which means you can be hired by the Executive Branch without going through the normal competitive hiring process. What's more, your Peace Corps time can be added to your 'time in service,' which basically means you can retire two years earlier! While Peace Corps is a valuable professional experience, for many it is much more than that. It is about service and building friendships across countries.

That said, if flying off to rural Benin isn't how you want to spend the next two years, don't fret: a career in international affairs is still a good fit and within reach. This career path can take many forms, which means that you can find the one that matches your interests and abilities. The point about Peace Corps, interning, fellowships or volunteering is just to get experience. Experience to build your résumé, make connections and figure out what you do (and do not) like working on. To find the right experience for you, visit *Annex One* for a list of volunteer opportunities, both abroad and at home.

GRADUATE SCHOOL

YOU'LL NEED AN ADVANCED DEGREE (an MA, MBA, law degree or PhD) for most jobs in our sector, but you certainly don't need to start your grad work right out of college. If you do, however, you'll be pleased to learn that some colleges and universities do offer a single-track bachelor's degree and master's degree in just five years! Most bachelor degree programs are four years, and master's degree programs are often two years, so if you combine the two you're saving a year's worth of tuition (which you'll probably just spend on all the coffee you'll need to make it through alive).

I worked for a year at Mercy Corps before going to graduate school. I was too busy writing my thesis and interning at Mercy Corps my senior year of college, so I didn't have time to study for the GRE (the standardized test that many grad schools require) or to even think about grad school applications.

In hindsight, I'm glad that I worked for a year because it gave me a bit more insight into the career that I was pursuing. A lot of graduate schools in international affairs actually prefer a student body that is a bit older for exactly this reason. Their real life experience brings a different depth to the classroom discussion and allows you to interpret what you're studying based on firsthand experience. In fact, a lot of international affairs grad programs prefer for their students to come in with a few years of work experience.

Graduate school allows you to take a deep dive into the issues you're passionate about, and develop your technical skills. So it's a time to figure out what you want to specialize in, right? Perhaps. Again, you don't have to have the right major in grad school in order to have a career in international affairs. I knew that I wanted to work on conflict issues and development, and that's why I got my Master's in International Peace and Conflict Resolution with a focus in International Development. I joined the Foreign Service as a Crisis, Stabilization and Governance Officer and I work for USAID, so in some ways what I studied in grad school did directly align with my career. But every career takes twists and turns. Today, I'm managing cross-sector teams on issues outside of my technical expertise. You're never going to stop learning; you're never going to stop growing; and you don't need to know everything on the first day of your new job.

My friend, Wendy Bolger, took a different approach. She says: "I did an MBA to ensure that my career would be diverse, and to keep my options open to move between the nonprofit and private sectors, and between international and domestic work.

Being flexible has been critical to managing a two-career marriage, and juggling the demands of raising a family. Since business school, I have had roles in high tech and in international relief and development, started my own consulting firm, and am currently working on domestic poverty issues—finding solutions for kids who withstand third-world-like circumstances in cities and rural communities here in the US. I stay involved with my first love of service leadership in international development by volunteering on the board of an international NGO, Prosperity Catalyst."

Ditto Jennifer Lawson, who today works for the Department of State as a Foreign Service Officer in France. Her entrée into the world of global affairs was a UN cultural exchange program to Bulgaria in the middle of the Cold War. Afterwards, she says: "curious about culture and committed to the arts, I went on to study anthropology and dance in college, working as a professional dancer and choreographer in the States and abroad for more than a decade after graduation. I later earned my Master's in education, focusing on transformational experiences."

Throughout my career, I've had the pleasure to work with many amazing people, many of whom turned to international affairs late in life. I met people whose previous careers were a singer, an accountant, a lawyer, a doctor, even a beer-brewing monk! That's why I say that you're never too young (or too old) to pursue your passion of global social justice.

I did my grad work at the School of International Service at American University in Washington, DC. It's a great program, with a younger student body (because they're happy to accept students right out of undergrad). Other good international affairs grad schools in DC are the School of Advanced International Studies (Johns Hopkins) and the grad programs at George Washington University, Georgetown and George Mason. In Boston, the Fletcher School of Law and Diplomacy at Tufts University is excellent and, in New York City, the School of International and Public Affairs at Columbia University is great. Over 80 percent of students at Princeton's Woodrow Wilson School of Public and

GLOBAL

International Affairs receive full scholarships, which means that even a prestigious school can be financially within reach.

The options don't end there, and each school has its own strengths, so do your homework in terms of which is the best fit for your interests. For example, some universities are great in public health, others in public affairs. How should you sift through all the options? If you're still in college, ask your career counselor or a respected professor to help you identify which graduate program is best for you. Or maybe someone you've met through your volunteering or interning might have advice. If you can't get advice from a real live person, then you should do an internet research to find the right program. You can even use websites such as LinkedIn to reverse engineer the problem: find people with the job you want in ten years' time and then see where they went to school!

Your choice of graduate school will also come down to location. I chose to go to grad school in DC because it would mean easy access to internships and networking opportunities. I even landed a job before I finished grad school. On the other hand, you can use summer internships in the same way, if your grad program isn't where the jobs are.

My friend Heidi Mihm (an International Development Consultant), offers another great piece of advice for people faced with a huge pile of grad school brochures: "Consider the student demographics of their international affairs focused degree program, as I greatly benefitted from a program that brought in students from all over the world." Remember, your tuition isn't just buying you access to great teachers and great classes—being immersed in a diverse student body can be just as valuable, because they will come with their own perspectives and experiences that might challenge your own assumptions about the way the world works.

Just like in college, you should go through much of graduate school thinking about what you're going to do next. Believe me: your two years will fly by, and more likely than not you'll be in debt, so getting a job is a high priority. See *Annex One* for a list of international affairs job websites and organizations you might want to work for. Another way to prepare for post-grad school life is to apply for fellowships (head to *Annex One* for info).

My own fellowship was a really effective 'way in' to government employment. This two-year program is called the Presidential Management Fellowship (PMF), and you apply during your second year of grad school. After the two-year fellowship, you automatically transition into being a permanent Civil Servant. The PMF is quite competitive, and includes a written application, as well as written and oral tests at the second stage. Once you pass, you are eligible to apply for PMF jobs (that's not to say you're guaranteed to get one; the application is just one big pre-screening mechanism). It's a grueling process, but ultimately worth it. To be honest, I wasn't sure that I would get a job as a result of passing the tests. As it turned out, the person who hired me at the Office of the Director of US Foreign Assistance took a chance on me, and that's how I got a job at the State Department. That said, the PMF isn't just for State—you could get the PMF and work in other US Government agencies related to international affairs such as USAID, DOD or even in a few programs at the Department of Justice, Commerce, Education, Treasury or Agriculture. Check it out!

BUILDING YOUR RÉSUMÉ

YOUR RÉSUMÉ IS THE FIRST THING that a potential employer will learn about you. So how are you going to nail it? Let's start with the obvious stuff. Presentation matters. That's because the person reading it will make a snap judgment about you in 30 seconds or less.

Here are my top tips. First, make sure that someone can skim your résumé very quickly and pull out relevant information (i.e. all those details that make you *perfect* for the job). List your professional experience first, and tailor how you write about each job to the specifics of the job opening. If being a waitress in a busy restaurant meant you fine-tuned the multi-tasking skills required for a potential new job, then say so. List your academic experience after your professional experience (even if you're still in school). Mention your IT and language skills, where relevant, and make sure your résumé isn't too long. Even with more than 15 years of experience, I keep mine to only two pages. Remember, your résumé will be in a huge pile, and whoever picks it up isn't going to read to the end if it's too long. Finally, make sure that you don't lose points for inconsistency, sloppy spelling or poor punctuation. I can't think of any job where attention to detail isn't important.

Great formatting also helps, but only if it doesn't get in the way of the content. A quick internet search for 'résumé template' will give you plenty of inspiration. And make sure to have someone you trust (your parent, friend, professor, supervisor, swim coach) proofread your résumé and cover letter.

I suggest that you look on LinkedIn for people who have jobs that you want and see the language on their résumés. If you're trying to break into the field of international affairs, see the language that these people use—how they describe their experience and mimic the language for positions you've had that could be relevant.

Of course, having a well-presented résumé is only half the battle. Substance matters too. (Actually, substance matters heaps more than style!) Building up your experience is crucial—and it doesn't have to be in the form of a paid position. It's never too early (or too late) to start volunteering or interning (providing your time for free to a cause or organization you care about). Internships are explicitly designed to give you hands-on professional experience, whereas people volunteer for all sorts of reasons (including meeting new people, or just doing something useful for the community on weekends). On the other hand, volunteering is a great way of demonstrating your civic engagement and strength of character, which any prospective school or employer would be glad to know about.

I volunteered at an elderly care facility when I was in the sixth grade. Had I put this on my résumé, it might have spoken to my community spirit, and that I was organized enough to get on the bus to the elderly care facility every week at the tender age of 11! Volunteering and interning are also a great way to start a career transition through hands-on experience and networking. If you're mid-career, volunteering can also help you decide whether you really do want to throw in the towel as a florist to become a grant manager for a women's rights organization, for example.

If you're in school, you can get great experience by being involved with student government, or other social clubs like your school's newspaper, literary journal, diversity club, etc. In high school, Todd Robinson (our Ambassador in Guatemala) was a member of the History Club and Student Government, and he also wrote for the school newspaper. He recalls: "Former Congressman, Donald Payne (D-NJ), was a family friend. Before he was elected to Congress, he had a number of community and civic action programs. One of them was designed for kids called Youth in Government. He took us to Trenton, New Jersey (the state capital) and to Washington, DC. I was elected to represent our Model UN program at the national event, which took place in South Carolina. It was great fun. I met a bunch of kids from all over the country, all of them interested in foreign affairs, like me. It was absolutely amazing."

When I first graduated from grad school, I listed my time on the editorial board of my school's academic journal. Victoria Stanski (an advisor to humanitarian NGOs) recalls how, during high school, she deepened her awareness of social justice issues. She says: "I was drawn to important causes like Amnesty International, HIV/AIDS peer education, multicultural clubs, etc. I immersed myself in these key causes to better understand the wider world, so when I went off to college, I was ready to dig deeper into my interests by studying anthropology and African studies. I took advantage of every internship opportunity to get outside the 'college bubble' and to better understand the world beyond my immediate surroundings."

Today, my friend Heidi Chase is the Director of the Innovation and Sight Program at the Seva Foundation. Interning was an important part of her career development, not just because of the experiences it provided her, but because of the doors it opened for her professionally. She says: "It was while doing my Peace Corps service in Uzbekistan when I met people who traveled and worked in other places outside of the US. I wanted to do that, too! So after Peace Corps, I spent a year teaching in Japan. As much as I loved finally seeing the places I'd only heard about from my exchange brother and sister, I wasn't satisfied. I wanted to go to a place that wasn't already full of big buildings and children attending schools—a place that gave me an opportunity to do some good in the world. When I started looking for jobs in these places, I realized I needed to go back to school. While pursuing my masters, a chance encounter led to an internship with Save the Children, an NGO that I admired. I went to a dinner with some friends and while there, talked with an acquaintance about my desire to work at Save the Children. It turned out that not only did he work there, his team was looking for a new intern. That internship turned into a job and a few years later I got the chance to go to a place with few buildings and even fewer roads—South Sudan."

So who should you intern for? Ideally, you would volunteer or intern at an international affairs institution that you would like to work for one day. But any volunteering activity (especially when you're less experienced) is a great résumé-builder. And you don't necessarily have to 'work' with a specific organization in a defined internal role. You can support organizations that you want to be involved with by creating your own opportunities (even if that organization is located far away from where you live).

For example, you can devise fundraising activities on behalf of an organization, such as holding a bake sale, a used book sale, or getting a part-time job and donating a portion of your income every week. With any of these, you can even try to get a matching donation from your parents, teachers, minister or librarian. If you enlist others to donate the same amount of money you raise, you'll multiply your impact! This is true even if you don't want to dedicate your career to international affairs. Donating money to organizations you believe in is a good way to have a positive impact.

Of course, organizations need more than just financial support. Supplies are important as well. For example, you might want to volunteer for an organization that disseminates supplies to refugees by running a food, clothing or blanket drive through your school, church, scout troop, community center, etc.

If you do happen to live near an organization working in international affairs that you would like to work with, call them to ask about volunteer and internship opportunities. Worried that your utter lack of experience will make them hang up the phone on you? Call anyway. The worst that they can say is 'no'. If there are no international affairs institutions near you, but you really want to get experience with an international organization, you could volunteer in another country during your vacation time off from school.

Volunteering or interning with a domestically-focused organization is also helpful for getting experience and building your résumé. You'll learn how to operate in a professional environment and help people at the same time. Better still, these sorts of opportunities are plentiful, and include homeless shelters, boys/girls clubs, elderly care facilities, food banks, or a domestic violence shelter. Here's Heidi Chase again: "Don't be afraid to ask for an internship at an organization you admire. If that is not an option, volunteer doing the type of work you want to do. Even if it is not internationally-focused, you can bolster your skills and learn new approaches. Even if it doesn't seem to be related to what you want to do, when a chance comes along, take it. You never know where the road may lead!"

You might even find ways of designing your own volunteer initiatives. Look around your community—what needs to be done? What needs are being overlooked? And how can you respond to those needs? Maybe the library in a nearby low-income community doesn't have enough children's books. Maybe a local homeless shelter wants to start a lending library. In either case, you could organize a book drive in aid of those organizations. Is there a litter problem in your local community park? Organize a weekend litter-picking and picnicking event. Being a community organizer is 'win-win-win': you get to design and carry out projects that match your schedule, your skills and your passions, you deliver benefit to the community, and you add depth to your résumé. Perfect!

GETTING A JOB

HAVING A JOB OFFERS ALL OF THE EXCITEMENT and challenge of an internship or volunteer position, with one important difference: a paycheck! Jobs come in every shape and size imaginable—my advice to the job-seeker is this: throw your net wide. You might have a 'dream job' in mind, but every job can be an important stepping stone, if you use it as a place to learn, grow your skills and network like a pro. And who knows? Your idea of what your 'dream job' actually is might just evolve once you get hands-on experience in the workplace.

In my case, I had passed the PMF test and was trying to find a PMF job when I took my job at InterAction. It took so long to find a PMF job and to pass the clearances that I was able to work at InterAction for a whole year before starting my job at the State Department. Thanks to InterAction, my year 'in limbo' was anything but!

Don't ever be discouraged that you're not 'qualified' enough to apply for a job. Once at a party in grad school, I heard some great advice from a woman who was a recruiter at an NGO. Her insight was this: job position announcements describe the ideal candidate, but no recruiter actually expects to find someone that ticks all the boxes. Really, they're just looking for someone who ticks as many boxes as possible—and if someone does come along who fits the bill perfectly, great!

Keep that insight in mind when you start applying for international affairs jobs. It's okay to fall short on having all the required qualifications. Who knows? You might have more of the required qualifications than anyone else applying, or there might be something else about your unique experience that is really relevant. So apply for the jobs you really want, not just the jobs you think you can get. Within reason of course! Don't apply for a job that requires 20 years of senior management experience if you have zero management experience! But do put yourself out there and aim high.

I'm especially talking to women here: research shows that women are much more cautious than men when they apply for jobs. In fact, women typically only apply for jobs they feel 100 percent qualified for, whereas men apply for jobs they feel only 60 percent qualified for.

146

Think of it this way: when you're young, jobs are supposed to be learning opportunities, and a chance for professional growth. If you're 100 percent qualified for a job, how much can you really expect to learn on the job? So don't ever be tempted to sell yourself short in the job application process. If you're missing an essential requirement, then use your cover letter to talk about how a different skill you have might be as equally valuable to the position, or how you're certain you can learn that particular skill on the job (and back up your point by talking about a time when you had to learn on your feet, and did so with aplomb).

Presumably, you'll send out a lot of résumés and applications before you land a job. People take different approaches to job hunting: some spend a lot of time on each application, researching the organization carefully, crafting the perfect cover letter, and adapting their résumé so that it's tailored to each position. This is great, but you'll send out fewer job applications than if you send out identical cover letters and résumés for each position. I always took the middle road: initially, I spent a lot of time crafting my résumé and writing a cover letter, asking friends to edit both to make sure they were flawless. Then, when it came to applying for a job, I would send out my standard résumé (in those days, I didn't really have enough experience to tailor my résumé to a position, so I put everything on there—even my internships and extracurricular activities from grad school). My cover letter was mostly standardized, but I would do quick research on the position and the organization so I could adapt the first and last paragraphs of the cover letter. That way, potential employers would know that I'd taken the time to consider the details of the position. By taking this approach, I was able to send out lots of job applications!

That doesn't mean that I landed loads of job interviews, however. I once heard someone claim that for every 20 job applications you send out, you'd be lucky to get one or two interviews. Don't be daunted, just get out there and apply for a lot of jobs!

* * * * *

AS YOU LOOK FOR A JOB, THINK ABOUT what type of institutions you might want to work at. I started my career working for international NGOs, and I think that NGOs are a great international affairs career option. With NGOs, you will implement projects and work directly with beneficiaries. You get to work on meaningful issues and see the impact that you're having in people's lives. However, a downside is that, if you're working in the field, it means you have to find a new job when your project is completed (likely every 3 to 5 years).

Of course, you can either work in a developing country or in headquarters. Most NGOs are headquartered in DC, some in New York and then some in random places like Portland, Oregon (the home of Mercy Corps; I interned with them because I'm from Portland and went to college there!) or Little Rock, Arkansas (home of Heifer International).

Another aspect of working with NGOs is that you have to deal with fundraising and donor relationships! Most US-based international NGOs receive a portion of their funding from a donor like USAID, and a portion from private donations or other sources. Some are less reliant on US Government funding, but may receive funding from other donors—like from the UK or Japan. Want to learn more about some of the different NGOs you could work for? *Annex One* is your friend!

Although I started out in the NGO world, I've worked for the US Government as an international affairs expert since 2006 (and I think it's a great gig!). If you're posted abroad working in an Embassy, then you get to work closely with host country governments to strengthen their relationship with the US. As a USAID official, you meet with them to ensure that you are being responsive to their development goals and to make sure that you have their buy-in for your projects. To further US strategic interests, you coordinate with the rest of the Embassy, diplomatic community and local civil society. And, as a USAID official, you get to design great projects and hire folks to make them happen.

If you're working on foreign policy from Washington, then you get to travel to interesting countries to support your Embassy colleagues in their diplomatic and development activities. Working from Washington, you get to formulate and implement important policy issues, and coordinate with the rest of the US Government in Washington to ensure that US foreign policy is being implemented abroad. In fact, you can end up working on a wide array of issues, from improving trade opportunities for American businesses to sharing US cultural experiences with other countries to helping US couples adopt children from overseas to fostering new technology to protecting the world's oceans to monitoring human rights issues—there's no such thing as a 'dull day in the office'!

Becoming a Civil Servant is hugely competitive, especially for State and USAID. While the PMF is one of the main ways to get hired as a Civil Servant, you can also apply directly for specific Civil Service jobs that are posted on usajobs.gov (and it's really no less competitive than going through the PMF).

There are other departments and agencies in the US Government that work on international affairs, including the Department of Defense, Department of Justice and the Department of Agriculture. Or you could always get your foot in the door with the Internal Revenue Service or the Department of Education and then try to transfer to State or USAID once you're in the system. Like I said, there are many paths to reach your goal!

Another option is to work for the US Government as a Foreign Service Limited (FSL), which is the closest thing to being a direct hire (Civil Servant or Foreign Service Officer). The position is time-bound, but you accrue government benefits and time in service. You could also join the government as a Personal Services Contractor (PSC). As a PSC you have some of the benefits of being a direct hire and similar roles and responsibilities, but you don't have the same retirement benefits or job security. You could also apply for government jobs as a third-party contractor, which is someone that works for a company, but is embedded within the government. They often have the same roles and responsibilities as direct hires, FSLs and PSCs, but different health and leave benefits.

Besides being a way to get a (hopefully) interesting job, a good thing about being a contractor is that it could potentially increase your chance of getting a Civil Service job. If a Civil Service position comes open and you have been basically doing the same job or a similar job while employed as a contractor, you are a much more competitive candidate for the job than you would be otherwise—because you already have the skills and the security clearance.

One big allure of being a direct hire are the benefits and the job security, which you don't have as a contractor. As a direct hire, once you pass specific requirements, you become tenured. This means that (unless you sell state secrets or something crazy like that) you are guaranteed a job for life. As a direct hire, the US Government also guarantees a retirement package if you reach the determined retirement requirements—for the USAID Foreign Service that means 20 years of service and being at least 50 years old. The retirement package is decent, but certainly doesn't mean retiring to a life of luxury, so many people pursue another career after retirement.

If you're interested in working abroad for the government (in an Embassy, Consulate or USAID Mission), you can apply for the Foreign Service. I am a USAID Foreign Service Officer and I love it! Foreign Service Officers can do tours in Washington, so you have the opportunity to work abroad or in DC. There are four different types of Foreign Service: the State Department, USAID, the US Department of Agriculture, and the Department of Commerce. There's a fifth type too: professional Peace Corps staff (not the volunteers) fits in the Foreign Service Category, but it's a limited appointment (typically five years). There's a book called *Inside a US Embassy* that explains more about the Foreign Service (worth a read!), and you can also head to *Annex One* to learn more about the application process.

The State Department Foreign Service is by far the biggest and best-known service. The State Department Foreign Service has different cones that you apply under (Political, Economic, Public Affairs, Consular and Management). These are considered Foreign Service generalists and are what most people probably think of when they think of the Foreign Service. There are also Foreign Service specialists in the State Department Foreign Service: these are mostly IT staff and secretaries. The specialist track has a different application process than the generalist track (see *Annex One* for more details).

To apply for the State Department Foreign Service as a generalist, you only need a bachelor's degree. The first step in the process is to register and take a written test that they offer all over the world, but that you can only take once a year. After you pass the written test, you submit a personal narrative. After that, if you are chosen, then you go to DC or San Francisco for an oral test. You also have to get security and medical clearances.

If you pass all of that, then your name gets put on a list of the people who have passed—which is ranked by your oral exam score. Having specific language skills gets you bumped higher on the list. Jobs are allocated starting from the top of the list as they become free, and your name gets dropped from the list if a position hasn't opened up within 18 months, which means you're back to square one and have to go all the way back to the beginning of the process if you want to reapply.

USAID Foreign Service Officers are technical experts, so to apply you need to have a master's degree. In the USAID Foreign Service, different technical areas are called 'backstops' (as opposed to State's Foreign Service, where they're called 'cones'). There are a lot more USAID backstops than State Department cones. The technical backstops are Crisis, Stabilization and Governance, Agriculture, Private Enterprise, Environment, Engineering, Health, Economics and Education. Other USAID backstops are functional: such as Financial Management Officers, Executive Officers (who deal with human resource issues), Regional Legal Officers, Contracting Officers or Program Officers (who manage the strategy, budget and reporting processes).

The application processes for the USAID and State Department Foreign Services are similar in some ways. For USAID, you complete an online application that includes questions about your technical expertise. When you pass, you go to Washington, DC for the oral and written exams. Once you pass that step, pass reference checks and get your medical and security clearances, your name is added to a ranked list and called in the order that positions in your backstop come open. Both State and USAID have six-week orientation classes to bring you up to speed on the Foreign Service—and both usually keep you in Washington doing language and other training for a year or two before heading out to your first assignment.

The State Department and USAID have the two largest Foreign Services, though State's is bigger (meaning it hires more officers!). With the State Department Foreign Service, you can be posted to any country with a US Embassy (i.e. most countries in the world). With the USAID Foreign Service, on the other hand, you'll only live in developing countries (given that we work on development issues). There are a few very senior USAID Foreign Service positions with the Combatant Commands in Honolulu and Germany, or with the UN in Rome, but they are few in number and super competitive! If you're a State Department Foreign Service Officer posted to a large enough country, you might work in a Consulate, which means that you live outside of the capital city. However, USAID Missions are only in capital cities.

You'll also find Foreign Service opportunities within the USDA's Foreign Agricultural Service and the Commerce Department's Foreign Commercial Service—you can find details on applying to both of those in *Annex One*. In addition, many US Government agencies and departments have representatives overseas. For example, several agencies under the Department of Justice (like the Federal Bureau of Investigations and the Drug Enforcement Agency), sometimes have representatives in US Embassies. The difference between being in one of the Foreign Services and being a US Government representative in an Embassy for a department (that doesn't have a Foreign Service) is that your overseas time isn't necessarily a continuous long-term thing, but rather could just be one three-year tour before you return to a domestic career.

When you're deciding where to apply for overseas jobs, here's one thing to keep in mind. If you work for the federal government abroad, you still have to pay federal taxes. Depending on which state you domicile in, you may or may not be exempt

GLOBAL

from state taxes. If you work abroad and don't work for the federal government, you're eligible for the foreign earned income exclusion, which means that you're still taxed on your worldwide income, but can exclude your foreign income up to a certain threshold (currently set at $100,800). You will still have to pay national taxes in the country where you're living, but at least you won't be taxed twice on the same income.

If you don't want to work for an NGO or the US Government, but still want to work overseas—you've got plenty of options. You could work for an international organization, such as the United Nations, the World Health Organization, the International Organization for Migration or the Global Fund to Fight AIDS, Tuberculosis and Malaria. Or, like my husband, you could teach in international schools around the world. You could work abroad in the private sector, like for an international bank, investment firm, corporation or consulting company. You could work in a social enterprise or as a social investor.

Or, you could always work in the US for a multinational corporation or a foreign-owned company, which would still expose you to a range of international economic or political issues. If you want to work for the private sector, it's a good idea to get a Master's in Business Administration (MBA). If you got a PhD, you could become a university professor and do research about international affairs.

You could also work for a think tank, where you could do research with the aim of influencing policy decisions. Foundations also offer opportunities for doing grant-making or investing in projects and organizations overseas.

And don't forget—you don't have to choose just one type of organization to work for, or even draw a hard line between 'working' and 'studying'. Listen to the experience of Victoria Stanski again: "After college, I spent the next seven years between Boston and DC, focusing on conflict resolution and peace building. I didn't follow a single track, but rather I gained greater exposure by working with a broad range of organizations. I worked for an NGO called

147

Peace First, a private foundation's initiative called the Institute for Inclusive Security, a think tank called the US Institute of Peace and a for-profit development company called Creative Associates. While working, I also went to graduate school for a Masters in International Conflict Resolution at American University's School for International Service. During this time, I focused on learning about key aspects of international aid like donor funding, policy, advocacy and communications—all the while building important skills like budget management, proposal writing, reporting and cross-cultural communication. At the same time, I traveled at any possible opportunity. This included a semester abroad in Tanzania in 1998, and later to Rwanda, Croatia, Brazil, Thailand, Vietnam, Cambodia, China, Jordan and more."

In short: you've got plenty of options. Head to *Annex One* for more details about what's out there for you.

CHAPTER 17
WORDS OF
WISDOM

FINDING YOUR PLACE IN THE WORLD, both in terms of where you live and what you do, can be one of the most exciting times in your life. For many, it's the first time you'll be expected to make major decisions, all by yourself, about your life. For that reason, it can also seem like a daunting time.

Take it from me: you're not alone. We've all been there. The nerves, the excitement, the fear, the anticipation. It's all part of the process. And no one – *no one* – expects you to have all the answers right now.

Luckily for you, you can tap into the insights of everyone that came before you. Like I said in the introduction: if you want to know the road ahead, ask those coming back. In this chapter, I've included words of wisdom from friends and colleagues that have, at one time, stood exactly where you find yourself today. Listen to their stories—and then go write your own!

FORGET THE GRAND PLAN

Elizabeth Bellardo: Humanitarian Policy Advisor, Office of US Foreign Disaster Assistance, USAID

In my sophomore year of high school, I took a world politics class that, looking back, set me on the course of a career in international affairs. I learned of the horrific recent history of Apartheid, read Nelson Mandela's autobiography and by that summer found a way to participate in a summer educational trip to South Africa. Even before that summer, my interest in people, cultures, food, history and politics outside of the US was certainly cultivated by our family trips abroad to places such as Germany, Greece and New Zealand.

After visiting South Africa in high school (my first international trip without my family) I was hooked. I identified two criteria for choosing where to go to college: a college that had an international affairs major and had an excellent study abroad program. Lewis & Clark College in Portland, Oregon, fit the bill perfectly. By the end of my four years there, I participated in two study abroad programs, in France and Senegal, and graduated with a double major in International Affairs and French studies.

Honestly, after graduation, I still didn't have a clue about what career within the field of international affairs I wanted to pursue. So, like many in the same situation, I decided to go to graduate school. Choosing a school in Washington, DC was the best move I made. I was able to take classes from professors and practitioners, and by proximity, landed a number of decent (though unpaid) internships. These internships helped to build my résumé, which made it easier for me to get a job when I graduated from grad school.

I didn't have a grand 10-year professional plan, but I felt compelled to apply for internships and then jobs which spoke to my personal values of equality, compassion and service. This roughly translated into the broad international affairs fields of human rights, civil society and humanitarian action. About six months after graduating from my master's program, I landed an entry-level position at InterAction, which is a coalition of NGOs working internationally on development and emergency response issues. I was saddled with student loan debt, had a master's degree and was making coffee and taking notes. I was grateful to have the job, but already thinking about my next move.

But then, three weeks after I started at InterAction in 2004, an earthquake in the Indian Ocean triggered a tsunami that killed over 230,000 people in 14 countries. The next few years were a whirlwind, and I marked time by disasters, not years. A cyclone in Burma, earthquake in China, Avian Influenza, earthquake in Haiti, war in Syria, war in South Sudan, Ebola outbreak in West Africa and on and on.

I was fortunate to move through a number of positions at InterAction, working on a cross-section of interesting issues. I worked with many amazing colleagues and had a chance to work in places like Haiti, Myanmar, Kenya, Ethiopia, Thailand and Vietnam. I stayed at InterAction for over 10 years, which was about nine years longer than I had intended. I realize now what a unique and lucky experience it was to have worked for a single organization for over a decade. I was able to witness the evolution of InterAction as an organization, the NGO community in the US and the entire international humanitarian community.

My experience working at InterAction was professionally and personally gratifying, but after 10 years I needed a new challenge. I knew I wanted to continue to work on humanitarian issues, and wanted exposure to another aspect of the system. After many chats over coffee with colleagues whom I respected and admired, and a bit of soul searching, I took a huge leap and accepted a position as a Humanitarian Policy Advisor for USAID's Office of US Foreign Disaster Assistance. Working for the government these past few months has not been without eye-opening experiences, challenging frustrations and a mountain of papers and emails. But most of all, I've found an excellent group of people who are passionate and dedicated to making the US contribution to humanitarian action as efficient and impactful as possible.

GRAB EVERY OPPORTUNITY TO LEARN ABOUT THE WORLD

Wendy Bolger, Director, Program Innovation Strategy, Share Our Strength

My career in international affairs actually started when I was selected to spend a week in Canada through an international exchange program at my grade school! It was not a very exotic experience, but at 10, I already felt like a worldly and independent person—and from then, on I kept my eyes open for other opportunities to see new places and learn about the world firsthand.

I was lucky that my neighborhood high school had an International Affairs magnet program. The curriculum was considered kind of a joke—you could go out to eat at a Chinese restaurant and write an essay about it to get the hours required for credit. But I had fun with the assignments and enjoyed the efforts to squeeze cultural experiences out of everyday life in my hometown, which wasn't very diverse at the time.

The real benefit of the school was the language electives available—in addition to French and Spanish, we could choose Japanese, German or Russian. I took four years of Russian with a very charismatic teacher. When I was 16, Mr. Poole bravely escorted 20 US teenagers behind the Iron Curtain for several weeks of language study and cultural immersion in what was still the Soviet Union.

We befriended real Russians who were our age but with vastly more complicated lives: a vet returned from wars in Afghanistan, as well as a young couple with a baby whose apartment was too small and not zoned to all live together. We had a blast playing 'diplomat', exchanging gifts and making toasts to peace at gala

'Friendship Celebrations' most every night. Several of my smart, ambitious 'fellow travelers' from that trip have gone on to be professors, three now live abroad and one has fulfilled a lifelong goal to work for the Foreign Service. The trip profoundly influenced us all, and we found ourselves in great company.

Home from the front lines of the Cold War, there was no stopping my international ambitions. A friend had spent a summer as a volunteer in Paraguay with *Amigos de las Americas* and came home with inspiring stories and pictures. The next summer, I raised funds required for *Amigos* from friends and relatives in lieu of high school graduation gifts, and got the opportunity to spend a month in Belize living with a Mayan family, building latrines for the community and teaching dental health to the kids. The villagers called me 'El Jefe,' as I strode through town in rubber boots, hauling a shovel or wheelbarrow, and rallying fellow volunteers and local families.

When the majority of the other volunteers on my program got sent back to the US in disgrace after being caught smoking marijuana, the leadership vacuum in international service work became an instant reality for me. Without a team of other students to help me, I had to rally the villagers behind me in a much bigger way to complete the project—it was community engagement in action! My leadership was recognized with the offer of a volunteer management role with *Amigos* the following summer.

Heidi Chase, Director of Innovation & Sight Program, Seva Foundation

When I was interning with Save the Children, I had the opportunity to live near the end of the 'development road'. I lived in a small community in South Sudan where we ran a health clinic, provided supplies to the school, and organized an early-education program. I saw firsthand the difference that these efforts made in the lives of local families.

Of course, there were challenges: The vital medicine that proved nearly impossible to clear through customs. The general who stood up during a condom demonstration and told the non-profit staff that they couldn't talk with the soldiers about safe sex and child spacing, only HIV/AIDS prevention. The women who still couldn't deliver their babies at the health clinic because cultural barriers didn't allow them to have a say in any decision-making.

But there were also moments of clarity and opportunity as a result of the work: children laughing and chasing each other in the morning as they made their way to the school building; families drinking clean water from the well; women working for the non-profit, earning money and having an increased status in their community.

RESPECT THE ITCH; TAKE A RISK

Kevin Grubb, International Affairs Specialist

I was living alone in a studio apartment in Portland, Oregon, working a job I loved, writing, exploring the natural beauty of the Pacific Northwest, going out with friends in the evenings. It was great. I had no responsibilities: no kids, no mortgage, not even a pet; and my life seemed to be in a good place for someone my age.

And yet, I was anxious. Some bug seemed to be itching at me from the inside, and I couldn't put a finger on it. As smooth and simple as life appeared to be, I felt somehow constrained and claustrophobic at times, isolated from the broader world. I had worked and lived in Russia for a couple of years in my 20s, taught in Kenya and I had fallen in love with international work: the multiculturalism, the feeling of a shared humanity regardless of one's nationality or circumstances.

One evening in Portland, I was out with a group of friends, when one of them went on a rant about our insular little world of over-privileged 20-somethings, sitting around talking about changing the world, but not ever doing anything about it. Too self-centered to actually act on our words and go out in the world and make the change. At one point, she stood up and mimicked a robot, moving her arms and legs robotically, blurting out, "Beep-bop-boop. I am a robot. ME. ME. ME." It hit me at the time that that was the root of my discontent.

It took me a few more years to get off my butt, but I did it. One day I decided I finally had to get back overseas and I quit my job, sold my stuff, moved out of my apartment and onto my little sister's couch (how humbling was that?), and looked for job opportunities abroad. I was offered an internship as a writer with Mercy Corps, which is based in Portland, and a few months later, I found myself in the uncharted territory of the former Soviet Republics of Central Asia: Uzbekistan, Tajikistan and Kyrgyzstan, the three countries that share the messy borders amidst the Ferghana Valley. (Kazakhstan and Turkmenistan are also part of Central Asia.)

I didn't arrive in the world of international affairs in the more traditional path that many take, but I did make some radical changes in my life that got me to a place I wanted to be in, working in concert with rural communities around the globe to help solve local issues with local resources. I took some risks, quit my job, and hopped on a plane to a foreign country for an unpaid internship. I wanted to work internationally, and I got there.

A lot of young people come to talk to me about how to get into international work or how to get a job overseas. I'm no longer surprised at how many of them crave the romanticism and adventure of what international work (trust me, it's not all romance and adventure), but are unwilling to actually go overseas. They have cats or a car lease, and it's all too daunting and complicated to take the leap. That's fine, but if you want to work overseas, the best way is to actually go overseas. Otherwise, what's the point?

TRY LOTS OF THINGS

Victoria Stanski, Program Advisor, Humanitarian NGOs

Identify what skills you bring and use them. Understand what you can do, develop that skill and use it within your work. International staff should add value when working abroad, but often our lack of language and contextual understanding make us a liability. Be clear and specific about what you can provide. It's good if you can nurture a particular skill like proposal writing, financial management or reporting, or if you can pursue a technical expertise that will contribute. Make sure it is respectfully grounded on advancing social justice.

Elizabeth Bellardo

My advice for someone interested in a career in international affairs is to try out different aspects and roles in the field of international affairs. You might be great at research, have a mind for logistics or have the passion for community organizing—there really are so many possibilities. Try to work for an organization or agency whose mission aligns with your values.

NETWORK LIKE A PRO

Brian King, Chief of Party, USAID Zrda (Growth) Project, Chemonics International, Georgia (the country!)

Network, network, network. If you're a consultant, it's the only way to get ahead. You need to know what firms are bidding on what projects and when and how to get in touch with the recruiters or proposal managers. Jobs in ongoing projects are rare, and you need to know how to navigate the proposal process. It's hard, especially when you interview for a job that doesn't actually even exist yet, because the firm may not win the project! A broad network helps keep you in the discussion for potential jobs. Do informational interviews and use your contacts at other companies to broaden your network. Be open and help other folks when you can, and doors will open for you.

Elizabeth Bellardo
A network of people who can vouch for your work and who know other people that could help you is the best route for professional advancement. I don't mean going to networking events and trying to meet as many people as you can. I mean taking the unpaid internship, doing your best work and really connecting with your supervisor and your colleagues. An investment in quality professional relationships will pay off.

FIND A MENTOR

Judi Heichelheim, Senior Regional Director, Latin America and the Caribbean, Population Services International
A common theme for me in this professional journey is that it is important to follow your passion, but also to listen and engage and seek out advice and mentoring from others. There is a world of need and opportunity out there, and no two career paths are the same. Find people to challenge your views and who can help you see how you can build yourself to make the difference you want to make professionally. And, most of all, never be afraid to jump in and try something new, even if it means picking up your life and moving into a new world full of uncertainties (because it will also be full of opportunities).

Brian King
Find a mentor in the industry. I was fortunate to have found a great mentor at my first stop in Romania—my boss at the time. Even though we've gone our separate ways and work for different companies, I know that I have someone to count on for advice anytime, anywhere from someone who knows the industry and has been through the same issues that I face every day. I can't express how valuable this has been.

Janell Wright, Public Health Specialist

While I wish my path had been smooth and easy, a lot of people helped me along the way. Find sponsors, champions and mentors. These are the individuals who are going to support your professional development and link you to your next job. The best way to do this is to find those people that you respect and start or foster the relationship by asking good questions and responding positively and openly to feedback. These people want to know that you are paying attention and the effort that they are spending on you is going to pay off.

IMMERSE YOURSELF

Heidi E. Mihm, International Development Consultant

My eyes were first opened to the wider world beyond the United States when I was in the fifth grade, and we spent eight months in Vienna for my dad's work sabbatical. I attended the international school and had classmates from all over the world. I had not spent much time overseas before and, at my elementary school in California, the focus on the world outside of the United States had been limited.

On my first day of class at the international school, my teacher announced that we would learn about geography and current events that year, and then she asked the South African student next to me to name the President of the United States. After she had answered correctly, the teacher turned to me and invited me to name the President of South Africa. I was incredulous and asked how she could possibly expect me to know that. She calmly replied that if my fellow student knew my president, then I should be aware of hers. Exasperated, I answered that everyone knew who the President of America was. Again, she patiently but firmly explained that if my fellow student knew my president, then I should know hers and that, when I said 'America', I was not even correctly naming a continent, let alone a country.

I was embarrassed, but also challenged. That year, my world-view was greatly expanded as I learned more about the rest of the world and where my fellow fifth graders came from. I also studied up and became the best in my class when it came to naming world leaders!

This awareness of, and interest in, the rest of world continued as I traveled across the border to Mexico and Central America during high school church group trips for short-term construction and other social projects.

As I entered college, I still wasn't sure about my career plans, but my earlier experiences had made me interested in the Peace Corps as an option after graduation. I knew I wanted a career focused on helping others and I went to Ecuador during my junior year for a semester abroad as part of a service-learning program. I took classes in the evenings, and during the days I volunteered at a girls' orphanage.

After graduating, I finally decided to take the plunge and apply for the Peace Corps, but I did not realize at the time that becoming a Peace Corps Volunteer would be my first real step in a career in international health and development. I always assumed that I would complete my two years of service and return home to work in domestic public health. However, working on health and sanitation in rural El Salvador was life-changing in so many ways!

Through life and work in a small Salvadoran village, I learned so much about myself on a personal and professional level. I realized that I could combine my desire to have a career in social justice with my interest in exploring new places and cultures and languages. I extended my Peace Corps service for a third year, working for a small NGO in the capital, which gave me some exposure to working in international development beyond life in the village.

Before the Peace Corps, I was not even aware that graduate programs in international development existed, but I ended up hearing about a Masters in Development Studies at the London

School of Economics and Political Science and started the program after my Peace Corps service ended.

While serving in the Peace Corps in El Salvador and later on working with a US NGO in Honduras, I had frustrating moments—but overall the work was gratifying because I was out in rural villages almost every day. I could see firsthand the difference my work was making in people's lives, whether I was working on a latrine construction project or teaching school children about the importance of hand-washing.

For those interested in international affairs as a career, I highly recommend looking for an experience where you are immersed in a different culture and a foreign language. While an extended volunteer experience like the Peace Corps may not be for everyone, I think any kind of grassroots field experience will not only make you a more attractive job candidate in any area of international affairs but will also provide you with skills that will make you more effective in your work. The insight I gained through learning and sharing in the daily lives of people in a culture and country different than my own has continued to serve me in positions where I wasn't traveling into the field (such as doing policy work in DC).

Having some real-world international experience before graduate school not only helped me pinpoint what I wanted to study, but also enabled me to take better advantage of my graduate education as I could contrast and compare the international development theory and policy I was learning about with my own hands-on experience. I also appreciated learning from my peers and hearing about their perspective based on their experience and backgrounds.

PACK YOUR 'SOFT' SKILLS

Jennifer Lawson, Foreign Service Officer, France, US Department of State

For anyone considering working in international affairs, particularly if moving out of the United States, I suggest bringing along flexibility, respect, curiosity, creativity and humor. Put them in your hand luggage, so they don't get lost along the way. Other things can be taught. You can be trained in foreign languages, computer applications, writing skills and protocol. Worry about those later.

You may also be surprised by which friends and family members visit you abroad and which don't. You may learn that it's harder to travel with pets than with kids. You may learn obscure facts about international maritime law that you couldn't imagine you'd ever need. That's great! Be open to the learning. And others will learn from you things they never thought they'd need either. For me, it's all in the name of becoming a more respectful, healthy, educated and inventive world community, while still cherishing and celebrating what makes us different... still building those idealistic yet real bridges of understanding.

Brian King

Working in development internationally requires a bit of a leap of faith and can be risky. Moving to a new country, especially with a family, is full of the unexpected—both positive and negative. You need to be flexible and positive, but also confident in your limits because frustrations can snowball quickly and you need to know your limits.

Be ready to live with uncertainty if you are working as a project implementer (like a consultant). Funding (and jobs) are project-based, which means 'time-limited'. Be prepared to search for a new job (and potentially a new country) every few years.

Todd Robinson, Ambassador, Guatemala, US Department of State

My best advice to those interested in a career in international affairs is to be ready to negotiate, to be flexible in getting to 'yes'—and to know your history, but to also cherish current events. History connects the dots of how we got from here to there, but in foreign affairs, you have to know what the current positions are, who is saying what and when and why. It's hard to keep up especially today with so many sources of information, but you have to do your best and try to formulate policy responses that offer flexibility all the time. I read, or scan, the media every day, and I communicate (maybe over-communicate!) with my colleagues regularly. I always want the latest information.

Landon Shroder, CEO, Applied Mathematics: Communications & Intelligence Laboratories

As you grow as a professional, you must not be scared to take professional risks that will place you outside the comfort zone of your colleagues. There is a dearth of creative solutions to the complexity gripping the world today, and these solutions will never be generated by acknowledging the status quo or the mediocrity of institutions that have led us to this point.

I would challenge you to engage and interact with people, cultures and traditions that are strange, foreign or otherwise distasteful. Attempt to understand the motivations of individuals whose beliefs might defy the very foundations of your own personal identity. Never stand on principle alone, always be flexible to circumstances that are beyond your ability to immediately assess. Become a subject matter expert in at least one thing, and use that expertise to shape the understanding of those around you. Immerse yourself in people, not policy. Understand how strategy and tactics can work to your advantage so that your worldview can evolve in a way that is robust and multifaceted.

But above all else, always speak truth to power. Inform your decisions based on what you know to be true, not what you know people want to hear. Anything short of this is why we continue to find ourselves in the intractable position we are in.

Victoria Stanski

Build teams and foster learning. One of the best aspects of humanitarian and development work is collaborating with motivated, engaged women and men who want to make a difference. From my experience, building a team to foster collaboration and learning is very powerful. It allows people to build analytical skills to question the norm, find solutions to problems, and expand their understanding outside their comfort zones. More recently, I've started to apply coaching within my management conversations by asking questions to facilitate learning and reflection, and it generates more meaningful engagement in a professional setting because it is tailored to each individual.

Be humble and generous—with a twist of humor. The best part of living and working abroad is meeting new people, navigating differences and exploring new ways of living. As a foreigner working abroad, understand that being kind, being patient, and having the ability to laugh at yourself in uncomfortable situations is the best way to live.

GO!

MY FRIEND DAVID RUBINO NAILS WHAT IT MEANS to grapple with the excitement and uncertainty that awaits you as you start your career. He says: "You'll probably face some version of the decisions that I faced. Do I take a risk? Do I leave everything that I know and love to pursue some half-formed vision of who I want to become? Or do I stay the course, choose an easier path and always wonder 'what if'? To me the answer is simple: Go. Go for a month, or a year or a lifetime—but if you are even considering the idea then just go! I guarantee it will change your life, and maybe, just maybe you can change the world a little bit."

Take it from me: it's a big world out there, and it needs your help. The problems facing global humanity are heart-breaking, urgent and far from inexorable. A career in international affairs will bring you face-to-face with that big, crazy, scary, inspiring and complicated world.

Every single decision that shapes the world is made by human beings. Ordinary people like you and me. A lot of these decisions make the world more humane, more equitable and more sustainable. Others, less so. We need more people standing on the side of social, racial, economic and environmental justice so we can make this world a more stable, peaceful and prosperous place. In other words: we need you.

If you're feeling small, if you're feeling insignificant compared to the scope of the challenges: you're not the only one. If you doubt your ability to actually make a difference, you're in good company. To you I say: you don't need to save the world. You just need to work on one small piece of the puzzle and have faith in strength in numbers. Think you can't do it? You'll never know if you don't try. So go out there and make your mark. Roll up your sleeves, and join the ranks of ordinary heroes doing extraordinary work to make the world a better place.

Go!

ANNEXES

ANNEX ONE
OPPORTUNITIES

THIS IS BY NO MEANS A COMPLETE LIST of all of the international job opportunities available, but it's a sampling across several sectors: government, international organizations, humanitarian development and relief organizations, foundations, social impact investors and think tanks. I've also included links to jobs in the private sector (which often have social impact or corporate social responsibility opportunities). Hopefully it will get you moving in the right direction. Also, check out the international organizations in *Annex Two*—you could work for one them too!

I've also listed some volunteer, fellowship and internship opportunities in this chapter. Though most of these sites are for jobs, any place that is hiring for a job is most likely also hiring for interns. I'd estimate that 99 percent of these places are looking for interns—even if they don't have internship positions listed. If you're interested in working somewhere, but you don't have enough experience yet to get a job, give them a call and try to set up an interview for an internship.

I think the reason why I got my first internship with Mercy Corps while I was in college was because I was persistent and kept calling until I got an interview and then the position. I got my internship in Indonesia by (again!) cold calling Mercy Corps and asking if they had any summer internships abroad. And voilà! The next thing I knew, I was on a plane to Jakarta for the summer.

The only thing to keep in mind is that, if you're volunteering or interning abroad, you may very well have to pay for your own expenses (I paid for travel and food expenses when I interned in Indonesia—Mercy Corps provided housing, but no salary). Or you may have to pay an organization to arrange the opportunity for you. But, if you can afford it, it's still a really great way to get international experience. It's good motivation to get a part time job or raise money from family and friends. There are even websites (like this one: volunteerforever.com) that help you raise money for volunteer opportunities.

Good luck and happy hunting!

JOB BOARDS

Council on Foundations: *jobs.cof.org*
Dev Ex: *devex.com/jobs*
Foreign Affairs: *jobs.foreignaffairs.com*
Forum of Regional Association of Grantmakers: *givingforum. org/jobs*
Global Corps: *globalcorps.com*
Global Impact Investing Network: *jobs.thegiin.org*
Global Jobs: *globaljobs.org*
Idealist: *idealist.org*
Indeed: *indeed.com*
International Affairs Jobs: *intjobs.com*
International Jobs Center: *internationaljobs.com*
LinkedIn: *linkedin.com/jobs*
NGO Job Board: *ngojobboard.org*
One World: *oneworld.org/jobs*

Philanthropy News Digest Job Board: *philanthropynewsdigest. org/jobs*
Relief Web: *reliefweb.int/jobs*
Simply Hired: *simplyhired.com*
Skoll Foundation: *skoll.org/community/jobs*
Thomson Reuters Foundation Job Market: *trust.org/ jobs-market*
UNjobs: *unjobs.org/non-un*
Work for Good: *workforgood.org*
Young Professionals in Foreign Policy: *ypfp.org/jobs*

US GOVERNMENT

Export Import Bank of the US: *exim.gov/about/careers*
Fed Biz Ops: *fbo.gov/index*
Homeland Security: *dhs.gov/homeland-security-careers*
Overseas Private Investment Corporation: *opic.gov/ who-we-are/careers*
Peace Corps: *peacecorps.gov*
State Department Foreign Service (Generalist): *careers.state. gov/officer/index.html*
State Department Foreign Service (Specialist): *careers.state. gov/work/foreign-service/specialist*
US and Foreign Commercial Service: *trade.gov/jobs/ world-of-opportunity.html*
USA Jobs: *usajobs.gov*
USA Jobs Pathways for Students & Recent Graduates to Federal Careers: *usajobs.gov/studentsandgrads*
USA.gov: *usa.gov/government-jobs*
USAID Foreign Service: *usaid.gov/work-usaid/careers/ foreign-service*
USDA Foreign Service: *fas.usda.gov/about-fas/careers*
White House: *apply.whitehouse.gov*

INTERNATIONAL ORGANIZATIONS

African Development Bank: *afdb.org/en/about-us/careers/current-vacancies*

Asian Development Bank: *adb.org/site/careers/current-opportunities*

Black Sea Trade & Development Bank: *bstdb.org/career/current-vacancies*

European Bank for Reconstruction and Development: *ebrd.com/careers-at-the-ebrd*

Global Fund to End Malaria, HIV/AIDS, and Tuberculosis: *the-globalfund.org/en/careers/current*

International Energy Agency: *iea.org/about/jobs*

International Finance Corporation: *ifc.org/careers*

International Labor Organization: *ilo.org/global/about-the-ilo/employment-opportunities/*

International Monetary Fund: *imf.org/external/np/adm/rec/job/howtoap*

International Organization for Migration: *iom.int/current-vacancies*

Organization for Security and Cooperation in Europe: *osce.org/employment/43284*

United Nations: *careers.un.org/lbw/Home*

UN Job List (external website): *unjoblist.org*

UNjobs (external website): *unjobs.org*

World Bank: *worldbank.org/en/about/careers*

World Health Organization: *who.int/careers/en*

World Trade Organization: *wto.org/english/thewto_e/vacan_e/vacan_e*

HUMANITARIAN & DEVELOPMENT ORGANIZATIONS/COMPANIES

Abt Associates: *abtassociates.com/Current-Opportunities*
ACCION: *accion.org/get-involved*
ACDI/VOCA: *acdivoca.org/work-with-us*
American Refugee Committee: *arcrelief.org/careers*
Amnesty International: *careers.amnesty.org*
Banyan Global: *banyanglobal.com/careers-php*
BRAC: *brac.net/work-for-brac*
CARE International: *care.org/careers*
Carter Center: *cartercenter.org/about/careers*
Catholic Relief Services: *crs.org/about/careers*
Center for Civilians in Conflict: *civiliansinconflict.org/
    who-we-are/our-team/join-our-team*
Chemonics: *chemonics.com/OurJobs*
Creative Associates International: *creativeassociatesinternation-
    al.com/why-creative*
Coffey: *coffey.com/en/careers/your-future-in/
    international-development*
Girls not Brides: *girlsnotbrides.org/about-girls-not-brides/jobs*
Global Communities: *globalcommunities.org/careers*
Global Impact: *charity.org/about-us/career-opportunities*
Equal Access: *equalaccess.org/about/career-opportunities*
Eurasia Foundation: *eurasia.org/CareerOpportunities*
Freedom House: *freedomhouse.org/content/
    career-opportunities*
Halo Trust: *halotrust.org/recruitment*
Heifer International: *heifer.org/about-heifer/careers/index.html*
InterAction: *interaction.org/about/job-openings-interaction*
The International Center for Not-for-Profit Law: *icnl.org/jobs*
International Center for Research on Women: *icrw.org/careers*
International Crisis Group: *jobs.crisisgroup.org*
International Foundation for Electoral Systems: *ifes.org/
    work-us/careers*

International Peace Institute: *ipinst.org/about/employment*
International Republican Institute: *iri.org/work-with-us*
International Rescue Committee: *rescue.org/careers*
Internews: *internews.org/careers*
IREX: *irex.org/careers*
John Snow, Inc.: *jsi.com/JSIInternet/Careers/jobpostings*
Madre: *madre.org/jobs-internships*
Management Sciences for Health: *msh.org/work-with-us*
Management Systems International: *msiworldwide.com/careers*
Médecins Sans Frontières (Doctors Without Borders): *msf.org/
     work-msf*
Mercy Corps: *mercycorps.org/careers*
National Endowment for Democracy: *ned.org/about/jobs*
National Democratic Institute: *ndi.org/careers*
Oxfam: *oxfam.org/en/work*
Path: *path.org/jobs*
Partners in Health: *pih.org/pages/employment*
Plan International: *plan-international.org/about-us/
     jobs-careers-plan-international*
Population Reference Bureau: *prb.org/About/Jobs*
Population Services International: *psi.org/careers*
Project Hope: *projecthope.org/about/careers*
Pro Mujer: *promujer.org/careers*
Promundo: *promundoglobal.org/about/careers*
RTI International: *rti.org/careers*
Save the Children: *savethechildren.net/jobs*
SEEP Network: *seepnetwork.org*
Tetra Tech: *tetratech.com/careers*
Vital Voices: *vitalvoices.org/careers-at-vv*
Women Care Global: *womancareglobal.org/about-us/careers*
Women Deliver: *womendeliver.org/about/careers*
Women's Refugee Commission: *womensrefugeecommission.
     org/about/employment*
Women for Women International: *womenforwomen.org/
     about-us/careers*

World Education: *worlded.org/WEInternet/workforus/ jobpostings*

World Learning: *worldlearning.org/connect/employment*

World Vision: *worldvision.org/about-us/job-opportunities*

FOUNDATIONS

Children's Investment Fund Foundation: *ciff.org/careers*

Clinton Foundation: *clintonfoundation.org/careers*

Ford Foundation: *fordfoundation.org/careers*

Gates Foundation: *gatesfoundation.org/Jobs*

The Gordon and Betty Moore Foundation: *moore.org/about/ careers*

Grameen Foundation: *grameenfoundation.org/careers-listing*

Humanity United: *humanityunited.org/about/careers*

Kering Foundation: *kering.com/en/talent/job-offers*

Kresge Foundation: *kresge.org/about-us/careers*

MacArthur Foundation: *www.macfound.org/about/employment*

MasterCard Foundation: *mastercardfdn.org/about/#careers*

Mott Foundation: *mott.org/about/OurOrganization/ employment*

NEO: *theneodifference.org/home/employment-at-neo*

Obama Foundation: *obama.org/opportunities*

Open Society Foundations: *opensocietyfoundations.org/jobs*

Packard Foundation: *packard.org/about-the-foundation/jobs*

Pan American Development Foundation: *padf.applicantstack. com/x/openings*

Peery Foundation: *peeryfoundation.org*

Skoll Foundation: *skoll.org/about/staff/#skolljobs*

William and Flora Hewlett Foundation: *hewlett.org/about-us/ careers*

WK Kellogg Foundation: *wkkf.org/employment*

GLOBAL

THINK TANKS

Atlantic Council: *atlanticcouncil.org/careers/employment-internships*
Brookings: *brookings.edu/about/positions-and-internships*
Carnegie Endowment for International Peace: *carnegieendowment.org/about/employment*
Center for Global Development: *cgdev.org/page/job-opportunities*
Center for Strategic and International Studies: *csis.org/about-us/careers*
Center for Strategic and Budgetary Assessments: *csbaonline.org/about/careers*
The Council on Foreign Relations: *cfr.org/about/career_opportunities*
The Dialogue: *thedialogue.org/careers*
German Marshall Fund: *gmfus.org/careers*
Institute for the Future: *iftf.org/iftf-you/jobs*
The Institute for the Study of War: *understandingwar.org/employment*
The Peterson Institute for International Economics: *iie.com/institute/jobs*
United States Institute of Peace: *usip.org/jobs*
Wilson Center: *wilsoncenter.org/job-openings-the-wilson-center*
Worldwatch Institute: *worldwatch.org/taxonomy/term/33*

SOCIAL INVESTORS

The Annie E. Casey Foundation: *aecf.org/about/jobs*
Blue Haven Initiative: *bluehaveninitiative.com*
Blur Orchard: *blueorchard.com/about-us/careers*
BNY Mellon: *jobs.bnymellon.com/jobs*
The California Endowment: *calendow.org*
The Case Foundation: *casefoundation.org*

Heron Foundation: *heron.org/enterprise/careers*
IDP Foundation: *idpfoundation.org*
Impact Community Capital: *impactcapital.net*
LGT Venture Philanthropy: *lgtvp.com/en/about-us/career*
J.P. Morgan: *careers.jpmorgan.com/careers/home*
Kois Invest: *koisinvest.com*
The Kresge Foundation: *kresge.org/careers*
Lumina Foundation for Education Inc.: *luminafoundation.org*
MCE Social Capital: *mcesocap.org*
The McKnight Foundation: *mcknight.org/about-us/job-openings*
Morgan Stanley: *morganstanley.com/people-opportunities/
students-graduates*
Omidyar Network: *omidyar.com*
Overseas Private Investment Corporation: *opic.gov/
who-we-are/careers*
Thriive: *thriive.org*
Tides: *tides.org/about/jobs*

PRIVATE SECTOR

Adidas Group: *careers.adidas-group.com/life-here/
without-borders*
Apple: *apple.com/jobs/choose-your-country*
Astellas Pharma: *careers.astellas.eu*
BAE Systems: *baesystems.com/en/careers*
Bank of America: *careers.bankofamerica.com/emea*
Bechtel: *jobs.bechtel.com*
Bloomberg: *bloomberg.com/careers*
BP: *jobs.bp.com*
Booz Allen Hamilton: *boozallen.com/careers*
Citi: *careers.citigroup.com/Careers*
Coca-Cola: *coca-colacompany.com/careers/
career-opportunities-job-search*
DDC: *ddcpublicaffairs.com/careers*
Deloitte: *careers.deloitte.com/jobs/eng-global*

GLOBAL

DHL: *dhl.com/en/careers*
Disney: *disneycareers.com*
Eurasia Group: *eurasiagroup.net/careers*
Facebook: *facebook.com/careers*
GE: *ge.com/careers/opportunities*
Google: *google.com/about/careers*
HSBC: *hsbc.com/careers*
IBM: *www.ibm.com/employment*
ICF International: *icf.com/careers*
IKEA: *ikea.com/ms/en_US/jobs/apply_now/international_jobs*
Instagram: *instagram.com/about/jobs*
JP Morgan: *careers.jpmorgan.com/careers/divisions/
    global-investment-management*
McKinsey: *mckinsey.com/careers*
Microsoft: *careers.microsoft.com/students/international*
Morgan Stanley: *morganstanley.com/people*
Nestle: *nestle.com/jobs*
Philips: *philips.com/a-w/careers*
Price Waterhouse Cooper: *pwc.com/gx/en/careers*
SAIC: *saic.com/about/careers*
Shell: *shell.com/careers*
Snapchat: *snapchat.com/jobs*
Sony: *sony.com/en_us/SCA/careers/overview*
Unilever: *unilever.com/careers*
Viacom: *viacomcareers.com*

VOLUNTEER & INTERNSHIP OPPORTUNITIES

A Broader View: *abroaderview.org*
AmeriCorps: *nationalservice.gov/programs/americorps*
AMIGOS: *amigosinternational.org*
Citi Volunteers: *citigroup.com/citi/volunteers/*
Corporation for National & Community Service: *nationalser-
    vice.gov*

Cross-Cultural Solutions: *crossculturalsolutions.org*
Do Something: *dosomething.org/us*
GIVE: *givevolunteers.org*
Global Leadership Adventures: *experiencegla.com*
Global Service Corps: *globalservicecorps.org*
Global Volunteer Network: *globalvolunteernetwork.org*
Go Abroad.com: *goabroad.com*
GVI: *gviusa.com*
Habit for Humanity: *habitat.org/ivp*
Hands On Network: *handsonnetwork.org*
Idealist: *idealist.org*
Idex: *goidex.com*
International Service Learning: *islonline.org*
International Volunteer Programs Association:
    volunteerinternational.org
ISV: *isvolunteers.org*
International Rescue Committee: *rescue.org/volunteer*
International Volunteer HQ: *volunteerhq.org*
Love Volunteers: *lovevolunteers.org*
Maximo Nivel: *maximonivel.com*
Naturally Africa Volunteers: *volunteerafrica.com*
National Youth Leadership Council: *nylc.org*
Network for Good: *networkforgood.org/volunteer*
Points of Light: *pointsoflight.org*
Projects Abroad: *projects-abroad.org*
The State Department: *careers.state.gov/intern*
Teach Away: *teachaway.com*
The Public Leadership Education Network: *plen.org*
Thinking Beyond Borders: *thinkingbeyondborders.org*
United Nations Volunteers: *unv.org*
United We Serve: *serve.gov*
United States Agency for International Development: *usaid.*
    gov/work-usaid/careers/student-internships
uVolunteer: *uvolunteer.net*
Volunteer Abroad: *goabroad.com/volunteer-abroad*

GLOBAL

Volunteer Match: *volunteermatch.org*
Volunteering Solutions: *volunteeringsolutions.com*
Volunteers for Peace: *vfp.org*
The Washington Center: *twc.edu/internships/
washington-dc-program*

Fellowships

AAAS Science and Technology Policy Fellowship: *aaas.org/
program/science-technology-policy-fellowships*
Asian Pacific American Institute for Congressional Studies
Congressional Fellowship: *apaics.org/congressional-fellows*
Boren Fellowship: *borenawards.org/boren_fellowship/basics*
Congressional Black Caucus Fellowship: *cbcfinc.org/fellowships*
Congressional Hispanic Caucus Institute Public Policy
Fellowship: *chci.org/programs/fellowships*
Department of Defense: *godefense.cpms.osd.mil/internships*
Donald M. Payne International Development Graduate
Fellowship Program: *paynefellows.org*
The Foreign Affairs Information Technology
Fellowship Program: *twc.edu/
foreign-affairs-information-technology-fellowship-program*
The Franklin Fellows Program: *careers.state.gov/work/
fellowships/franklin-fellows*
Fulbright-National Geographic Storytelling Fellowship: *us.ful-
brightonline.org/fulbright-nat-geo-fellowship*
Fulbright Program: *eca.state.gov/fulbright*
The Global Health Fellows Program: *ghfp.net*
The Minority Access National Internship Program: *minorityac-
cess.org/ndiip*
The Native American Congressional Internship Program: *udall.
gov/OurPrograms/Internship/Internship*
Pamela Harriman Foreign Service Fellowship: *wm.edu/offices/
dccenter/additional/harriman*
Presidential Management Fellowship: *pmf.gov*

Reagan-Fascell Democracy Fellowship: *ned.org/fellowships/
reagan-fascell-democracy-fellows-program*
The Thomas R. Pickering Foreign
Affairs Fellowship Program: *twc.edu/
thomas-r-pickering-foreign-affairs-fellowship-program*
White House Fellowship: *whitehouse.gov/participate/fellows*
The Women's Research & Education Institute Congressional
Fellowship Program: *wrei.org/Fellows*

ANNEX TWO
ORGANIZATIONS

●┈┈┈┈┈┈┈┈┈━━━●━━━┈┈┈┈┈┈┈●

THE UNITED NATIONS

The United Nations (un.org) is the world's largest and most powerful global multilateral organization. It's not a perfect organization, but in a world with no supranational government, the UN is how the governments of the world try to create order out of the anarchy that is the international system. It was also one of the world's first international organizations. The UN grew out of the League of Nations, which was created in 1919 after the First World War. It was created as an attempt to foster coordination and collaboration among member states in order to avoid another world war. The US didn't join the League of Nations and, with 58 member states, it obviously didn't succeed in preventing another world war. In the 1930s, World War II broke out with Nazi Germany, Japan and Italy on one side, and the US, Russia and the rest of Western Europe on the other. After Germany and its allies lost WWII, the UN was created as another effort to foster a more productive relationship among 51 initial member countries attempting to prevent a third world war. This time, the

US joined the UN and now it has 193 member states, which is almost every country in the world.

The UN's annual budget is roughly $5.5 billion, and each member state pays dues (money) to the UN. The US has been its largest financial supporter. It's hard to estimate exactly what percentage of the UN budget that the US pays for, but historically it's been estimated at almost a quarter. 148

The goal of the UN is to "maintain international peace and security; to develop friendly relations among nations based on respect for the principle of equal rights and self-determination of peoples, and to take other appropriate measures to strengthen universal peace; to achieve international cooperation in solving international problems of an economic, social, cultural or humanitarian character, and in promoting and encouraging respect for human rights and for fundamental freedoms for all without distinction as to race, sex, language, or religion; and to be a center for harmonizing the actions of nations in the attainment of these common ends." 149

The UN is very large and has a complex structure. To see an overview of the structure and to learn more about specific elements, visit un.org/en/aboutun/structure. The UN has several organizing committees, two of which, the General Assembly and Security Council, play the biggest role in international relations.

The *General Assembly* is made up of all 193 members of the UN and is the main policymaking and representative organ of the UN. It's where decisions about peace and security, admission of new members and budgetary matters are decided. Each country has one vote and, in order to make a decision, there needs to be a two-thirds majority. The General Assembly is used as a way for countries to be able to speak with one another collectively and to resolve issues together, thus ideally preventing the need for military force.

The *Security Council* takes decisions about peace and security even further. Through the Security Council, members make decisions about UN peacekeeping operations, the establishment of international sanctions and the authorization of military action. It is also the only part of the UN that has the authority to issue binding resolutions to member states. The Security Council has 15 members, five of whom are permanent members, which are China, France, Russia, the UK and the US. The remaining 10 members are elected for two-year terms, but the five permanent members can veto any substantive resolution. The Security Council can mandate peacekeeping missions, which are comprised of volunteer staff from member states, and they try to create peace and order in unstable countries. It's a way for countries to respond to the needs of other countries through a multilateral effort to create peace and security. These efforts work to a varying degree, but are the best approach that the international community has figured out so far.

The UN also has many programs that work on a myriad of issues from alleviating poverty and suffering to improving the rights of women to reducing the spread of crime and the drug trade. These programs, which include the UN Development Program (UNDP), the UN Children's Fund (UNICEF), the World Food Program, the UN Population Fund and many other programs, work in developing countries around the world to create peace and prosperity for the world's poor. They work on poverty reduction, creating good governance, improving health and education, reducing hunger and responding to humanitarian crises. These programs work with host country governments and NGOs to undertake activities that will help the world's poor.

In addition to the annual operating budget, donors also give the UN money to help implement projects. I've worked closely with several UN organizations in my career in international affairs. Here in Armenia, USAID works with UNICEF to implement a child welfare reform to get kids out of orphanages and back to their families or into a newly-created foster care. And, along with the EU, British and Germans, USAID supported UNDP in a project to utilize voting technology to try to reduce voter fraud for Armenia's Parliamentary (like the US Congress) elections. In Tajikistan, USAID gave money and worked closely with UNICEF to provide nutritional supplements to pregnant women and babies to reduce child and maternal mortality. While I was there, USAID also coordinated with UNDP to strengthen local government's ability to govern well and respond to citizen's needs. In Guatemala, my first USAID Foreign Service tour, we worked with the UN Office on Drugs and Crime to reduce trafficking in persons.

Under the UN system, there are also organizations like the International Organization for Migration, International Labor Organization and the World Health Organization. These organizations are affiliated with the UN and help to fulfill the UN's mandate.

OTHER MAJOR INTERGOVERNMENTAL ORGANIZATIONS

There are many other types of intergovernmental organizations in addition to the UN. The majority of these organizations are focused on economic or security cooperation or on development and poverty alleviation. And, of course, there's a lot of overlap between the areas that they focus on. The US is a member state of most of these international organizations, which means that it supplies both funding, often as the largest financial contributor, and political power. This is not an exhaustive list, but many of the main international organizations are broken down by category below.

International financial institutions

International financial institutions (IFIs) are international organizations that are like banks, but that are created by multiple governments to lend money to and help other governments. IFIs include regional and sub-regional development banks and global development banks that lend money to their target countries. Here is a list of the biggest IFIs:

The African Development Bank Group (afdb.org) was founded in 1964 and its mission is to promote sustainable economic growth and to reduce poverty in Africa. It's comprised of the African Development Bank, the African Development Fund and the Nigeria Trust Fund. It has 80 member countries, 54 of which are from Africa and 26 of which are not in the region, including the US. Through loans and grants, it undertakes activities to promote sustainable economic growth and reduce poverty in Africa by improving infrastructure, human capital, financing, agriculture

150 and rural development, mining and other industries.

The Asian Development Bank (adb.org) was founded in 1966 and its mission is to alleviate poverty in Asia and the Pacific. It has 67 member countries, 48 of which are from Asia and the Pacific and 19 of which are not in the region, including the US. Through loans, grants and technical assistance, it works to alleviate poverty by improving infrastructure, education, health, access to clean drinking water, reducing environmental degradation and

151 increasing economic opportunities.

The Inter-American Development Bank (iadb.org) was founded in 1959 and its mission is to reduce poverty and inequality in Latin American and the Caribbean—you see a trend here! It has 48 member countries, 26 of which are from Latin American and the Caribbean and 22 of which are not in the region, including the US. Through loans and grants, it works on climate change and renewable energy, improving equity and social welfare and

152 increasing economic integration.

The Islamic Development Bank (isdb.org) was founded in 1975 and its mission is to foster the economic development and social progress of member countries and Muslim communities. It has 56 member countries ranging from the Middle East to Africa to Central Asia to South Asia. Through loans and grants, it helps to fund economic and social development projects, the promotion of foreign trade and helping Muslim countries conform to

153 Shari'ah law, which is Islamic (not secular) law. This last goal sets it

apart from the other IFIs because none of the other ones have a stated religious objective.

The World Bank (worldbank.org) is like the regional development banks, in that it's an IFI that provides loans to developing countries, but it has a global geographic focus and is much larger than the regional IFIs. It was established in 1944 at the Bretton Woods Conference, which was a gathering of Allied Nations (the winners) after World War II as an attempt to create international institutions (such as the United Nations) that would help ensure international peace and stability. The World Bank's initial goal was to help reconstruct Europe after World War II and, once that was accomplished, its mandate expanded to the newly independent developing countries. The World Bank has 189 member countries.

The World Bank is comprised of two institutions, the International Bank for Reconstruction (IBRD) and the International Development Association (IDA). The IBRD funds projects through loans to middle-income governments to improve transportation, infrastructure, education, the environment, energy, health care, food security, access to clean water and sanitation. Meanwhile, the IDA funds project to the world's **154** poorest governments and provides more funding to the poorest countries than any other single entity. Like the IBRD, IDA projects focus on developing infrastructure, improving education and healthcare, increasing access to clean water and food security and protecting the environment.

The International Monetary Fund (IMF) (imf.org) was also a creation of the Bretton Woods Conference in 1944 and is the main organization for international monetary cooperation. Like the World Bank, the IMF has 189 member countries. Its stated goal is to protect the stability of the international monetary system, which is the system of exchange rates and international payments that allows for international trade. The IMF tries to achieve this stability by providing policy advice, research, loans, technical assistance and training to governments and central banks.

The European Bank for Reconstruction and Development (ebrd.com) is different from the other IFIs in that it works with the private sector (businesses and companies) instead of the public sector (sovereign governments). It was founded in 1991 and has 65 members from around the world, most of which are countries, but some of which are multilateral organizations like the European Union and the European Investment Bank. Through loans and grants it works with private sector entities (banks, industries and businesses) who couldn't take out loans from com-

155 mercial banks and it provides technical advice.

Economic organizations

Economic organizations are international organizations that intend to help their member countries manage their economic relationships. This is achieved through establishing and enforcing trade regulations and policies, sharing information and creating coordination.

The World Trade Organization (WTO) (wto.org) is another baby of the Bretton Woods conference after World War II, though at that time it was called the General Agreement on Tariffs and Trade (GATT). The GATT became the WTO in 1995 and it is now the global regulatory body for international trade. This means that it's the international organization in charge of creating and enforcing the rules of economic trade between countries – though countries can also still have separate bilateral (between two countries) and multilateral (between several countries) trade agreements. Countries have to apply to be a part of the WTO and, as of 2017, there are 164 member countries.

In 2013, while I was living there, Tajikistan became the 159th country to join the WTO. USAID helped the Tajik Government with its WTO accession process. Over 96 percent of both world trade and GDP are accounted for by WTO members, as is over

156 90 percent of the world's population. This means that the WTO manages the vast majority of trade agreements around the world

and, as an international organization, is very powerful.

The Organization for Economic Cooperation and Development (OECD) (oecd.org) is another international economic organization, which also grew out of World War II. There is a definite theme here – a lot of today's international institutions were a product of lessons learned in the international arena from the world wars. The OECD started in 1948 and used to be called the Organization for European Economic Cooperation, which was created to help administer the Marshall Plan. Remember – the Marshall Plan was the US's foreign assistance to help rebuild Europe after World War II. Today the OECD has 35 member countries, many of which are from Europe (though not all EU countries are part of the OECD), but some from around the world, including the US. The OECD's goal is to promote policies that improve economic and social well-being around the world by providing a forum for governments to coordinate and resolve shared problems.

Security

The North Atlantic Treaty Organization (NATO) (nato. int) is an intergovernmental military alliance of 28 western countries' militaries. Founded in 1949 and headquartered in Brussels, NATO was initially established as a response to the Soviet Union's perceived initial Cold War aggression. NATO is meant to protect its members through political and military cooperation. Basically, the idea is that NATO allies will protect one another militarily; an attack against one of the members is an attack against all of them. Member states commit to spend at least two percent of their GDP on their defense budget.

The Organization for Security and Cooperation in Europe (OSCE) (osce.org), which was created during the Cold War as a form of communication between western and eastern powers, is the largest security-orientated multilateral organization. The OSCE has 57 participating states, which span Europe, Central Asia and North America. The OSCE takes a comprehensive approach to security, so it doesn't only focus on security-building measures like counter-terrorism and arms control, but also on human rights, minorities, democratization and economic issues. The OSCE is also well known for their trained election monitors.

REGIONAL INTERGOVERNMENTAL ORGANIZATIONS

All regional intergovernmental organizations have a similar goal, which is to create prosperity and stability in their regions through economic and political cooperation. The goal is also to create a unified voice by which to communicate with the rest of the world – whether it's with other regional intergovernmental organizations, other international organizations or bilateral governments – by speaking together, the intergovernmental organizations give the member countries more power than they would have individually. One difference among them is that some organization's budgets, like the European Union, come solely from member country's financial dues. Whereas most of the other regional intergovernmental organization's budgets are comprised of member's dues, but are also very dependent on donor's contributions, which means that other countries outside of the region help pay for their budget.

The European Union (EU) (europa.eu) is an economic and political union. Like many other international institutions it grew out of the end of WWII as a way to increase cooperation in Europe and decrease the possibility of another European war. The inception of the EU was a more modest endeavor, the European Coal and Steel Community. This initial organization, started in 1952, grew into the EU, which currently has 28 member countries, mostly in Western Europe and some in Eastern Europe. There are another five countries that are candidates to join the union (Albania, Macedonia, Montenegro, Serbia and Turkey). The citizens of the EU don't need passports to travel to other countries in the union and most countries in the EU have the same currency, the Euro. Member states of the EU are still sovereign nations with their own economies and laws, but, by being part of the EU, they also have to abide by the rules and regulations of the EU. The EU is the gold standard of regional political and economic integration and even won the Nobel Peace Prize in 2012 for advancing peace, reconciliation, democracy and human rights in Europe. The EU was dealt a major blow in 2016, when the United Kingdom (UK) voted to leave the union. The UK has a large economy and has long been considered a leader in Europe, so its 'exit' will have ramifications on the rest of Europe, though it's too soon to fully understand what those ramifications will be because exiting the union is a long process, and the UK is still considered to be a full member with the corresponding rights and responsibilities. Hopefully, when it does actually exit the EU, this won't spell the demise of the rest of the union.

The Organization of American States (OAS) (oas.org/en) started in 1948 and its member states are all 35 states in the Americas with permanent observer status of 70 other states, including the European Union. The OAS's goal is to create peace, **157** justice and cooperation among its member states through democracy, human rights, security and development. The OAS is a mechanism for the governments in the Americas to work together to resolve disputes between them, to create political and economic cooperation and to try to eliminate poverty and insecurity in the region.

The Association of Southeast Asian Nations (ASEAN) (asean. org) is an economic and political organization that was founded in 1961 and has ten member countries in Southeast Asia. ASEAN works toward creating economic growth, security, social progress, environmental protection and development in Southeast Asia. ASEAN is working on creating regional economic integration by facilitating free trade in the region. Like other regional organizations, the fact that ASEAN brings the separate countries together to speak with one voice means that it can be more powerful, economically and politically, than the separate member countries.

ASEAN receives financial support from the US, the EU, Australia and other donors.

The African Union (AU) (au.int) is a social, economic and political union that was started in 2002 to replace the Organization of African Unity, which had been Africa's largest organizing institution since 1963 and had 32 member countries. The AU is comprised of 55 countries, which is every country in Africa (even its newest country, South Sudan). Morocco recently rejoined the AU after a 33-year absence, during which time it had a special status within the union and participated in AU events, but wasn't an outright member. This is because the disputed territory that it lays claim to, Western Sahara, is a member, but in early 2017 Morocco nonetheless rejoined the AU. The AU's goal is to create coordination across the 55 countries (including Western Sahara) of the African continent in order to move past the crippling legacy of colonization and to move into an era of stability and prosperity for the billion people that live there.

The League of Arab States (lasportal.org) was formed in 1945 and is the oldest multilateral regional organization in the world. It has 21 members from the Middle East and North Africa. The league used to have 22 members, but it suspended Syria's membership in 2011 because of the brutal tactics used by the government in response to its political opponents, which has now mired the country in an ongoing civil war. The goal of the Arab League is to create political, economic and security coordination among member states.

GROUP OF EIGHT

The Group of Eight (G8) (g8.utoronto.ca) does not quite fit into one of the above categories and it's not technically an international organization, but it is still an important international entity. The G8 is an apparatus for eight of the world's most powerful heads of state to come together to discuss important issues. It's a mechanism by which the world's most economically and militarily powerful industrialized countries can coordinate and use their collective power to respond to shared problems. Starting in 1975, the G8 has used an annual summit for coordination to discuss important issues, mostly economic and political in nature. In the last few years, a lot of the discussion has been around food security and the global food supply. The G8 started as the G6 and was comprised of the heads of state of France, the US, Britain, Germany, Japan and Italy, then it grew to the G7 when Canada joined, and now it's the G8 because Russia participates.

ECONOMIC FORUMS

Economic organizations are another way that governments work together to create coordination. There are different types and one example is the organization called the *Asia-Pacific Economic Cooperation* (apec.org), which is an economic forum intended to further trade in the Asia Pacific region. It has 21 members mostly from the region, and also the US, Russia, Canada, Peru and Mexico. Another example is the *Organization of the Petroleum Exporting Countries* (opec.org), which is a powerful organization that coordinates petroleum policies of 12 of the world's main national producers of oil and gas.

Annex Three
Information

For your reading list…

A Problem from Hell by Samantha Powers
The Blue Sweater by Jacqueline Novogratz
The Bottom Billion by Paul Collier
Building Social Business by Muhammad Yunus
Capital in the 21st Century by Thomas Piketty
Confessions of an Economic Hitman by John Perkins
Dead Aid by Dambisa Moyo
Development as Freedom by Amartya Sen
Doughnut Economics by Kate Raworth
The End of Poverty by Jeff Sachs
The Fortune at the Bottom of the Pyramid by CK Prahalad
Getting Beyond Better by Roger L. Martin and Sally Osberg
Globalisation and Its Discontents by Joseph Stiglitz
Half the Sky by Nicholas Kristoff and Sheryl WuDunn
How Europe Underdeveloped Africa by Walter Rodney
King Leopold's Ghost by Adam Hochschild
The Life You Can Save by Peter Singer
Making Globalization Work by Joseph Stiglitz
Nickel and Dimed by Barbara Ehrenreich

Pathologies of Power by Paul Farmer

Poor Economics by Abhijit Banerjee and Esther Duflo

The Price of Inequality by Joseph Stiglitz

The Rent Collector by Camron Wright

Sex and World Peace by Valerie M. Hudson and Bonnie Ballif-Spanvill

The Shock Doctrine by Naomi Klein

Stuff: The Secret Lives of Everyday Things by Alan Thein Durning and John C. Ryan

Understanding Power by Noam Chomsky

Wars, Guns, and Votes by Paul Collier

We Wish to Inform you that Tomorrow we Will be Killed with our Families by Philip Gourevitch

White Man's Burden by William Easterly

Why Nations Fail by Daron Acemoglu and James Robinson

The World is Flat by Thomas Friedman

RESEARCH, DATA AND STATISTICS

A Roadmap for Promoting Women's Economic Empowerment: *womeneconroadmap.org/sites/default/files/WEE_Roadmap_Report_Final.pdf*

Fragile State Index: *fsi.fundforpeace.org*

Freedom in the Word: *freedomhouse.org/sites/default/files/FH_FITW_Report_2016.pdf*

The Global Partnership for Sustainable Development Data: *data4sdgs.org*

The Global Slavery Index: *globalslaveryindex.org*

International Aid Transparency Initiative: *aidtransparency.net*

The Institute of Development Studies: *ids.ac.uk*

NGO Aid Map: *ngoaidmap.org*

UN Human Development Reports: *hdr.undp.org*

Reporters without Borders World Press Freedom Index: *rsf.org/en/ranking*

State Department Human Rights Report: *state.gov/j/drl/rls/hrrpt*

GLOBAL

State Department Trafficking in Persons Report: *state.gov/j/tip/rls/tiprpt*
UNDP's Human Development Reports: *hdr.undp.org/en*
US Government's National Action Plan for Women, Peace and Security: *usaid.gov/sites/default/files/documents/1868/National%20Action%20Plan%20on%20Women%2C%20Peace%2C%20and%20Security.pdf*
USAID Civil Society Index for Africa: *usaid.gov/africa-civil-society*
USAID Civil Society Index for Europe and Eurasia: *usaid.gov/europe-eurasia-civil-society*
USAID Storytelling Hub: *stories.usaid.gov*
Voices against Violence Handbook: *unwomen.org/~/media/Headquarters/Attachments/Sections/Library/Publications/2013/10/VoicesAgainstViolence-Handbook-en%20pdf.pdf*
Women, Business and the Law: *wbl.worldbank.org*
World Factbook: *cia.gov/library/publications/the-world-factbook*
World Bank Data: *data.worldbank.org*
World Bank World Development Indicators: *data.worldbank.org/data-catalog/world-development-indicators*
World Bank Gender Portal: *datatopics.worldbank.org/gender*
World Bank Little Data Book on Gender: *data.worldbank.org/products/data-books/little-data-book-on-gender*
World Economic Forum Global Gender Gap Report: *reports.weforum.org/global-gender-gap-report-2015/*
World Economic Outlook: *imf.org/external/pubs/ft/weo/2016/update/01/*
World O Meters: *worldometers.info*
World Poverty Clock: *worldpoverty.io*

NEWS & REPORTING

All Africa: *allafrica.com*
Brookings: *brookings.edu*
Center for Strategic and International Studies: *csis.org*
Council on Foreign Relations: *cfr.org*

314

Dev Ex: *devex.com*
Fuller Project: *fullerproject.com*
Global Voices: *globalvoices.org*
The Guardian: *theguardian.com/world*
The International Crisis Group: *crisisgroup.org*
Jinha: *jinha.com.tr/en*
The New York Times: *nytimes.com/pages/world/index.html*
The Nonprofit Chronicles: *nonprofitchronicles.com*
RYOT: *ryot.org*
Thomson Reuters Foundation News: *news.trust.org/humanitarian*
UN Wire: *smartbrief.com/un_wire/index.jsp*
United States Institute of Peace: *usip.org*

COOL ORGANIZATIONS

The Advocates for Human Rights: *theadvocatesforhumanrights. org*
Care2: *care2.com*
Center for Global Development: *cgdev.org*
Civicus: *civicus.org*
End Violence Against Women International: *evawintl.org*
Farming First: *farmingfirst.org*
The Global Gratitude Alliance: *gratitudealliance.org*
Half the Sky Movement: *halftheskymovement.org*
The Life You Can Save: *thelifeyoucansave.org*
Malala Fund: *malala.org*
Mona Foundation: *monafoundation.org*
NoVo Foundation: *novofoundation.org*
Slavery Footprint: *slaveryfootprint.org*
Society for International Development: *sidint.net*
Spacehive: *spacehive.com*
Think Impact: *thinkimpact.com/students*
Transparency & Accountability Initiative: *transparency-initiative.org*
United Nations Association: *unausa.org*
Women in International Security: *wiisglobal.org*

GLOBAL

World Youth Alliance: *wya.net*
Young Nonprofit Professionals Network: *ynpn.org*

ENDNOTES

1. The US Energy Information Administration (EIA) is a great place to go for the latest stats: eia.gov/tools/faqs/faq.php?id=32&t=6

2. For any stats related to health, the World Health Organization should be your first port of call. Here's data on drinking water: who.int/mediacentre/factsheets/fs391/en/

3. I'm not making this up. It's not the survey results that are interesting, but the discussion around privacy: washingtonpost.com/news/wonk/wp/2014/04/23/1-6-million-americans-dont-have-indoor-plumbing-heres-where-they-live

4. Human Rights Watch publishes useful annual reports on the trouble-spots of the world. Here's one on Guatemala: hrw.org/world-report/2013/country-chapters/guatemala

5. It's easy to search online for voter turnout statistics. I like the PBS website for this: pbs.org/newshour/updates/voter-turn-out-2016-elections/

6. So says the hiring pages for Foreign Service Officers at State. Check it out here: careers.state.gov/work/foreign-service/officer

7. Here's the website for non-career positions in the government: apply.whitehouse.gov

8. The Embassy Page for the US lists all diplomatic and consular missions in the US, and all US diplomatic and consular offices abroad: embassypages.com/usa

9. Americans for Informed Democracy publishes really useful articles, like this one: aidemocracy.org/programs/development/us-foreign-assistance/

10. Here's James Surowiecki's 'In Defense of Philanthrocapitalism' in The New Yorker: newyorker.com/magazine/2015/12/21/in-defense-of-philanthrocapitalism

11. Food for thought from Forbes, McCarthy, Niall in 'The World's Biggest Employers,' June 23, 2015: forbes.com/sites/niallmccarthy/2015/06/23/the-worlds-biggest-employers-infographic/#3af4d-4c251d0

12. *Ibid.*

13. Here's a great report from the Office of the Under Secretary of Defense for Acquisition, Technology and Logistics, 'Department of Defense Base Structure Report FY 2015 Baseline,' acq.osd.mil/ie/download/bsr/CompletedBSR2015-Final.pdf

14. Embrace your inner data geek! For economic data, always head to the World Bank's Databank—it's your best source, and freely available. Here are the GDP stats I talked about: databank.worldbank.org/data/download/GDP.pdf

15. The Peter G. Peterson Foundation has some serious data visualization game. Check out this one on defense spending: pgpf.org/Chart-Archive/0053_defense-comparison

16. The World Bank publishes an excellent annual 'Ease of Doing Business' survey, which ranks 190 countries along several indices (starting a business, dealing with construction permits, getting hooked up to utilities, paying taxes, etc.) A high ranking means the regulatory environment is more conducive to starting and running a business. doingbusiness.org

17. Tim Worstall's Forbe sarticle does a good job at articulating both sides of the issue: forbes.com/sites/timworstall/2017/02/07/us-trade-deficit-rises-to-502-billion-for-2016-not-that-it-matters-in-the-slightest

18. Here's a complete list of government trade agencies: ustr.gov/about-us/trade-toolbox/us-government-trade-agencies

19. Here's a list of Business Insider's top 25 MNCs to work for: businessinsider.com/the-25-best-multinational-companies-2011-10?op=1

20. From Foreign Policy (a good international affairs news website), here's a Fletcher School of Law and Diplomacy's (which is Tufts University's excellent graduate school for international affairs) professor's top ten favorite books about the global economy: foreignpolicy.com/2009/07/27/the-top-ten-books-to-read-about-international-economic-history

21. The Guardian published a great set of graphics to show which targets have been achieved: theguardian.com/global-development/datablog/2015/jul/06/what-millennium-development-goals-achieved-mdgs

22. Learn about the Sustainable Development Goals here: undp. org/content/undp/en/home/sdgoverview/post-2015-development-agenda.html

23. It was a good time to be a flag designer. Read up on the history here: history.state.gov/milestones/1945-1952/asia-and-africa

24. The World Economic Forum publishes some great articles. Start with this one on whether democracy is good for growth: weforum. org/agenda/2014/05/democracy-boost-economic-growth/

25. There is a lot of controversy around whether the IFIs actually help countries or are just tools of neo-colonization and I'm not going to get into that. Read Confessions of an *Economic Hit Man* and *The Shock Doctrine*, and form your own opinion.

26. This Brookings Institute article makes for sobering reading: brookings.edu/articles/odious-debt-when-dictators-borrow-who-repays-the-loan

27. It makes your blood boil: jubileeusa.typepad.com/blog_the_ debt/2012/12/lending-to-dictators-bad-loans-good-business

28. United Nations Water, 'Facts and Figures: An Increasing Demand,' unwater.org/water-cooperation-2013/water-cooperation/facts-and-figures

29. *Ibid.*

30. Water.org, 'Global Water Crisis: Water and Sanitation Facts,' water. org/water-crisis/water-sanitation-facts.

31. The measure is calculated using purchasing power parity; that means equalizing the purchasing power of two currencies by taking into account the cost of living and inflation differences. It's kind of a hard concept to get your head around. For a more amusing way of thinking about the relative value of currencies—check out The Economist and its Big Mac Index, which tracks how many units of currency are needed to purchase the famous hamburger in different countries over time.

32. The report is worth a read and can be found here: oxfam.org/ sites/oxfam.org/files/file_attachments/cr-even-it-up-extreme-inequality-291014-en.pdf

33. Bernadette D. Proctor, Jessica L. Semega, Melissa A. Kollar, 'Income and Poverty in the United States: 2015,' United States Census Bureau, September 13, 2016, census.gov/library/publications/2016/ demo/p60-256

34. The World Health Organization publishes great factsheets on every aspect of the health justice agenda: who.int/mediacentre/factsheets/fs114

35. The Centers for Disease Control is a leading voice on health justice in the US: cdc.gov/flu/fluvaxview/coverage-1415estimates

36. who.int/mediacentre/factsheets/fs094

37. who.int/features/factfiles/malaria

38. This is an awesome organization! nothingbutnets.net/the-solution

39. bbc.com/news/world-africa-28755033

40. worldbank.org/en/topic/health/brief/world-bank-group-ebola-factsheet

41. HIV, the virus that leads to AIDS, is the human immunodeficiency virus and AIDS is the acquired immunodeficiency syndrome.

42. ART is actually several antiretroviral medicines given at the same time, hence why it's called a therapy and not a medication.

43. who.int/gho/hiv

44. *The Lancet* is perhaps the most well-known academic health journal; here's an article on mothers and children: thelancet.com/series/maternal-and-child-nutrition

45. Check out the work of this awesome organization: thousanddays.org/the-issue/why-1000-days

46. popcouncil.org/uploads/pdfs/2012PGY_GirlsFirst_Health.pdf

47. Humanosphere, 'How Discrimination at the Dinner Table Leads to 'Missing Women' in Asia,' October 3, 2013, humanosphere.org/basics/2013/10/how-discrimination-at-the-dinner-table-leads-to-missing-women-in-asia

48. *Ibid.*

49. World Health Organization, 'Maternal Mortality,' November 2015, who.int/mediacentre/factsheets/fs348/en

50. World Health Organization, 'Skilled Attendants at Birth,' who.int/gho/maternal_health/skilled_care/skilled_birth_attendance_text/en

51. Helping moms helps kids. Full stop. ncbi.nlm.nih.gov/pubmed/26100131

52. World Health Organization, '10 Facts on Obstetric Fistula,' who.int/features/factfiles/obstetric_fistula/en

53. That's why USAID is working on this critical issue: usaid.gov/what-we-do/global-health/family-planning

54. unesco.org/new/en/unesco/events/prizes-and-celebrations/celebrations/international-days/world-radio-day-2013/statistics-on-youth/

55. Huffington Post, 'The Global Search for Education: Girls,' March 5, 2013, huffingtonpost.com/c-m-rubin/girl-rising_b_2808728

56. Tariq Khokhar and Hiroko Maeda, 'Four Charts on Gender Gaps we Still Need to Close,' The World Bank, January 20, 2016, blogs. worldbank.org/opendata/four-charts-gender-gaps-we-still-need-close?cid=ISG_E_WBWeeklyUpdate_NL

57. United Nations Girls Education Initiative, 'End School Related Gender Based Violence,' ungei.org/resources/index_5903

58. timesofindia.indiatimes.com/india/70-cant-afford-sanitary-napkins-reveals-study/articleshow/7344998

59. No one likes talking about periods, but that's got to change. Period. theguardian.com/global-development-professionals-network/2015/may/28/we-need-to-talk-about-periods-why-is-menstruation-still-holding-girls-back

60. ilo.org/global/about-the-ilo/multimedia/maps-and-charts/WCMS_369618/lang--en/index.htm

61. dol.gov/ilab/reports/pdf/2013TVPRA_Infographic.pdf

62. Read up on how the issue of child labor is addressed by Fair Trade standards: fairtrade.net/programmes/child-labour

63. Check out the report by the World Bank here: doingbusiness.org/reports/global-reports/doing-business-2017

64. pubdocs.worldbank.org/en/992371492706371662/Migrationand-DevelopmentBrief27.pdf

65. Read more here: theguardian.com/sustainable-business/2016/nov/08/dispelling-the-myths-why-the-gender-pay-gap-does-not-reflect-the-choices-women-make

66. reports.weforum.org/global-gender-gap-report-2016/infographics

67. Taylor Timothy, 'Unpaid Care Work, Women, and GDP,' Conversable Economist, October 12, 2015, conversableeconomist.blogspot.am/2015/10/unpaid-care-work-women-and-gdp

68. Mayra Buvinic, Rebecca Furst-Nichols and Emily Courey Pryor, 'A Roadmap for Promoting Women's Economic Development,' United Nations Foundation, womeneconroadmap.org/sites/default/files/WEE_Roadmap_Report_Final.pdf

69. United Nations Women, 'Facts and Figures: Economic Empowerment,' April 2015, unwomen.org/en/what-we-do/economic-empowerment/facts-and-figures

70. thenational.ae/business/industry-insights/economics/gender-pay-gap-in-middle-east-between-20-40

71. time.com/3836977/un-women-wages-and-careers

72. businessinsider.com/countries-with-the-biggest-gender-pay-gap-2016-3

73. reports.weforum.org/global-gender-gap-report-2016/infographics/

74. wbl.worldbank.org/~/media/WBG/WBL/Documents/Presentations/WBL2016-CSO-powerpoint.pdf?la=en

75. blogs.worldbank.org/europeandcentralasia/armenia-economic-pie-smaller-it-should-be

76. data.worldbank.org/country/armenia

77. reports.weforum.org/global-gender-gap-report-2016/infographics/

78. ub.edu/ubeconomics/wp-content/uploads/2014/02/308-Web.pdf

79. theguardian.com/business/2016/oct/25/gender-pay-gap-170-years-to-close-world-economic-forum-equality

80. Food and Agriculture Organization of the United Nations, 'The State of Food and Agriculture 2010–2011,' fao.org/docrep/013/i2050e/i2082e00.pdf

81. The Global Alliance for Improved Nutrition (GAIN) is an international organization that was launched at the UN in 2002 to tackle the human suffering caused by malnutrition. gainhealth.org/knowledge-centre/fast-facts-malnutrition/

82. World Hunger has really useful resources on this topic, as you might expect: worldhunger.org/africa-hunger-poverty-facts

83. United States Department of Agriculture, 'Food Security in the US: Key Statistics & Graphics,' September 8, 2015, ers.usda.gov/topics/food-nutrition-assistance/food-security-in-the-us/key-statistics-graphics

84. You can learn more about Feed the Future here: feedthefuture.gov

85. Betty A. Reardon, Women and Peace, Albany: State University of New York Press, 1993

86. J.J. McCullough, 'Female World Leaders Currently in Power,' January 22, 2015.jjmccullough.com/charts_rest_female-leaders

87. WorldWide Guide to Women in Leadership, 'Female Presidents,' guide2womenleaders.com/Presidents

88. Gender quotas are complicated. Just because a law states that women have to hold office doesn't mean they'll run for office, or win. Read more, and make up your own mind: theatlantic.com/international/archive/2014/10/do-quotas-for-female-politicians-work/381320

89. International Labor Organization, 'Forced labor, modern slavery and human trafficking,' ilo.org/global/topics/forced-labour/lang--en/index

90. Don't think for one moment that we've put slavery in a museum: globalcitizen.org/en/content/these-5-countries-58-worlds-slaves

91. You can read it to learn more about individual country's experience and response to TIP: state.gov/j/tip/rls/tiprpt

92. You can find the State Department Human Rights Reports online here: state.gov/j/drl/rls/hrrpt

93. Read more about the 'resource curse' and its effects here: dissentmagazine.org/article/beyond-conflict-minerals-the-congos-resource-curse-lives-on

94. See more here: theguardian.com/global-development/2013/feb/18/girl-soldiers-battle-civilian-life

95. United Nations, 'Background Information on Sexual Violence used as a Tool of War,' un.org/en/preventgenocide/rwanda/about/bgsexualviolence

96. Jo Adetunji, 'Forty-Eight Women Raped every Hour in Congo, Study Finds,' The Guardian, May 12, 2011, theguardian.com/world/2011/may/12/48-women-raped-hour-congo

97. unwomen.org/en/what-we-do/peace-and-security/facts-and-figures

98. If you're not already hooked on Ted talks, you soon will be. Start here: ted.com/talks/zainab_salbi

99. pdf.usaid.gov/pdf_docs/Pnadl089.pdf

100. Ibid.

101. Ibid.

102. Jessica Valenti, 'Worldwide Sexism Increases Suicide Risk in Young Women,' The Guardian, May 28, 2015, theguardian.com/commentisfree/2015/may/28/worldwide-sexism-increases-suicide-risk-in-young-women

103. theguardian.com/business/2016/oct/25/gender-pay-gap-170-years-to-close-world-economic-forum-equality

104. state.gov/documents/organization/258703.pdf

105. usaid.gov/sites/default/files/GBV-Infographic.pdf
106. United Nations, 'Ending Violence against Women and Girls,' un.org/en/globalissues/briefingpapers/endviol
107. Max Novendstern, 'Half the Sky,' Harvard Political Review, April 16, 2010, harvardpolitics.com/online/hprgument-blog/half-the-sky
108. John Bongaarts and Christophe Guilmoto, 'How Many more Missing Women?' thelancet.com/journals/lancet/article/PIIS0140-6736(15)61439-8/fulltext
109. United Nations Children's Fund, 'A Statistical Snapshot of Violence against Adolescent Girls,' October 2014, unicef.org/publications/files/A_Statistical_Snapshot_of_Violence_Against_Adolescent_Girls.pdf
110. Geeta Anand and Jaeyeon Woo, 'Asia Struggles for a Solution to its 'Missing Women' Problem,' Wall Street Journal, November 26, 2015, wsj.com/articles/asia-struggles-for-a-solution-to-its-missing-women-problem-1448545813
111. RAINN, 'Scope of the Problem: Statistics,' rainn.org/statistics/scope-proble
112. rainn.org/statistics/campus-sexual-violence
113. C.M. Rubin, 'The Global Search for Education: Girls,' The Huffington Post, March 5, 2013, huffingtonpost.com/c-m-rubin/girl-rising_b_2808728
114. United Nations Women, 'Half of Men Report using Violence and a Quarter Perpetrate Rape according to UN Survey of 10,000 Men in Asia-Pacific,' September 10, 2013, unwomen.org/en/news/stories/2013/9/half-of-men-report-using-violence-and-a-quarter-perpetrate-rape-according-to-un-survey
115. Tulip Mazumdar, 'Almost a Quarter of Men Admit to Rape in Parts of Asia,' BBC, September 10, 2013, bbc.com/news/health-24021573
116. United Nations Women, 'Half of Men Report using Violence and a Quarter Perpetrate Rape according to UN Survey of 10,000 Men in Asia-Pacific,' September 10, 2013, unwomen.org/en/news/stories/2013/9/half-of-men-report-using-violence-and-a-quarter-perpetrate-rape-according-to-un-survey
117. The study is called 'Why Do Some Men Use Violence against Women and How Can We Prevent It?' and you can read the whole thing here: unwomen-asiapacific.org/docs/WhyDoSome-MenUseViolenceAgainstWomen_P4P_Report.pdf

118. new.mankind.org.uk/wp-content/uploads/2015/05/30-Key-Facts-Male-Victims-Mar-2016.pdf

119. cdc.gov/violenceprevention/intimatepartnerviolence/teen_dating_violence

120. Katie Sanders, 'Steinem: More Women Killed by Partners Since 9/11 than Deaths from Attacks, Ensuing Wars,' PunditFact, October 7th, 2014, politifact.com/punditfact/statements/2014/oct/07/gloria-steinem/steinem-more-women-killed-partners-911-deaths-atta

121. International Center for Research on Women, 'Child Marriage Facts and Figures,' icrw.org/child-marriage-facts-and-figures

122. United Nations Children's Fund, 'End Child Marriage,' unicefrosa-progressreport.org/childmarriage

123. *Ibid.*

124. *Ibid.*

125. Huffington Post, 'The Global Search for Education: Girls,' March 5, 2013, huffingtonpost.com/c-m-rubin/girl-rising_b_2808728

126. *Ibid.*

127. International Center for Research on Women, 'Child Marriage Facts and Figures,' icrw.org/child-marriage-facts-and-figures

128. United Nations Children's Fund, 'A Statistical Snapshot of Violence against Adolescent Girls,' October 2014, unicef.org/publications/files/A_Statistical_Snapshot_of_Violence_Against_Adolescent_Girls.pdf

129. unfpa.org/resources/female-genital-mutilation-fgm-frequently-asked-questions

130. Food and Agriculture Organization of the United Nations, 'The State of Food and Agriculture 2010 – 2011,' fao.org/docrep/013/i2050e/i2082e00.pdf

131. Carla Sarrouy 'Four Key Reasons why Climate Change Adaptation and Mitigation need a Gendered Approach,' Exchanges: the Warwick Research Journal, 2014, exchanges.warwick.ac.uk/index.php/exchanges/rt/printerFriendly/45/151

132. Laura Bailey, 'In Armenia, is the 'Economic Pie' Smaller than it Should be?,' World Bank, September 22, 2016, blogs.worldbank.org/europeandcentralasia/armenia-economic-pie-smaller-it-should-be

133. NBC News, 'Gender Inequality Costs Sub-Saharan Africa $95 Billion: UN,' August 28, 2016, nbcnews.com/news/world/gender-inequality-costs-sub-saharan-africa-95-billion-un-n638966

134. McKinsey Global Institute, 'How Advancing Women's Equality can add $12 Trillion to Global Growth,' September 2015, mckinsey.com/global-themes/employment-and-growth/how-advancing-womens-equality-can-add-12-trillion-to-global-growth

135. National Geographic, 'Planet Earth: By the Numbers,' Feb. 2015 Issue, page 10.

136. Worldometers, worldometers.info

137. livescience.com/27692-deforestation

138. National Geographic, Wallace, Scott, 'Last of the Amazon,' environment.nationalgeographic.com/environment/habitats/last-of-amazon/#page=1

139. *Ibid.*

140. National Geographic January 2016 by Charles C. Mann, 'Riding the Rubber Boom,' pages 123–133.

141. unesdoc.unesco.org/images/0024/002439/243938e.pdf

142. Growing Blue, 'Environmental Implications,' growingblue.com/implications-of-growth/environmental-implications

143. nationalgeographic.com/environment/global-warming/sea-level-rise

144. National Geographic, 'Planet Earth: By the Numbers,' February 2015 Issue, page 127.

145. National Geographic, 'Rising Seas,' September 2013 Issue, page 31.

146. I'm not making this up. Read more at: hbr.org/2014/08/why-women-dont-apply-for-jobs-unless-theyre-100-qualified

147. A career abroad means becoming an expert in filling out foreign earned income statements every year. Find out more here: irs.gov/individuals/international-taxpayers/foreign-earned-income-exclusion

148. Congressional Research Service, 'United Nations Regular Budget Contributions: Members Compared, 1990-2010,' January 15, 2013, fas.org/sgp/crs/row/RL30605.pdf

149. United Nations, 'Charter of the United Nations: Purposes and Principles,' un.org/en/documents/charter/chapter1.shtml

150. African Development Bank, 'Annual Report 2012,' May 2013, afdb.org/fileadmin/uploads/afdb/Documents/Publications/Annual%20Report%202012.pdf

151. Asian Development Bank, 'Annual Report 2012,' April 2013, adb.org/sites/default/files/adb-financial-report-2012.pdf

152. Inter-American Development Bank, 'Annual Report 2012,'

March 2013, idbdocs.iadb.org/wsdocs/getdocument.aspx?doc-num=37614856

153. Islamic Development Bank, 'Annual Report 2012,' March 28, 2013, isdb.org/irj/go/km/docs/documents/IDBDevelopments/Internet/English/IDB/CM/Publications/Annual_Reports/38th/AnnualReport38.pdf

154. World Bank, 'Annual Report 2012,' issuu.com/world.bank.publications/docs/annual_report_2012_en?e=1107022/2001324

155. European Bank for Reconstruction and Development, 'Financial Report 2012,' February 26, 2013, ebrd.com/downloads/research/annual/fr12e.pdf

156. The World Trade Organization, 'Handbook on Accession to the WTO,' August 2007, wto.org/english/thewto_e/acc_e/cbt_course_e/preface_e

157. Organization of American States, 'Who We Are,' oas.org/en/about/who_we_are

red